2013

DISCARDED

Parking Spaces

Parking Spaces

A DESIGN, IMPLEMENTATION, AND USE MANUAL FOR ARCHITECTS, PLANNERS, AND ENGINEERS

Mark C. Childs

McGraw-Hill

New York   San Francisco   Washington, D.C.   Auckland   Bogotá
Caracas   Lisbon   London   Madrid   Mexico City   Milan
Montreal   New Delhi   San Juan   Singapore
Sydney   Tokyo   Toronto

Library of Congress Cataloging-in-Publication Data

Childs, Mark C.
    Parking spaces : a design, implementation, and use manual for
architects, planners, and engineers / Mark C. Childs.
      p.   cm.
    Includes bibliographical references and index.
    ISBN 0-07-012107-9 (alk. paper)
    1. Parking lots—Design and construction. I. Title.
TL175.C47 1999
711'.73—dc21   98-48077
                                          CIP

McGraw-Hill

A Division of The **McGraw·Hill** *Companies*

1 2 3 4 5 6 7 8 9 0 DOC/DOC 9 0 3 2 1 0 9 8

ISBN 0-07-012107-9

*The sponsoring editor for this book was Wendy Lochner, the editing supervisor was Christine Furry, the
editing liaison was Patricia V. Amoroso, and the production supervisor was Tina Cameron. It was set in
Matt Antique by North Market Street Graphics.*

Printed and bound by R. R. Donnelley & Sons Company.

This book is printed on acid-free paper.

McGraw-Hill books are available at special quantity discounts to use as premiums and sales promo-
tions, or for use in corporate training programs. For more information, please write to the Director of
Special Sales, McGraw-Hill, 11 West 19th Street, New York, NY 10011. Or contact your local book-
store.

To the Queen of Commas,
My Literary Rose,
Professor Quin,
and
in memory of
my father

Contents

Foreword

How would the pioneers of modernism react if they were to visit an American metropolitan city today? Their revolutionary urbanist agenda was based on four principles that are now coded into planning manuals and commonplace in practice all around us: a call for universal car ownership and the radical restructuring of cities to accommodate the resulting boundless automobility; a strict separation of uses in space and the invention of new, larger, and universal building types to accommodate them; the dissolution of formed, urban public space and its replacement by a free-form, naturalistic landscape; and the relentless imposition of engineering solutions to the perennial human task of controlling natural forces and processes (e.g., water, sewage, climate, daylight). Fifty years of rigid application of these ideas has generated the greatest crisis in the quality of human life worldwide since the beginning of civilization. Would they be surprised?

What would Le Corbusier think of his highly rational and technical drawings of freeways transformed into their common current reality as instruments of urban sprawl, urban decay, and traffic congestion? How would he respond to his idealistic drawings of a radiant city of slabs and towers in nature morphed into a nightmare of buildings mired in seas of parking?

How would Frank Lloyd Wright respond to his vision of a Broadacre City in balance between architecture and nature trashed by unprecedented areas of asphalt paving and purposefully ugly buildings? The miles upon miles of big boxes, malls, strip retail, and other highway-related businesses respond, after all, to the car culture he so admired and promoted.

How would the founders of CIAM and signers of the Charter of Athens react to car-induced levels of visual, sound, air, water, and soil pollution unprecedented in the history of the world? Would they reverse their vision of city making that is now driven by beaurocratic fiat, linear thinking, optimization, and mechanical solutions? Would they acknowledge the role of their theory and practices in the current chaotic state of the built and natural world?

Not surprisingly, the dominant, conventional view of urban development here and abroad is still based on modernist urbanism, and that despite the catastrophic evidence of its effects on the City and on Nature. The historical fact is that the great modern masters died unrepentant, and their heirs and apologists continue unfazed and unapologetic in their support of the modern dogma. I guess we will never know the modern masters' answers to these questions.

It falls on us, their intellectual heirs, to deal with the sprawling mess we have inherited and to work to reclaim cities as humane places to live and nature as the medium that sustains all of us in life. To this end, we need to be thinking and acting simultaneously in two directions.

Theories of urban development must be invented that circumvent the four poles of modernism. Such theories should be cast in support of cities that promote human interaction, experience, and prosperity. An example of such global thinking and ambition is the New Urbanist movement. As a coalition of people and a set of ideas, it is poised to radically redefine the terms of urban growth and promote the conservation of nature in the world.

Thoughtful, topical, and specific suggestions must also be developed on how to ameliorate the universe of sprawl that we currently inhabit. An example of this focused thinking is books such as the one you are holding in your hands. *Parking Spaces* offers welcome advice on how to humanize the world around us incrementally and irreversibly. Both the global and topical modes of thought and action are essential to architecture and urbanism in the coming decades.

Cars will not and should not go away. They play a vital role in giving us unprecedented mobility and access. In our country they are promoted and virtually identified with the idea of freedom itself. Yet we need to stop building roads, reduce the number of trips we generate each day, and redirect our attention toward enhancing the quality of life at the beginning and at the end of every trip. The origins and destinations of car trips must become places of serious consideration for designers.

In a world of senseless automobility, pedestrian pockets in our towns and cities are the places where people interact most intensely. Places where people can park once, abandon their cars, and carry out multiple tasks on foot are the locations that we identify as having both high social and economic value. The points of arrival and departure, parking lots, parking garages, and street parking become critical design elements in promoting the idea of a high quality of urban life.

Mark Childs's book is an affirmation of the importance of addressing all these residual and unglamorous places in our midst, but also a pattern book full of suggestions toward appropriate and constructive design. His remedies to ugly and desolate car-dominated land and buildings are not generated through narrow ideological prescriptions. His patterns are offered as ingredients to be combined according to the needs of individual contexts and projects. His ideas are backed up by research and detailed engineering considerations that allow the reader to judge the utility of each pattern to the problem at hand. His approach and his book are generative. Questioning on the part of the reader can lead to further creative investigation. Acceptance can promote design with authority.

The book champions the cause of designing existing or proposed parking facilities as valid places in themselves. It is particularly rewarding that this book does not deny the value and importance of public space in the city. As a matter of fact, many of the patterns are presented in a manner that supports the forming of such public space through the propitious design of parking facilities. This point emerges as the principal theme of the book and as the ultimate social objective for all urban design.

Many ideas that can result in the generation of traditional urban and architectural form are also suggested. The full integration of cars into pedestrian-dominant buildings, blocks, and streets, although never an explicit agenda item, is clearly the central architectural interest of the author.

In order to minimize the environmental harm caused by parking, the book suggests a crusade in favor of landscape, architectural, and environmental design initiatives. Water harvesting, climate-specific planting, and carefully designed paving are all ideas whose time has come. Their application in concert could change the quality of our everyday life more than the change of any other design standards.

Alternative modes of transportation are also championed. Intelligent arguments are made in favor of walking, bicycling, and using transit through the design of parking places and traffic arrangements that encourage their use. Prudently, the maintenance and security of such parking places are encouraged as clearly as their design.

In conclusion, *Parking Spaces* is valuable reading for all those with a role in affecting the form of development and redevelopment in our country. Professionals, elected officials, administrators, and developers can learn a great deal by consulting its pages. The book's ultimate value is in the argument that properly built places can and will change the way people live, and there are simple and generative patterns that can be used to get us from here to there—that is, from the age of sprawl and social alienation to a country full of towns and cities that support values under which families endeavor to live and prosper.

Stefanos Polyzoides
May 1, 1998

Acknowledgments

For years, I have wondered about the purpose of acknowledgments. Certainly, acknowledgments are to thank those who generously helped the writer, but why don't writers simply send letters to their benefactors or buy presents for their long-suffering spouses? What do acknowledgments have to say to the general reader? The reader, unacquainted with the author's community of support, may well ask: Why take up space with a declaration of the author's debts? I offer three reasons for doing so.

First, acknowledgments provide the aspiring writer with a glimpse of the process and business of writing. I thank Professor Andy Pressman, who graciously showed me how to put a book proposal together, the reviewers of my book proposal, Everett Smethurst, who refined and presented my book proposal to McGraw-Hill, and Wendy Lochner, my editor at McGraw-Hill, for their willingness to take a risk on me and for their professionalism in helping me learn the business of writing a book.

Second, books are part of the public realm. They are a component of the public dialogue, and they rest on the works, ideas, and skills of others. Copyright notices, references, and notes reveal to some degree how this book rests on previous work. However, other intellectual support is not reflected in such notes. I thank a small army of friends—Ann Annella, Joel Condon, Patrick Doherty, Douglas Eberhart, Davidya Kasperzyk, Rocky Piro, Sue Mortier, Mark

Savage, Maura Glynn-Thami, Dorothy Thomas, and Jane Thurber—for reading and correcting draft chapters. Professor David Driskill, Director of the Children's Resource Lab for Architecture at Texas Technical University, offered his expertise about children's play, and Professor Richard Longstreth of George Washington University offered assistance in obtaining illustrations. The public realm, too, has made absolutely essential contributions to this book. The University of New Mexico librarians and librarians at the American Automobile Association, the American Institute of Architects, and the United States Department of Transportation have provided excellent assistance. I urge the reader to support our educational infrastructure.

Finally, these acknowledgments invite the reader to be part of my community. I ask you to bear witness to my acknowledgment of a personal debt: I thank my wife for her uncounted hours of editing and, more important, for her sharp intellect and hours of conversation about work far from her field of medicine.

Note on Metric Measurements

Metric equivalents are provided throughout the text. Generally, measurements are given to two decimal places. However, some measurements are rounded either up or down according to the context. These measurements are generally preceded by the symbol "~." In many cases, the reader should use these measurements as guides only. A better solution may be to recalculate formulas with input information in reasonable metric increments (e.g., 8.5 m instead of 8.456 m).

Introduction

No artifact is a work of art if it does not help to humanize us.

—BERNARD BERENSON, 1952

Parking lots are critical to the fate of modern cities. Despite their general lack of architectural design, parking lots are significant public spaces that cover anywhere from 6 to 40 percent of the land in American cities.[1] (See Figure I.1.) Important parts of our lives take place in parking lots. Skateboarders, tailgate partiers, and lovers have made the parking lot significantly more than a place to store automobiles, and public festivities such as the small-town carnival, the farmers' market, the high school car wash, and the Model T rally lay claim to the parking lot as part of the public realm. Society has occupied this public space despite the standard parking lot design.

We cannot afford the standard cheap parking lot design. Typically, zoning codes, banking practices, and real estate norms result in a surfeit of stalls. Empty parking spaces are not only a waste of land and money, but by separating buildings from one another with uninhabited spaces, they undermine the ability of cities to be social places.

When we see parking lots as social spaces, then we understand that the term *parking lot* refers to a variety of

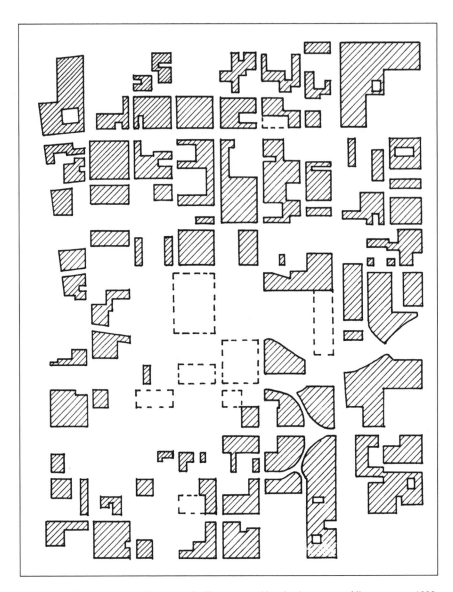

Figure I.1 Figure-ground diagram of off-street parking in downtown Albuquerque, 1996. Hatched areas are surface lots and dashed boxes are major garages. On-street parking and small garages are not shown.

places. The front-yard driveway, a shopping mall's asphalt field, and curbside parking are very different places, yet they share characteristics beyond accommodating storage of the automobile. They may be places of the ceremonies of arrival and departure, and they may be, in varying shades and colors, common ground in which we meet, talk, work, play, or dance as members of society.

The typical design of parking lots as simply a monofunctional expanse of cheap asphalt and a net of white lines is wasteful and destructive. This land, which should be vital and delightful, is often unsafe, environmentally unsound, underpopulated, and ugly. The standard design aims to provide for the safety of cars and their drivers, but once drivers step from their vehicles and become pedestrians, the lot turns into an unfriendly place. Despite their built-in supply of people, parking lots are often barely inhabited and thus are places ripe for crime. Neighbors will not linger long to converse over their grocery carts if the lot has no real shade, if cars continually threaten them, and if there is no place to sit, to get a drink, or to eat a snack.

Because they have been designed simply to hold cars and not to support their use as public space, parking lots have eaten away cities in the United States like moths devouring a lace wedding gown, and they are now moving on to the cities of Russia, Asia, and South America. Unlike the openings of parks and plazas that help define the weave, the holes left by our "functional" parking lots destroy the fabric of a city. Instead of being places to enjoy, parking lots are dull spaces to pass through. When a barren parking lot interrupts a pleasant window-shopping street, it replaces the joy of strolling with the task of moving along and erodes the environment on which the businesses depend.

The public life of parking lots should not be ignored in the suburbs, small towns, or rural centers. Suburbs and smaller settlements are often in even greater need of public places than are cities, and studies in these settings indicate that both municipal parking requirements and the actual supply of stalls far exceed demands.[2] The frequently made argument that pedestrian facilities are not required in the suburbs is assailable on four grounds. First, despite the insults and obstacles, suburbanites and small-town residents *do* walk and *do* "hang out." Second, providing for the automobile does not preclude providing for the pedestrian, bicyclist, and bus rider, and these may provide a secondary clientele for a business. After all, children, bicyclists, and otherwise carless people all buy groceries. Third, better facilities will, according to economic and advertising theory, promote more use. Better facilities are built project by project. Finally, the suburban grocery store lot often already serves crudely as a public square where neighbors meet, community notices are posted, and local public celebrations are held. Much of the environmental and social criticism of suburbs[3] could be addressed by starting with the parking lot.

By advocating more thoughtful design of parking lots, I am not making the cultural criticism, often implied by urban designers, that the car is the sole cause of the unraveling of our cities. During the century since the creation of the automobile, we have made many intertwined changes in how we live together, and we have continually remodeled and rebuilt our settlements. Nor is my aim to promote the use of the automobile. We live in a time that is overinvested in and overdependent on the car. The United States now has more motor vehicles than licensed drivers (Pisarski 1996, 32). However, for better or for worse, the places of cars are key components of our cities. It is the role of architects, landscape architects, urban designers, planners, and other design professionals to make the most of the resources at hand and to add value to building through thoughtful design. I aim to show that parking lots provide a golden opportunity to make silk purses out of a surfeit of sows' ears.

Adding value is not simply a matter of convincing clients to spend more money, but of illustrating how a well-designed parking lot will yield more value for their investment. Designers must show not only that they can provide a judicious supply of parking, but that (1) the space can be used for multiple purposes, including revenue generation,

(2) the attractiveness, safety, and security of the site for clients and employees will be improved, and (3) neighborhood and governmental acceptance of proposed developments can be increased.

Furthermore, it is the design professional's responsibility not just to build for the client at hand but to protect and enhance the commonwealth. Careful design can decrease the environmental harms produced by parking lots and enliven the public realm.

Nevertheless, no matter how well designed our parking lots become, at some point there are too many spaces and not enough buildings to make a city. In many cities, the zoning codes require that new shops devote more land to parking than to the building's actual floor area.[4] The environmental movement's hierarchy of action—reduce, reuse, recycle—should guide our planning and design of parking lots.

We can reduce our need for parking by building compact and mixed-used cities with walkable neighborhoods (like many pre–World War II towns), providing public transportation and high-quality bicycle facilities, sharing transportation, and telecommuting. Furthermore, as design professionals we can report problems with such things as existing sidewalks, curb parking zones, and bike lanes to municipal agencies. Shared parking facilities (Chapter 12), in which, for instance, a church lot is used by a school during the week, allow us to recycle a facility. The patterns in this book are suggestions about ways to reuse parking lots for multiple purposes. Parking garages present significantly different engineering, architectural, and social issues than do parking lots. Thus, although much of this book is applicable to garages, and occasionally garages are discussed, it does not focus on the design of multilevel parking structures.

After a brief history of the automobile and parking lot and a review of the art of making public space, I offer a collection of design patterns to transform the basic parking lot into a delightful public space. Finally, several chapters provide technical information on security and safety, environmental considerations, parking demand analysis, and dimensions for facilities.

Two features of the book are designed to allow quick reference. First, in boldface type at the beginning of each pattern is a brief summary of recommendations. These summaries can be used to skim the patterns and to refresh one's memory. The body of the pattern provides supporting material for the recommendations. Second, technical reference information is assembled into tables.

A recipe's directions and list of ingredients are not sufficient to produce an excellent meal. Likewise, architectural patterns and engineering standards cannot replace design judgment. Public space must be integral with its context, and appropriate recipes must be chosen and seasoned according to the places in which they are used. The design of each parking court or driveway will raise its own questions. What, for example, should be the spirit of the parking lot for a pilgrimage church? Is it appropriate to paint parking stalls at a library with scenes from children's books? To help inform this judgment, I have provided a historical perspective and a rhetorical stance as well as illustrations and technical references. However, there are many aspects of parking that are inadequately studied, and I may have overlooked significant contributions to this poorly indexed field of study. The patterns and tables in *Parking Spaces* should be viewed as my opinion and should in no way relieve the designer of proper care and judgment.

This book is about farmers' markets and public speech, alley basketball and public safety, children's chalk drawings and civic art. This book is about parking lots.

Parking Spaces

An Auto Century

The rise of the automobile industry and the socio-
economic impact of the road and the car are central
to the history of the advanced capitalist countries in
the twentieth century, and explain an especially
large part of the history of the American people.
— JAMES J. FLINK, 1990

The December 11, 1912, issue of *Horseless Age* reported that the mayor of Chicago suggested the establishment of municipal parking lots somewhere along the lakefront to relieve downtown traffic. In 1916, the owner of a livery stable and auction block in Freehold, New Jersey, bequeathed about one and a half acres in the business area for permanent free parking. He also provided an endowment for maintenance of the lot (Sammis 1948). In 1917, a Mr. Goldberg had a shop selling seat covers in Detroit. It was a convenient location, and a customer suggested he could charge for all-day parking (Miller 1988, 10). These milestones mark the beginning of organized parking lots.

A number of researchers have discussed the coevolution of road-building techniques and vehicle design (McShane 1994, Flink 1990, Rae 1971). Better road materials have repeatedly allowed the improvement of vehicle design, and better vehicles have created a demand for smoother roads. Clay McShane, in *Down the Asphalt Path,* interjects a third creature into this relationship: public space.

Streets were once the prime public space of a city, where children played, businesses operated, and people flirted and fought. The rise of automobile traffic required that Americans change their conception of the street from a public room to a place to drive. McShane makes the case that the automobile arose when it did in part because the creation of the first suburbs created an increased demand for the vehicular use of the street. "Automobile technology emerged in the United States not just because of the refinement of internal combustion engines in the late 1890s but because American urban culture changed" (McShane 1994, x). He backs this argument with evidence from the prior half-century of urban resistance to the use of streets (public places) as roadways (traffic arterials).

Since the adoption of the automobile, we have seen that there are many more partners in this evolutionary dance. The supermarket and its parking lot, for example, evolved with the car (Mayo 1993). The automobile street and the parking lot are such dominant species that we have experienced the rise of entirely novel civic ecosystems such as twentieth-century Los Angeles and Phoenix.

Automobile parking is an invasive new species in the 6000-year history of the ecosystems called cities. There are some precursors of the species, and parking has undergone at least four generations of adaptation. A comprehensive natural history of the parking lot would be a fruitful addition to our knowledge of urban dynamics. The following is a brief outline.

B.C. (Before the Car)

The wheel and axle came into use at least 5000 years ago. Existing archaeological evidence places the origin of wheeled vehicles in the region south of the Caucasus Mountains (Rae 1971, 3). The vehicle is perhaps responsible for the road, as the concentration of weight on the wheels demands a "made" surface in a manner that foot and animal traffic does not (Rae 1971, 1).[1]

We know that wheeled vehicles were an important part of early cities. A depiction of a cart found in Ur in Mesopotamia dates from 3000 B.C. (Miller 1988, 3), and archaeological digs show that street corners in Ur were rounded to facilitate turning (Kostof 1995, 52).

The word *parking* traces its origins to the medieval Latin word *parricus,* meaning an enclosure (*Oxford English Dictionary*). The most well-known uses of chariots within Roman cities were the races within the circuses and the triumphal parades celebrating victorious generals. However, Roman cities also incorporated extensive facilities for everyday use of vehicles. In Rome, parking facilities were provided in order to get the chariots off the streets (Miller 1988, 6). In Pompeii, streets had sidewalks, stepping-stone crosswalks (presumably to keep pedestrians above stormwater and manure), watering troughs (Adkins and Adkins 1994, 134), and raised stones that may have marked off parking spaces (Eno Foundation 1942, 14). However, foot traffic and not vehicular traffic was the main means of transportation, and in Roman cities vehicles were banned from daytime use of the city streets in the first and second centuries (Adkins and Adkins 1994, 186).

Nineteenth-Century Antecedents

From the birth of the city until the end of the nineteenth century, pedestrians dominated the use of the street, and walkways frequently occupied as much as half the right-of-way of nineteenth-century eastern seaboard city streets (Pushkarez and Zupan 1975, 15). Boston's citizens, for example, owned only 145 wheeled vehicles in 1798 (Rae 1971, 13), and streets were not only passages but also public space where vendors sold goods, children played, and neighbors met.

This use of the street as a public place was an essential part of the city, and the invasion of vehicles was strongly resisted. In 1769, the first self-propelled highway vehicle was launched down the road by French artillery officer Nicolas-Joseph Cugnot (Rae 1971, 10). By 1835, American railroads used steam power on routes between cities, but attempts to run steam engines on city streets resulted in riots. In 1839, New Yorkers fought against a steam line, and in 1840, residents of Philadelphia rioted against an attempt to construct a steam railroad on streets in the Kensington neighborhood. Major eastern cities banned steam engines and restricted street railroads to horse power. The New York Supreme Court in 1843 supported this ban on steam vehicles, calling them a public nuisance (McShane 1994, 1–13).

From the 1870s to 1900 the 10 largest American cities doubled in population. The accompanying exodus of the middle class to suburbs changed the political calculus on the value of city streets. A significant demand arose to use streets as arteries facilitating traffic from the suburbs to downtown regardless of the consequences for inner-city neighborhoods. An 1890s engineering periodical was the first to use the term *artery* in reference to a street (*Oxford English Dictionary*). Governments shifted from defending the street as public space to promoting suburban travel. For example, the Commonwealth of Massachusetts mandated that if passengers purchased monthly tickets, the railroads should commute part of the fare. Thus was born the "commuter" (McShane 1994, 13). The elevated railway, the electric streetcar, the safety bicycle, and the carriages of the wealthy captured the inner-city streets. The latter two, in particular, paved the way for the automobile.

In *The Automobile Age,* James Flink writes, "Apart from its impact on road improvements in the United States, no preceding technological innovation—not even the internal-combustion engine—was as important to the development of the automobile as the bicycle" (1990, 5).

The modern geared, low-wheeled "safety bicycle" was introduced by James Kemp Starley of Coventry, England, in 1885. The bicycle craze then swept America in the 1890s. Bicyclists were part of the social battle for vehicular use of the street. They were frequently regarded as a menace to public safety and accused of "scorching" (speeding past pedestrians).[2] In return, children stoned bicyclists, and in 1896 the *New York Times* reported that the roads of Long Island were littered with tack-studded strips of leather (Smith 1972, 190). Bicycle groups lobbied to protect their members from harassment and for good roads so that they would not have to ride on the sidewalks (Rae 1971, 29).

In 1897, at the peak of the bicycle craze, New York City passed the nation's first comprehensive traffic code including parking regulations (Smith 1972, 202, and McShane 1994, 51). In the same year, Chicago began taxing and licensing bikes to pay for improved roads (Smith 1972, 224). Although evidence is scant, bicyclists likely established customs about parking machines. The bike, unlike animal-powered vehicles, can be left indefinitely without tending.

Bicycle manufacturers pioneered mass assembly and a host of technical inventions and techniques such as steel frame tubing, ball bearings, chain drive, differential gearing, and the pneumatic tire. Bicycle dealerships were often the first to sell automobiles (Rae 1971, 28), and a number of the early automobile manufacturers were originally bicycle manufacturers (Flink 1990, 5).

The carriage, obviously, also set the stage for the horse-less carriage. Two examples follow. The neighborhood shopping centers that arose in the turn-of-the-century suburbs were often set back from the street behind a grass lawn. A carriage drive allowed the dropping off and picking up of customers. This lawn and drive later transformed into parking lots (Liebs 1985, 30). The parkway, as first proposed by Frederick Law Olmsted in 1868, was a street for the exclusive use of carriages. It provided romantic pleasure drives for the wealthy "carriage set." Because the number of cross streets was limited, and trolleys, bicycles, and other traffic were banned, the parkway also provided fast access across town. The city-owned park on both sides of the street prevented adjacent property owners from having right of access because they did not abut the street (McShane 1994, 34). Olmsted also proposed that homes along the parkway should be detached "villas" with plenty of room behind them for stables.

The parkway and the rise of the early suburbs initiated the transformation of the city street from a social place to vehicular space. The bicycle craze reinforced the vehicular use of the street and provided the technological and entrepreneurial resources for the refinement of the automobile. The infrastructure needed for the carriage—macadam pavements, parkways, livery stables, carriage houses, carriage drop-offs and porte cocheres—provided the environment for the emergence of the automobile.

Four Generations of Automobility

In *The Necessity for Ruins,* J. B. Jackson outlines the history of the residential garage in three phases. The first stage, the Romantic Garage, reflects the early use of the automobile as a toy of the wealthy. These buildings were often architect-designed structures placed well away from the main house, often with a second-story apartment for the chauffeur. The Practical Garage emerged in force around the time of World War I and coincides with the adoption of the car by the middle class. These were often premanufactured sheds just large enough to cover a car and usually placed in the rear of the yard. Finally, after World War II, the Family Garage, attached and integrated into the house with an interior door, began to dominate.

A fourth generation of automobility must be added to

extend J. B. Jackson's phases to the present. From the 1980s to the present, the car has served as a mobile living room or an office. As the car has become more weather-resistant, the residential garage has begun to relinquish its role of regularly housing the car. Garages are often becoming home offices, meeting rooms, repair shops, and other extensions of the world of work.

This classification of residential garages works well to organize the history of other places for the car—with the caveats that important subthemes exist, periods overlap, and aspects of previous periods persist through later developments. For example, the Brimmer Street garage in Boston of the 1980s is a reincarnation of the original turn-of-the-century automobile garages, with valet parking, waxing service, and attendants to gas up your car.

The Experiment, circa 1895 to circa 1910

The first wave of automobility was washed onto American shores by the press. The Paris to Bordeaux to Paris automobile race of 1895 received extensive coverage and sparked the imaginations of many. About 500 patents relating to the automobile were filed that summer, and the magazines *Horseless Age* and *Motorcycle* were first published by the end of the year (Flink 1970). In 1900, the trade magazine *Automobile* observed, "The unprecedented and well nigh incredible rapidity with which the automobile industry has developed . . . is largely due to the fact that every detail of the subject has been popularized by the technical and daily press . . ."

The horseless carriage was at first an ultra-elite version of the elite carriage. The early purchasers of motor vehicles were mainly wealthy businessmen. The Automobile Club of America, founded in 1899, was said to have more millionaire members than any social club in the world (Flink 1970). In 1907, the Club opened an eight-story clubhouse and a 300-car garage in New York City (Flink 1970). Downtown garages were necessary because most cars did not have tops and early car paint needed to be protected from the weather. In the garages, cars were washed, repaired, tuned, and most important, simply stored—for within the cities and suburbs there were few other places to keep them.

The invasion of the public street by the wealthy in their automobiles continued the battle for control of the streets begun by the bike and carriage. In 1901, a Wall Street chauffeur killed a two-year-old playing in the street. Neighborhood residents assaulted the chauffeur, whom they considered to have invaded their territory. In 1903, children in a New York City neighborhood stoned a wealthy woman's car, knocking her unconscious (McShane 1994, 176).

Figure 1.1 The necessity to remove play from the street is reflected in this November 1907 cartoon.

(*Harper's Weekly,* Nov. 1907, p. 1611.)

William Eno, a man of independent wealth, had for years devoted himself to a crusade to organize street traffic. Based on his "rules of the road," in December of 1903, New York City adopted an extensive traffic code that included assigning the roadbeds to vehicles and the sidewalks to pedestrians. These rules codified the occupation of the public realm by the car, and the government began clearing other uses from the street. (See Figure 1.1.)

By 1909, new places for the variety of outdoor activities that had previously taken place on the street were emerging. Off-street food markets started replacing on-street public markets, and an extensive transformation of the private home had begun. The article "Converting Back Yards into Gardens: The Happiness and Economy Found in Cultivating Plants and Vegetables" in the April 1909 issue of

Craftsman, for example, extolled the virtues of transforming the backyard from a work yard into a garden oasis—a place to enjoy nature and for children to play.

The movement to keep one's car at home, however, had also begun. On October 23, 1902, *Motor World* urged the construction of home garages: "In contradistinction to a horse stable, an automobile house can always be made attractive. . . . Consequently its proximity to the house is an advantage rather than a drawback." Architects were hired to design these automobile houses. They were often elaborate buildings with an apartment for the chauffeur and repair facilities such as a pit and overhead hoist (Figure 1.2). By 1910, most of the domestic garage types had been established. All of the garage door types we use today— hinged, accordion, horizontal track, and overhead—had been refined, and the carport, the semiattached garage with

Figure 1.2 Detached garage with chauffeur's quarters designed by McCreary, Wood, and Bradney, before 1911.

breezeway, the drive-through garage, the porte cochere, and the detached, attached, and integrated garage had all been designed by architects (Gebhard 1992).

Parking at destinations followed the manners of the horse-drawn carriage. Cars were either parked along the curb, or the owners were dropped off and picked up by the driver. By 1905, many livery stables offered temporary storage and even rented automobiles.

However, even while the germination of automobility was dominated by the elite, the roots of middle-class adoption of the car were strong. Physicians were the best-represented group of early automobile owners because, as *Automobile* observed in 1908, "First and foremost, the doctor invests in an automobile for business use." The auto was more reliable and went farther and faster than the carriage, and thus was a great benefit to doctors on their rounds of home visits. There was resistance to elitist control and widespread belief that the car would soon be the main means of transportation. For example, *Motor World* in 1901 wrote in reference to the actions of the millionaire-dominated American Automobile Club, "No club, no matter how rich or exclusive its membership may be, can arrogate to itself the right to pose in any way as supreme ruler of the present or future of the motor vehicle."

The press helped in other ways to promote middle-class adoption of the car. Numerous "reliability" races were sponsored by manufacturers and newspapers. Perhaps the most audacious of these was the 1908 New York to Paris auto race. The route across the United States, the wilds of Siberia, and the capitals of Europe was considered by many patently impossible. No car had ever driven across Alaska or Japan or Siberia. Six cars entered, five finished (Fenster 1996). This race and others settled the issue of automobile reliability and, more significantly, captured the hearts of many Americans. As J. M. Fenster wrote of the race, "Something had changed during the running: timid people had come to realize that a car itself was a road, in dreams, and that it might lead anywhere at all" (1996, 77).

The Liberator and the Parking Problem, circa 1910 to World War II

One of the four definitions of the word *parking* in the *American Heritage Dictionary* is "kissing or caressing in a vehicle stopped in a secluded spot." One of the two definitions of *parking lot* is "a traffic jam." Both of these slang usages arose during the second generation of American automobility when the middle class took up the car.

By the time the Ford Motor Company opened its Highland Park Plant on January 1, 1910, to make Ford's "car for the masses," the middle-class market for cars was established. The practicality of cars had been by then adequately demonstrated. The most dramatic demonstration was the 1906 San Francisco earthquake and fire. To meet that crisis, military and civic officials drafted about 200 private cars for emergency uses. Automobiles took over where horses had died, ran with few failures, delivered food and aid, and helped keep civic order.

More subtle proofs had also been made. Motorized fire patrols, ambulances, and police cruisers had been purchased by many cities during the first decade of the century, and by 1908, New York City had built the first municipal garage. In 1909, President Taft replaced the White House horses with autos, and the U.S. Postal Service began its first substantial use of autos (Flink 1970).

As Ford's Model T rolled off the Highland Park production line in ever increasing numbers, automobility began to transform Americans and their cities. New mores and manners gave rise to new or vastly expanded types of places, both for activities driven from the public streets by use of the automobile and for car-related activities themselves.

By the teens and twenties, the public space of the street belonged in law and deed to vehicles. As streets became arteries, playgrounds were built, public markets were removed from the streets, and vendors were banned from the public right-of-way. Most "City Beautiful" plans of the early twentieth century advocated playgrounds (McShane 1994, 223). The removal of public food markets from the street had begun in the streetcar era. By the 1920s most of the street markets were gone, and the off-street public market was well on its way to becoming the suburban supermarket (Mayo 1993).

While places for activities dislocated from the street burgeoned, places for the automobile also proliferated. In 1927, the United States Senate built the first underground garage, which included a tunnel to let Senators go from office to car protected from the weather and the public (Hackman and Martin 1969, 1–3). Lovers' lanes, motor courts, and gas stations appeared. The latter two set the stage for the car to escape the arteries and invade the tissue of the city.

Before World War I, adventurous motorists began to travel the country camping along the road. After the war, so many people began auto-camping that landowners began to object to the litter and invasion of privacy. Towns, eager to capture tourism, responded by establishing free tourist camps with off-street parking and restrooms. These facilities in turn gave way to cabin camps and then to motor courts. Chester Liebs argues that these motor courts with their cabin-side parking were prelude to post–World War II suburbs: "The little cabins offered individual housing in a mini-suburban setting—enabling depression-era city dwellers to rent a freestanding, grass-surrounded dream cottage" (Liebs 1988, 181).

The gas station also invited the car off the street and set the precedent for other drive-in services. In 1905, the first gas station with a hosed dispenser and paved drive-through off-street lot opened in Saint Louis, Missouri (Vieyra 1979, 4) and began replacing the livery stable and private garage as the place to fuel. By the 1920s, the big oil companies were operating their own gas stations. These buildings departed from the normal city pattern of street-oriented buildings that filled their sites and touched each other along property lines. Gas stations have traditionally been separated from their neighbors by a ring of asphalt parking and designed not as part of the street but as independent sculptures. Stations of the 1920s included one that looked like the airplane the *Spirit of Saint Louis* and ones that were meant to be space stations. At the same time, some stations were built as stand-alone "miniatures" reflecting the City Beautiful movement. Beacon Oil Company, for example, built a set of "classical" stations with domes recalling Jefferson's University of Virginia buildings (Vieyra 1979).

This new-fashioned city created by the automobile also created modern problems. The *Saturday Evening Post* coined the phrase "traffic jam" in 1910 (McShane 1994, 193). By the summer of 1915, morning and afternoon rush-hour gridlock overtook every large American city. On-street parking received much of the blame. "Newark . . . reported a 48 percent increase in traffic between 1913 and 1915 at its major downtown street intersection, now reduced in travel lanes because of shopper and commuter parking. In Washington D.C., where parked cars occupied 30 percent of the downtown street space, rush hour speeds declined below 6 mph" (McShane 1994, 194). Two types of solutions were proposed: (1) street widening and construction and (2) providing off-street parking. (See Figure 1.3.)

Urban street widening and construction has continued unabated since then and is one of the major stories of the modern American city. It is interesting to note that a 1907 article in *Municipal Journal and Engineer* observed that street improvements had not eased traffic mobility but resulted in exactly the opposite. The 1925 authoritative book *Street Traffic Control* demonstrated that "any reasonable increase in street capacity . . . will not reduce the den-

Figure 1.3 Lamppost parking.

(Cartoon from the *Los Angeles Times,* 29 February 1920, II-1, courtesy Richard Longstreth.)

sity of traffic" (McClintock 1925, 4).

In 1921, 90 percent of the passenger cars were still open models with no tops (Miller 1988, 9). Thus, for long-term parking, covered garages were necessary. For the wealthy, the earlier system of private garages and chauffeurs continued. A 1929 *Architectural Record* article on garages states, "It is now necessary in large city garages to provide a lounging room for chauffeurs, equipped with games and with reading tables." In any case, the majority of the garages had valet parking. Lonnie Hackman and Norene Martin date the creation of the self-park garage to 1926 (1969, 1–2).

For much of the middle class, however, the curb provided downtown parking. Organizing this haphazard abandonment of cars along the curb into the well-regulated system of curb parking we have today was one of the first major traffic management tasks. In 1916, a Cleveland study recommended parking regulations, including parallel parking within 6 inches of the curb and 30-minute time restrictions (*American City Magazine* 1916, 702). (See Figure 1.4.) A significant portion of the 1925 *Street Traffic Control* is devoted to regulation of the "Standing Vehicle," and it strongly deplored the continued practice of backing to the curb. Parking meters did not join this system until 1935, when they were installed on the streets of Oklahoma City.

The idea of organized parking lots spread rapidly in the teens. Auto commuters wanted to take over public spaces for parking. Cadillac Square in Detroit and market squares in Dallas, Boston, and Newark were taken over for parking

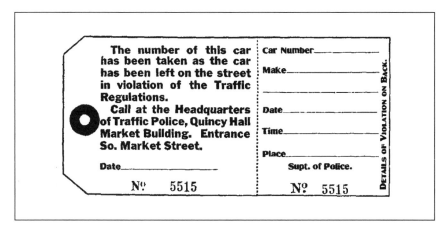

Figure 1.4   1920s Boston parking ticket.
(*The American City Magazine,* July 1920, p. 32.)

lots. There were proposals to carve parking lots into Washington D.C.'s Mall and to build a 30,000-car parking lot in Central Park (McShane 1994, 206).

But all of these efforts—building garages, regulating curb parking, and converting public spaces to parking lots—did not sate the demand for parking. In 1923, Columbus, Ohio, was the first city to require off-street parking in its zoning ordinance (Miller 1988, 10), and parking first appeared as its own category in the index of *American City* in 1927. The 1928 Radburn Garden City development incorporated attached garages on cul-de-sacs, and a 1929 *Architectural Record* article promoted "A House for the Motor Age." (See Figure 1.5.)

Thus cars captured the street and public squares and invaded building

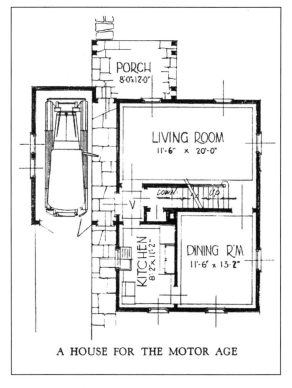

A HOUSE FOR THE MOTOR AGE

Figure 1.5   A House for the Motor Age.

(*Architectural Record,* Feb. 1929, p. 197. Copyright 1998 by the McGraw-Hill Companies. All Rights reserved. Reproduced by permission of the publisher.)

lots. Still, parking remained an unsolved puzzle. In the February 1929 issue of *Architectural Record,* Ernest P. Goodrich wrote, "The place of the garage in City Planning is one of the most troublesome of all planning problems." The years of depression and war in the 1930s and 1940s did little to settle this problem.

The Car as Companion, World War II to circa 1980

After World War II, the working class entered the car market. Cars had become common conveyances, not toys for the rich, and the assistance of servants was no longer a given. Traffic engineering texts of the late 1940s and 1950s describe valet parking as the old system and self-parking as the coming wave (Burrage 1957).

By 1956, only about 16 percent of parking spaces in big cities were along the curb (although these spaces served 50 percent of the parking demand) (Burrage 1957, 135). The idea of the arterial route had become more refined, so that even parking was no longer a legitimate use of the street. In the 1957 book *Parking,* Burrage and Mogren wrote, "Streets are primarily intended for travel, and a basic policy should be that whatever part of the street is needed for free movement of traffic must not be used for parking."

To remove parking from the street, so-called blighted areas had been demolished for parking lots; new housing often incorporated the "domesticated" attached garage that had been advocated in the 1920s; and a whole set of descendants of the drive-in gas station, such as drive-in banks, restaurants, and movie theaters, were built.

The suburban shopping center adrift in a sea of parking is another of the gas station's progeny. Highland Park Shopping Village in Dallas (1931) was the first suburban center with stores turned away from street, but it wasn't until the 1950s Northgate in Seattle that the classic mall took hold (Flink 1990, 155). In *Main Street to Miracle Mile,* Chester H. Liebs chronicles the rise of other drive-in buildings.

This massive dedication of land to the automobile failed to relieve traffic congestion or to solve what engineering textbooks called "the parking problem." Nonetheless, it did generate other parking difficulties. With more and more land and money dedicated to the automobile, pedestrian and public transit systems deteriorated. Buildings became isolated functions instead of part of an overlapping ecosystem of places, and the streets and courtyards of the city became mere mechanisms for driving and parking.

As early as the 1930s, the urban design consequences of parking lots were widely discussed. A 1937 article in *Architectural Record* described Los Angeles as "a series of parking lots interspersed with buildings," and *American City* ran an article in 1938 entitled "A Parking Lot That Is Not an Eyesore." By the 1950s, the automobile gave rise to the expansive suburb and the commercial strip, and parking had completely transformed or destroyed many downtowns and city neighborhoods.

Architectural Forum observed in 1950 ". . . the shopper could be pulled almost anywhere . . . by what the downtown district so signally lacked—a place to park the car" (Liebs 1988, 28).

The average number of parking spaces in medium-size towns and cities (5000 to 100,000 population) increased fivefold between 1972 and 1980. In small towns there were more than 12 times as many stalls in 1980 than just eight years before (Miller 1988, 1). In 1960, there was 1 car per 3.8 Americans. In 1990 the ratio increased to 1 car for every 1.8 people (Hanson 1995, 18). Surface parking now covers 30 to 40 percent of the downtown area of many smaller cities (Miller 1988, 1).

Beginning in the 1970s, some cities have begun to tame parking with caps on the number of downtown stalls (e.g., Portland, Oregon, and Boston, Massachusetts), waivers of the number of stalls otherwise required by zoning (Boulder, Colorado), and financial incentives not to provide employee parking (California). The parking problem is no longer how to provide enough stalls, but how to reclaim the city from the parking lot.

The Car as Room, circa 1980 to the Present

The car has become a well-appointed room, with digital sound, office equipment, passenger VCRs and game tables for child care, and an infinitely variable view. The number, variety, and sophistication of businesses operated primarily from trucks have grown—delivery services have boomed, architects have established branch offices in vans, and small shops repairing everything from broken windows to copy machines rove our streets.

As the automobile itself is becoming more of a place, a small movement to civilize the parking lot is also emerging. One approach has been to find ways to hide the parking lot. Underground garages and alley lots are seen as ways to have

Figure 1.6 Billed as "an interesting innovation in automobile parking stations," this 1924 parking lot included a terra-cotta gas station, a glass conservatory for the sale of flowers, and a stage for "the use by the city or any other civic organization for evening, Sunday, or holiday band concerts, or other civic entertainments."

(*The American City Magazine,* December 1924, p. 588.)

your car and your city, too. The original era of valet garages is also making a comeback. In Boston, New York, and Chicago, condominium garages offering valet parking, shuttle service, and car care are arising in wealthy urban neighborhoods.

A parallel approach of enriching the places of parking is also emerging. In the early 1980s, Columbus, Indiana, sponsored the Carscape Competition for the innovative design of a downtown parking lot and, with the Irwin-Sweeney-Miller Foundation, published *Carscape: A Parking Handbook.* Since then, there have been articles in *Landscape Architecture* and *Planning* documenting "parking lots that are not eyesores." This movement, of course, has historical precedents. Stately residential garages, complete with chauffeurs' quarters, well-regulated curb parking, and parking lots with civic facilities (Figure 1.6) were built in the first era of the automobile. Perhaps these are the seeds of a new generation of civil parking.

CHAPTER 2

The Art of Public Space

When civilized people require a cup of coffee it is not because they need to drink coffee but because they have felt the need to renew their contacts with humanity.

—DE CRESCENZA, 1988

Public Space

The London Coffee House was established in 1754 in Philadelphia, Pennsylvania (Figure 2.1). The house, a great streetside shed, and the street itself were the places where many of the instigators of the American Revolutionary War gathered and debated. The *Pennsylvania Journal* was published from the Coffee House. After the Declaration of Independence was first publicly read, the king's arms, taken down from the chambers of the British Supreme Court in Philadelphia, were carried in procession and burned in the middle of the street in front of the coffeehouse (Scharf and Westcott 1884). This was a public place.

Two hundred years later, parking lots are prime candidates for public space. The First Amendment to the U.S. Constitution aims, in part, to protect the life of such public places. The freedom of speech and the right of the people to peaceably assemble are essential aspects of the public realm. The First Amendment, however, simply limits the government's actions and protects actions essential to public space. It leaves open the questions of what constitutes

Figure 2.1 Woodprint of the London Coffee House.
(Scarf and Westcott 1884.)

public space, how public spaces are created, and what makes a great public place. This book rests on two major assertions in answer to these questions.

The first assertion is that public places are created by public life. All the world is a stage—*when* people act on it. The public realm is wherever people may, and do, come of their own initiative to speak and act together. It is a place to see and be seen, to listen to whomever is there, and to speak to whomever will listen. It is fundamentally an occasion taking place, not a space, that dictates behavior. Thus, a city-owned space that is used only to hurriedly walk through is not manifesting the public realm. A discussion that takes place over grocery carts in the parking lot is in the public realm.

The customs and rights of landownership, however, may disrupt or support the practice of the public realm. Ideally, the places for public activity are held in common, with all citizens having full rights of access and unabridged freedom of speech. This is rarely the case. It is questionable, for example, whether U.S. citizens may now freely assemble on publicly held land in the middle of a busy city street and burn the British flag.

Nevertheless, despite constraints, the public realm does function for many purposes, under less-than-ideal conditions. Even a parking lot restricted to company employees and hidden from general public view may host the public realm. It is collective space in which members of a society casually or formally meet each other and engage in un-planned or planned conversations. The U.S. Supreme Court, for example, has held that employers must allow employee organizational activities on company property under certain conditions.[1] A later federal case expanded this right to allow outside organizers to dispense leaflets at a shopping center parking lot.[2] I will use the term *civic space* to mean both the ideal public space and a place where the public realm is con-strained to a limited group or to a limited set of rights yet still functions as public space.

Because it rests on communication and direct contact, the public realm is primarily a pedestrian activity. However, as drivers, we do occasionally participate in public dialogue. People parked in their cars often lean out their windows and partake in conversation; drivers honk in support of pick-eters; and "cruising" may be seen as an elaborately cos-tumed public promenade.

When people regularly come together in a particular place, the place itself begins to signify the public realm. It becomes a place to go if you want to run into people and talk. The place develops a character that evokes previous public meetings and actions. When the place starts to show physical signs of public occupation, such as artwork, deco-rations, or furnishings supplied by the public or accommo-dations for the props of public festivals or markets, then the public has begun a kind of permanent claim to the space and its meaning.

Figure 2.2 Public space—Santa Fe Farmers' Market, 1997. The farmers' market turns a parking lot into an active public space. Citizens are using this manifestation of public space to protest expansion of a parking lot at the Santa Fe ski area.

The common activity of people is the primary creator of civic space. Thus, rather than relying on their ability to form new spaces that will then hopefully create civic space, architects should first search for places that already show signs of being civic space. Instead of abandoning the parking lot as a prospective civic place, designers should support its inherent features as a place of arrival and gathering. (See Figure 2.2.)

The second assertion is that architectural design can provide choice ingredients to make a more inviting public realm. The physical design of a place can increase the access to and recognition of a space as a civic place, and it can increase the feasibility, ease, and pleasantness of using the space for public activities. The American Revolution could readily have happened without the London Coffee House. Perhaps, however, if the meetings, discussions, and rallies had to take place in and around a private home or the chambers of the British Supreme Court, the character and eloquence of the Declaration of Independence would have suffered.

Furthermore, design should not simply *allow* public use, but should facilitate public use and reflect the fundamental dignity of civic space. As Kevin Lynch wrote, "Spaces should not merely support the activities that occur within them—they should visibly support them" (Lynch 1984).

In their book *People Places,* Clare Cooper Marcus and Carolyn Francis (1990, 6) offer extensive criteria that summarize research on what makes successful civic plazas. They conclude that the best places are accessible oases designed as both comfortable social settings and as visual art. These places (1) are woven into the city and sidewalk, (2) give the message that the place is open and available, (3) promote the sense of belonging necessary to make it a good place to hang out, (4) have temperate microclimates, and (5) offer sensory complexity. Greater detail on each aspect follows.

City Weaving

Public commons are successful for the same reason that any real estate development is successful—they fulfill a public desire in a prime location. That is, they thrive in the appropriate habitat.

The most frequently used plazas are in the areas of greatest land-use density (Whyte 1988) and diversity (Chidister 1986). This density and diversity of uses must be within about 900 feet of the plaza, as that is their primary pedestrian catchment, although their influence often extends up to a five-minute walk, or approximately 2000 feet (Figure 2.3). They also benefit from integration with the pedestrian system (Marcus and Francis 1990, 18). A commons on a busy street corner makes an active meeting place for two sidewalks. Plazas that link the sidewalk to an active pedestrian source such as a subway entrance or parking lot can also be well used.

Open and Available

The freedom to enter a space is not simply a legal matter. In *Defensible Space,* Oscar Newman (1972, 63) outlines a number of symbolic architectural signs that can be used to define private space—gateways, a short run of steps, and changes in the texture of the pavement. Plazas must avoid creating these kinds of barriers. From his studies of plazas in New York City, William Whyte concludes that what is most important in the success of a plaza is the location of the space (as close to the busiest part of the city as possible) and its relationship to the street. He writes, "A good space beck-

(a)   (b)

Figure 2.3   Plaza catchment. (a) Santa Fe Plaza, circa 1846: 900-foot (~275-m) and 2000-foot (~610-m) catchment radii from the plaza. The core is within the 900-foot radius, and the bulk of the settlement is within the 2000-foot radius. (Base map: J. F. Gilmer, U.S. Army Corps of Engineers.) (b) Santa Fe Plaza, 1995: 900- and 2000-foot catchment radii. Note that the core of downtown, the majority of large hotels, and the only parking structures are near the 900-foot radius and that the government buildings and most large buildings are within the 2000-foot radius. Single hatch denotes parking structure; crosshatch denotes large hotel; 1 = state capitol; 2 = post office and federal building; 3 = city hall; 4 = county building.

ons people in, and the progression from street to interior is critical in this respect. Ideally, the transition should be such that it's hard to tell where one ends and the other begins" (1988, 130).

It is important to note that this ease of psychological access is a subtle matter. Places like Waterfall Park in Seattle that are designed as roofless buildings have walls along the sidewalk, and yet, as evidenced by their popularity, they are open and inviting. Waterfall Park's entry is wide and unobstructed, and a passerby can easily see into a delightful place occupied by seating, sunny planting beds, and people eating. These clues may be culturally specific, and a designer should carefully observe local examples to see how they function.

Plazas below the grade of the sidewalk are well used only if there is a major attractor (e.g., ice skating) and if the levels are composed as part of one integrated space. For example, sunken plazas may be designed as outdoor theaters with viewing balconies, stairs made for seating, and lampposts or other elements that rise from the plaza level above the street level to connote a ceiling.

In addition to symbolic barriers, physical barriers must be considered. Public space must be accessible to the elderly, the handicapped, and children. Particular care must be taken with the design of the ground surface. Trips and falls make up almost 75 percent of liability claims in parking lots (Ellis 1996).

In the design of space open to the world, there is often a concern about the activities of "street people" and off-hours vandalism. Jane Jacobs's observation that "eyes on the street" provide the foundation for public safety has been corroborated by other researchers (e.g., Newman 1972) and has become a basis of community policing. Places actively used and watched over by the community are not likely targets for crime. Squares should have caretakers, be well lit, not have hidden back corners, and in some cases should be able to be closed during the night (see Chapter 10).

Hanging Out

Once you have successfully invited people into a public space, it should be a good place to be. Ninety percent of plaza use is for hanging out—sitting, watching, and listening, often combined with eating or reading (Marcus and Francis 1990, 9). These uses are "edge uses" rather than "field uses." That is, people hang out along the edges of spaces, and anchors such as seats, walls, poles, or trees enhance good "edge" sites (Joardar and Neill 1978, 489).

Parking is a "field use" and can complement a public square as long as it doesn't dominate the space and is placed to increase the amount and variety of edge places. The car hood is often the best seat.

Three design elements shape a place's role as public hangout: seating, activities, and size.

Seating is, perhaps, the most critical aspect of public space design. Seats are major props on the public stage and thus should be designed to enhance a variety of interpersonal interactions. William Whyte writes, "Ideally, sitting should be physically comfortable. . . . It's most important, however, that it be socially comfortable. . . . Choice should be built into the basic design" (1980, 28).

To accomplish this there should be lots of seats. San Francisco's 1986 Downtown Plan requires 1 linear foot of seating for each linear foot of plaza perimeter. The seating should offer a variety of types (e.g., chairs, ledges, grass), orientations, and groupings. About half of the places to sit should be informal seating (planter edges, stairs, mounds of grass, etc.)—places that do not look like empty seating when not in use (see Sitting and Leaning in Chapter 6).

Activities should be programmed for the space. The presence of other people and food are the great attractors. Sidewalk cafés, hot-dog vendors, and farmers' markets bring people to a place and provide an excuse for them to stay and initiate conversations with strangers. Food is the basis of civilization in more ways than one.

Other things that enliven a place include concerts and political rallies, street artists, and entertainment for children and adults such as water-related activities, interactive public art, rollerblading, and game areas (chess tables, boccie courts). Support functions such as newspaper racks, drinking fountains, automated teller machines, bulletin boards, telephone booths, and mailboxes can give a steady flow of life to a square during nonpeak hours. The Project for Public Spaces recommends that a minimum of 50 percent of the rooms facing a communal space directly serve that space (entries, stores etc.). Where the facade is not open to the inside but is a blank wall, the plaza space in front of the wall should be made into an exciting part of the commons (fountain, sunny sitting area, trees, etc.).

Research has not been able to establish recommended sizes and shapes for public space. I believe that this is because a good sense of enclosure, although taking many forms, is dependent on the social use of the place, the urban context, and the details of the place. The dimensions of a baseball park would be inappropriate for an outdoor café. What constitutes a strong sense of enclosure remains an architectural judgment. Square and Courtyard in Chapter 4 discusses factors that inform such a judgment.

Microclimate

A temperate microclimate is the range of local weather conditions physically pleasing to a person who is in casual clothes. Sunlight, temperature, humidity, and wind are the main components of microclimate. Public space should be a sheltered space that has a more temperate ambiance than the surroundings.

In northern climates, access to sunlight is critical. In hot climes, sunlight needs to be carefully shaped. Above about 55°F (12.7°C) there is a considerable increase in the use of public spaces. Above about 75°F (23.8°C) shade is required for comfort. In arid climates, the sound, smell, or virtually any sign of water increases comfort. Rain, however, dampens outdoor activity, but the active street life of London, Paris, and Seattle indicates this is not insurmountable. Umbrellas, awnings, glass roofs, arcades, and quick-drying furniture help make outdoor spaces viable in wet climates. Winds in excess of 7 to 8 miles per hour (~12 kph) disturb hair, flap clothing, and make sitting uncomfortable (Marcus and Francis 1990, 25–27). Noise control and balanced lighting are also critical ingredients of the climate.

Sensory Complexity

The smell of food, the music of street performers, the rustle of trees, the aroma of flowers, the feel of sunlight, and a view of people going past are some of the joys of being out in public. Commons succeed based on how harmoniously they provide an environment of pleasing sensory complexity. Various studies have shown that bare, monotonous plazas are poorly used (Marcus and Francis 1990, 19). Sensory complexity is built of three elements: the placement of the space in the landscape, the square's materials and forms, and the flow of activities.

A plaza can be set in the landscape to provide views of a city and its lands. Parking lots from lovers' lanes to sunset beaches have become public spaces simply by virtue of the view. Views of human activity such as ice rinks, the parade of the sidewalk, and boat docks also bring life to a public space.

The form and furnishing add to the sensory depth of a commons in two manners. Colors, forms, textures, and patterns create the sculptural landscape, and chairs, interactive fountains, game courts, platforms, and other props provide social stages for impromptu play.

As described under Hanging Out earlier in this chapter, scripted uses, such as the morning chatter of vendors, mail delivery, lunch concerts, the rounds of meter maids, and the evening performances of street artists, provide a rhythm of life to public places. Designing and budgeting for these scripts is part of creating successful urban commons.

Even the most crowd-loving of us, however, can be overwhelmed if the sensory complexity of a place greatly exceeds our ability to make sense of it. This ability varies from person to person and time to time. Thus a plaza should not be verging on riot all the time. Part of the joy of a public festival is drinking a quiet cup of coffee the following morning among the fallen confetti.

Nicias said to the Athenian soldiers on the beach at Syracuse, "You are yourselves the town, wherever you choose to settle . . . it is men that make the city, not the walls and ships without them."[3] In the design of civic space for a democracy, an architect should follow the collective practices of the people. Wherever they freely come together is public space. The architectural art of public space aims to provide comfort for and proclaim the dignity of citizens talking together. When this art is applied to the parking lot, we can create vital civic places.

The following chapters contain patterns of design that support the creation of civic places. They all rest on the following beau ideal:

The Car Commons Pattern

People naturally meet and talk where they park their cars. Therefore, design parking lots as car commons that are symbolically and physically accessible urban outdoor rooms, are delightful places to talk, have a full palette of sensory experiences, and include a comfortable microclimate. Provide for the comfort and dignity of the citizen as pedestrian and as driver.

CHAPTER 3

Parking Ecosystem

No new feature such as this typical twentieth-century device [the automobile] can come into our lives without making a place for itself, causing readjustments in our scheme of things.
—JOHN TAYLOR BOYD JR., 1917

Parking lots are keystone species of our cities. They not only are indicative of the health and character of cities, but they are also critical components that constrain and sometimes dictate the form of buildings and streets. Large, individually owned, streetside parking lots are, for example, emblematic of suburban commercial development. More fundamentally, typical zoning code requirements for suburban parking, along with the precedent of adjacent complexes, make it nearly impossible to develop a building that varies significantly from the suburban type.

Niche

Each species of parking, from curb to courtyard, has its niche. In other words, the various types of places to park interact with each other, with other means of transportation, and with buildings and the street. The interaction is complex.

Competition between the automobile and other means of transport is perhaps the most obvious type of interaction.

Doubling the daily downtown parking charge, for example, can increase use of transit for work trips by one-half (Hanson 292), but as the widespread success of park-and-ride lots demonstrates, transit and parking may also work synergistically.

Furthermore, the fitness of any species depends not only on its integration with adjacent buildings and streets but on the type of parking provided nearby. If, for example, four rows of parking separate the sidewalk from its buildings, curb parking loses much of its utility. Likewise, off-street lots may be reduced or eliminated if parking-row streets can be established. I conducted a survey of a 1940s-vintage shopping center with parallel curb parking, angled curb parking, a parking courtyard, and a typical off-street lot, all of which have direct pedestrian access to the shops. I found the following hierarchy of parking preferences: The courtyard and the parking street had the highest occupancy; curb parking stalls along the busy streets were occupied nearly as frequently; and all had significantly more use than the parking lot.[1] Detailed review of the data suggests that distance from the driving lane (i.e., curb parking is closest to the driving lane, and stalls that require multiple turns from the driving lane are far away) strongly influences the preference for parking spaces. Additionally, directness of pedestrian access, which was roughly equivalent among types in the study, is a critical factor. Thus, the stalls of a streetside parking lot were often occupied before curb stalls when curb parkers would have to walk across the lot to get to the buildings.

Building types and parking have also adapted to each other. The drive-in theater, which arose with the domestication of the car, is a prime example. The fast-food joint, the suburban bank, and the three-car-garage tract home are also products of the coevolution of cars and buildings.

Social use and form also influence each other. In the previous chapter, "An Auto Century," I outlined the interaction between public space and traffic facilities. A second illustration is the interaction between the form of parking and the social class of ownership. As the middle class became car owners, the majority of parking facilities changed from valet parking to self-parking. Changes in design standards have also generated new social uses. For example, smooth asphalt pavements with slopes to area drains have unintentionally led to the use of parking lots as prime sites for skateboarding.

Habitats

Districts or ecosystems (e.g., the commercial strip, main street, the office park) have a characteristic balance of these interactions that is not simply a sum of the individual buildings, streets, and lots. New proprietors continually remodel buildings, new buildings are built, and old ones are torn down, yet the form and character of these districts persist.

Districts endure because they represent an investment in a way of doing things and because the parts reinforce each other. For example, a successful store on Main Street attracts customers. These customers park their cars along the curb or walk from their offices and penthouses and pass other stores which, if they cater to pedestrians, then benefit from this pedestrian traffic. Along the suburban strip, a successful store attracts drivers. These drivers pass other stores which, if they cater to drivers, then benefit from this auto traffic. For this reason, it is very difficult to have a successful neighborhood walk-in restaurant in the midst of the commercial auto strip.

Yet districts do change. The most substantial sources of change come from incremental evolution due to changes in society's values and the incremental invasion of the district by buildings and uses associated with a neighboring district. For instance, the wharves of Boston, San Francisco, and Seattle, built as industrial areas, are now commercial and residential districts. Occasionally, outside forces such as fires or urban renewal cause massive change. The current beauty of Santa Barbara, California, arose from the conscious reshaping of the city after the 1925 earthquake, and modern Chicago arose from the ashes of its great fire of 1871.

However, in many of these cases there is remarkable resilience. Chicago, after its fire, retained its street pattern. London, perhaps, gives one of the best-known examples. Despite significant efforts to the contrary, London was rebuilt in its own image after the great fire of 1666 (Kostof 1991, 113). In *The Architecture of the City,* Aldo Rossi gives numerous examples of the permanence of form. This permanence suggests that (1) because these ecosystems are persistent we should keep long-term consequences in mind when developing new districts, and (2) to reform existing areas we must understand their internal dynamics and make incremental catalytic revisions. The perceptive and persistent nudge is, particularly in the absence of crisis, more effective than the revolutionary vision.

Some types of districts have proven to be remarkably well rooted in American cities and conducive to "good city life." Following are some that I believe offer a fruitful balance between public space, types of access, and parking while leaving room for a variety of architectural and social characteristics. Attention to the distribution, pattern, and type of parking areas is critical to the vitality of these ecosystems. A pedestrian shopping street such as State Street in Santa Barbara or "The Ave" in Seattle may appear to function with little parking, yet an examination of adjacent streets shows the success of the district rests on curb parking and an integration of parking into back lots and structures. The pattern of parking is critical to the creation and vitality of a district.

The Walking City

Recognize that within vital downtowns the majority of trips are on foot and that a significant number of vehicular trips are by bicycle and local public

transit. Build generous and delightful walkways with a minimum of curb cuts for vehicles. Provide bicycle parking, bike lanes, and bike-activated traffic signals. Give mass transit priority over car traffic with bus malls or subways. Provide curb parking and public garages or alley lots to support pedestrian access.

"In cities such as Chicago, Philadelphia, and New York, from 70 to 80 percent of all intra-downtown trips are walking trips. In addition, a significant percentage of the total trip length of all trips by car is also by walking. Yet, approximately 50 to 70 percent of the downtown is devoted to vehicles" (Federal Highway Administration 1978, 2).

Not only is the land area devoted to cars disproportionate to their market share, but the investment in pedestrian facilities in terms of public money and regulation of private property often pales in comparison to automobile infrastructure. Newman and Kenworthy, in *Cities and Automobile Dependence* (1989), postulate a correlation between the attractiveness of a central city area (i.e., a place for rich and easy encounter, a place of exuberance and exaltation of the human spirit) and the amount of parking. New York, Toronto, and San Francisco, for example, have higher attractiveness ratings and fewer parking spaces per person than Detroit and Houston. Perhaps, if parking areas are made more social and pleasant places, then the apparent conflict between parking and enjoyment of the city can be reduced.

I do not advocate banning the car from downtowns, but rather suggest that cities invest more in what they do best—provide a public place for people to meet. Many cities have developed downtown design guidelines. Portland, Oregon's 1983 Downtown Design Guidelines provide a strong example of actions that can protect and enhance the pedestrian system.

Provisions for the pedestrian may mean that the traffic capacity and speed of downtown streets should be reduced. Establishing wider sidewalks where pedestrian use is high

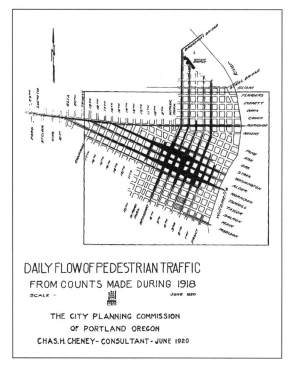

DAILY FLOW OF PEDESTRIAN TRAFFIC
FROM COUNTS MADE DURING 1918
SCALE -   JUNE 1920

THE CITY PLANNING COMMISSION
OF PORTLAND OREGON
CHAS.H.CHENEY- CONSULTANT- JUNE 1920

Figure 3.1 1918 pedestrian density map for Portland, Oregon.

(*The American City Magazine,* July 1921, p. 48.)

may require reclaiming space from traffic lanes. (See Figure 3.1.) Long walk cycles at intersections give pedestrians priority and slow down cars. On-street parking reduces traffic speed—and streets are considerably safer when that traffic is slow. "In successful downtowns, [general car] traffic," Toronto urban planner Ken Greenberg says, "should move at the speed of a horse and buggy" (Mitchell Pacelle, *Wall Street Journal,* May 15, 1997). Neighborhoods like New York's Greenwich Village and downtown Santa Fe, New Mexico, are lively, prospering places because they are pedestrian environments in which the car is forced to travel at about 20 miles per hour. Some great pedestrian shopping streets such as the Champs-Élysées in Paris and Michigan Avenue in San Francisco have faster speeds and more traffic, but they also have very wide and well-designed sidewalks.

As the patterns in the following chapters suggest, parking is part of, and may be integrated with, the rest of the pedestrian realm.

Christopher Alexander and others suggest that when the land area devoted to parking cars is greater than about 9 percent, the storage of cars begins to dominate over the perception of the city as a place for people to be in public (1977, pattern #22). Only about 1.8 percent of midtown Manhattan was used for surface parking lots in 1969 (calculated from Pushkarev and Zupan 1975, 57), but some 1980s' estimates of other American cities indicate that 30 to 40 percent of downtown land is given over to parking (Miller 1988). Albuquerque in the 1990s has over 50 percent of its downtown dedicated to parking. Research is needed on the extent to which the percentage of land devoted to parking, and/or other measures of parking density in a district, correlates with land costs, occupancy rates, volume of business activity, trips by transit or foot, measures of citizen and tourist preference, and other indices of the vitality of a downtown.

Local Main Streets

(Re)establish and/or add to the vitality of neighborhood main streets. Eliminate curb cuts and provide curb parking along the main street. Provide diagonal curb parking along side streets, and establish hidden parking lots off the alleys.

Many of the neighborhoods or districts of our cities were once independent towns with their own governments, neighborhoods, and main streets. The founding structure of these "captured towns" is an asset that should be built upon rather than submerged. In newer neighborhoods, efforts

Figure 3.2   Curb farmers' market along downtown street in Lancaster, Pennsylvania.
(Postcard from the collection of David K. O'Neil.)

should be made to emulate the advantages of captured towns. An unofficial but ceremonious government may be established to promote, perpetuate, and shepherd the public life of the town. The main street should continue as the forum, civic center, market, and parade ground. To serve in this role, parking must support but not overwhelm the street. Side streets could provide diagonal curb parking (see Slow Streets, Chapter 4); curb parking could line the main street (see Figure 3.2); and parking lots could be hidden off the alleys (Hidden Parking, Chapter 4) and used for weekend markets, summer outdoor movie festivals, and street hockey competitions (Chapter 8).

Rail Suburbs

Build a walking district around rail stations. Provide neighborhood facilities at the core and pastoral amenities at the periphery. Walkways, bicycle parking, and automobile drop-offs should have direct access to the station. If a large park-and-ride lot is necessary, it should double as fairgrounds, farmers' market, and/or other public gathering place and include an orchard or other garden. (See Figure 3.3.)

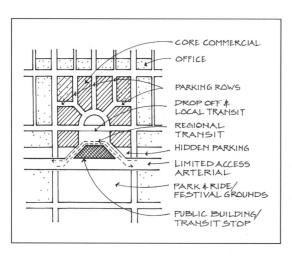

Figure 3.3 Diagram of parking for core area of a rail suburb.

The earliest American suburbs were built around rail stations, with local shopping and community facilities near the station and access to the countryside at the edges of the development. Commute trips were by rail, and intrasuburb trips were by foot, bicycle, or carriage.

The ideal of the suburb was expressed by the Garden Cities movement in the early part of the twentieth century. In the book *Garden Cities of Tomorrow,* Ebenezer Howard wrote, "Human society and the beauty of nature are meant to be enjoyed together." The ideal rail suburb provides access by train to a large urban downtown, has a local commercial and social district around the rail station, and is surrounded by farms and other open space. Both the urban core and the pastoral edge should be within walking distance of the houses. This cultural root is deep in the United States. Even Thoreau's cabin on Walden Pond was near a commuter train line providing him access to the commuting society of Boston (McShane 1994, 14).

Peter Calthorpe's transit-oriented development as presented in *The Next American Metropolis* is an updated version of these early satellite and garden cities that admits the automobile in place of the carriage.

The pedestrian, bicycle, and carriage roots of the rail suburb should be primary design considerations, with automobile parking woven in as a supporting characteristic. Thus walkways, bicycle parking, and drop-offs (Kiss and Walk, Chapter 4) should provide the main access to the station. If necessary to promote transit over driving to center city, provide side streets with diagonal parking rows and perhaps a park-and-ride lot. The park-and-ride lot should be landscaped with an orchard or other garden and serve as a large public gathering space for farmers' markets, fairgrounds, and other events (see Calming the Seas, Chapter 4). Care should be taken to give psychological primacy and actual physical ease of access to pedestrians, bicyclists, and people dropped off over those parking at the park-and-ride.

Streetcar Streets

(Re)establish streetcar lines or bus streets. Particularly with bus service, make physical improvements to the street—bus shelters, timed signals, bus lanes, or electric bus lines—to demonstrate a commitment that service will remain on the route. Eliminate driveways across the streetcar street's sidewalks, and provide parking on side streets and alleys. (See Figure 3.4.)

(a)

(b)

Figure 3.4   Streetcar streets. (a) SW Morrison Street, Portland, Oregon, circa 1900. (Oregon Historical Society Neg. OrHi 9937, used by permission.) (b) SW Morrison Street, Portland, Oregon, 1994. (Oregon Historical Society Neg. Lot 824-44, used by permission.)

From Richmond, Virginia, to Boston, Chicago, Seattle, and Los Angeles, many of our cities' close-in neighborhoods were founded as streetcar suburbs. Unlike rail lines and subways, streetcars and buses may pick up and let off passengers at many points along the line. Thus, instead of having a focal point like the rail suburb, streetcar streets form lineal neighborhoods.

Trolleys have been reintroduced in places like Galveston, Texas, to reinforce the character of a historic district and to entertain tourists. However, trolleys can do more than provide amusement. In 1997, Royal Oak, Michigan, established trolley service expressly to help alleviate a parking problem by providing service between various parking lots and businesses. Businesses along the line can purchase a trolley stop for $1500. It's estimated that the fees from 10 such stops, fares, and ad space on the trolleys will cover the cost of operating and maintaining them (*The Parking Professional,* September 1997).

Parking along a trolley line does not need to be concentrated near a station but can be spread in small increments along intersecting side streets and alleys. If at all possible, alleys should be provided, parking along the main street should be allowed only where it does not interfere with transit service, and streetside driveways should be eliminated to reduce their interference with transit service and pedestrian traffic. The amount of parking can be reduced from the amount otherwise required because the transit service provides access to the main street and circulation from shop to shop along the street. A continuous band of land approximately 2000 feet deep along the street is within walking distance. (See Catchment, Chapter 6, for walking distance information.)

In order for developers and remodelers to reduce their reliance on parking because of the transit service, they must be assured that the service will remain on the street. A bus route, for instance, can easily be moved to another street. Literally, they must be able to bank on the continued presence of transit service. Trolley tracks, electric bus lines, bus shelters, wide sidewalks, and other structural investments in improving the street for transit can provide tangible evidence of a commitment.

In addition to the transit service, organizational support can help businesses along a streetcar street reduce their reliance on parking. Pedestrian and transit ridership counts can build the case for reduced parking. Street improvement districts can organize shared parking and raise taxes to improve sidewalks, provide transit stops, and supply bicycle parking.

Streetcar streets can expand a pedestrian district beyond the limits of Americans' willingness to walk, provide tangible proof of a civic commitment to public transit, maximize the opportunities for reduced and shared parking, and attract people to a district.

Modifying the Strip

Work to (re)introduce the pedestrian into existing commercial auto strips. Provide and connect pleasant sidewalks from complex to complex to encourage people to park and walk to multiple stops. Provide pleasant walks and bike paths from adjacent neighborhoods to encourage those nearby to walk. Alter zoning regulations to eliminate minimum parking requirements, place parking to the side or rear of buildings, allow mixed-use and multistory development, and require pedestrian, bicycle, and (where possible) bus facilities. Look for existing nodes of pedestrian-friendly buildings and encourage their growth.

We cannot afford to ignore the existing miles of auto-dominated commercial strip developments. They are significant parts of our economic and cultural landscape, in which much is invested, and we cannot expect to abandon or massively reconstruct them. We can, however, seek to incrementally improve them.

Despite poor and discouraging facilities, some people do walk, ride bikes, and take the bus to and along the auto strip. Many more would do so if the facilities were graciously developed. Site development plans should be specifically reviewed for the connectivity of sidewalks—people should be able to walk directly, safely, and pleasantly from store to store and to adjacent neighborhoods (Chapter 6).

Parking lots should be (re)developed to support walking and as places for outdoor events (Chapters 4, 6, and 8). In new developments, parking should be placed to the side or rear of buildings, and zoning should allow mixed-use developments that may share parking among the various uses.

On many older strip streets, there are remnants of older commercial districts with buildings fronting the sidewalk and parking to the side or rear. Cities should improve the sidewalks and other infrastructure of these nodes, place bus stops to serve them, revise zoning regulations, and otherwise support their growth.

Campus

Build car-free gardens and grounds that house a set of buildings for an institution. Construct a well-defined edge to the campus but do not isolate it from the city or countryside with a ring of parking lots. Instead, edge the campus with streetcar streets, local main streets, or neighborhoods with live-end streets. Provide hidden parking and courtyard parking in pockets outside of and within the campus. Provide many parking and transportation options and coordinate services with the adjoining neighborhood. (See Figure 3.5.)

The word *campus* was first used to describe the grounds of Princeton and comes from the Latin for "field" (*Oxford*

Figure 3.5 From *Cable on Academe,* by Carole Cable. Copyright © 1994. Reprinted by permissions of the author and the University of Texas Press.

English Dictionary, 3910). It has come to be loosely applied to collections of buildings such as office parks, medical complexes, and so forth. For the purposes of this book, I define a campus as a set of buildings of an institution collected within the bounds of a pedestrian precinct and set among landscaped grounds.

Campuses should not be confused with compounds or cloisters, which are closed and set apart from the city. Thus, the pedestrian world of the campus should be integrated with and flow easily into the pedestrian system of the surrounding city. Parking lots should not create a moat around the campus. Instead, the edge of the campus should be primarily buildings and gardens, and on-campus lots should be courtyards and gardens served by generous pedestrian pathways.

If parking is hidden on the side of a streetcar street opposite the campus, then local businesses will be supported by those who park and walk past on their journeys to and from campus. Additionally, trolley ridership will be promoted because riders will have shorter walks than drivers.

The campus should be connected to adjacent residential areas by pedestrian and bicycle paths integrated with the residential street system. Neighborhood traffic-calming measures and neighborhood parking districts that restrict non-resident parking are often needed so that campus parkers do not overwhelm the neighborhood.

On many university campuses, space for parking is becoming scarce, there is no room to grow into adjacent neighborhoods, and there is little money to subsidize structured parking. Thus alternatives to simply providing more parking spaces are required. Susan A. Kirkpatrick, parking administrator for the University of Michigan, suggests that the scope of campus parking services be expanded in two ways: (1) Provide a menu of transportation services, from high-cost reserved parking to low-cost park-and-ride service to bicycle lockers and well-designed and maintained walkways; (2) coordinate with the adjacent municipality, neighborhoods, and businesses to share and integrate transportation systems (Kirkpatrick 1997). The excess parking capacity of shopping malls, for example, can be used by students if business-hours bus and after-hours taxi service is provided.

Districts with Live-End Streets

Compose residential districts with a grid of pedestrian and bicycle paths, but with limited through routes for automobiles. Provide local transit service (streetcars or buses) along the edges of the district. Park cars along the streets and the alleys, leaving the sidewalks free of curb cuts.

In the interest of better living conditions, England's Public Health Act of 1875 established the Bye-Law [*sic*] street ordinance. It required wide and straight paved streets and banned cul-de-sacs. By 1906, in the interest of better living conditions, Raymond Unwin convinced Parliament to pass the Hampstead Garden Suburban Act, which suspended parts of the Bye-Law ordinance and allowed the creation of cul-de-sacs. This conflict about the fitness of the cul-de-sac continues to the present. In the spring 1995 issue of the *Journal of the American Planning Association,* Robert Cervero and Roger Gorham present data supporting the transit-supportive nature of a grid of streets. In the same issue, Oscar Newman supports the formation of cul-de-sacs by closing through streets to support neighborhood security. Lost in this battle are a range of intermediate solutions (Childs 1996).

Residential districts that are composed as a network of streets can be strategically closed to automobiles but allow passage of pedestrians, bicyclists, and emergency vehicles—"live-end" streets. Traffic-calming techniques such as 90° parking and shared streets (Slow Streets, Chapter 4) should be used along entranceways to define the district as a place

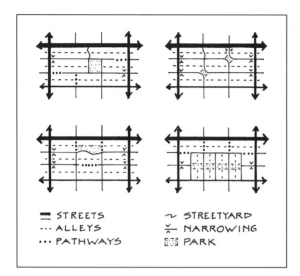

STREETS
ALLEYS
PATHWAYS
STREETYARD
NARROWING
PARK

Figure 3.6   Network of streets allowing pedestrian, bicycle, and alley access, but calming automobile traffic.

where cars are guests. Likewise, "knotting" the streets in a neigborhood (reducing the number of ways to go straight through a neighborhood) can discourage through traffic while retaining multiple access points (Figure 3.6). Either system provides quiet neighborhood streets and gives human-powered transportation direct routes of travel.

Sidewalks should be provided unless the streets are clearly developed as streetyards where the pedestrian has right-of-way. The Federal Highway Administration (FHWA) reported that residential areas *without* sidewalks had a highly disproportionate share of pedestrian collisions (Knoblauch et al. 1988). In order to encourage sidewalk use and reduce the significant hazard of driveway backing-out accidents, leave the sidewalks free of curb cuts by parking cars along the slow residential streets, at the street closures, and off alleys. Build narrow streets and use the saved resources for generous sidewalks and planting strips and to lower the cost of the houses (Southworth and Ben-Joseph 1997, chapters 5 and 6). Provide local transit service (streetcars or buses) along the edges of the district and make the farthest house no more than 2000 feet by sidewalk to a bus stop.

Industrial Spines

Compose industrial districts along main transportation routes such as freeways, rail lines, and ports. Provide factory outlets, restaurants, and other support services along intersecting local roads. Concentrate truck parking in work yards along the industrial road, and place well-forested employee parking as a buffer to adjacent districts. Share use of the employee lot with the factory outlets and other retail uses. (See Figure 3.7.)

In earlier eras, industry tended to concentrate along ports and rail lines. The flexibility of access offered by the truck has tended to disperse industries to cheap land across the suburban landscape. Unfortunately, this also distributes truck traffic and the concomitant large roads and other industrial infrastructure in an uncoordinated fashion throughout a region.

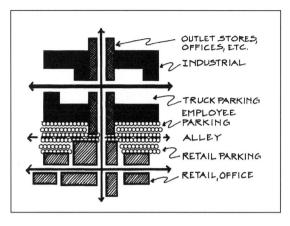

Figure 3.7 Use parking to transition from industrial areas to other districts and to serve as multiple-use areas.

Industrial areas, on the other hand, should not be treated as menacing alternative worlds and segregated into large compounds. The edges of industrial areas can serve as interfaces to the community with factory outlets, restaurants, banks, and other support services. Employee parking lots can then be used in the afternoon and on weekends for shoppers and/or company-sponsored sports (Chapter 8).

Car Commons

This basic idea of city planning is the clear recognition of the fact that no one can accept responsibility for any smallest element in the complex unit that we call a city without participating also in the joint, undivided, and complex responsibility for the future excellence or inferiority of the city as a whole.

—FREDERICK LAW OLMSTED,
THE AMERICAN CITY MAGAZINE, 1913

Ninety percent of the time, private cars are not transporting us down the road but are parked somewhere. There are approximately seven parking stalls for every car in an American city. The cumulative effect of all these stalls can rip the fabric of a city apart and make it wearisome to walk. The large parking lot is often a disorienting no-place, separating fragments of the city. However, some thought about the character and the location of parking lots can reduce their tendency to disjoint a town.

Parking should be placed to support, rather than replace, the pedestrian life of the city. The following patterns suggest places that may help integrate parking with the fabric of the city. To be successful, the particulars of the site and surroundings must shape the details of the design. Building entrances, the continuity of window and sidewalk shopping, curb cuts, sidewalk widths, bus stops, and the other features of the pedestrian infrastructure need to be respected and improved.

Provide parking to support the city rather than simply individual buildings.

Figure 4.1 Parking tucked away underneath a bridge approach.

Nooks and Crannies

Unused spaces under bridges, along levees, and in odd parcels can house a few cars in what otherwise would be a weed patch. A small car commons can improve these spots and keep the cars from claiming valuable building or street space. (See Figure 4.1.)

Because cars can be housed in places unsuitable for other uses, this should be the first place we look to put them. Care should be taken, however, not to think about this as sweeping them under a rug. Landscaping, lighting, and other amenities should be provided to improve a derelict space and weave it into the fabric of the city.

Public agencies such as the Federal Highway Department and the city power company own a fair amount of residual land. The space near and under power lines, the underside of bridges, and the fragments of land around freeway interchanges can all be used for parking without taking up land that can be put to better use.

Figure 4.2 Curb parking—Carmel, California, 1996.

Meter Made

Provide curb parking wherever possible. Design for emergency vehicle access and pedestrian and traffic safety. Give priority to vehicles based on their ability to generate pedestrian traffic. (See Figure 4.2.)

The curb is the most efficient place for parking in terms of time it takes to park, utilization of stalls, and amount of land per stall. In 1997, the average vacancy rate for metered spaces in the

United States was 6 percent (Kuzemka 1997). Burrage (1957, 80) reported that in large cities curb parking provided 16 percent of the stalls yet met 50 percent of the parking demand. Curb parking minimizes the number of intersections of pedestrian paths and auto lanes and provides a barrier between pedestrians and traffic lanes. Metered curbs also provide revenue. On average, meters return $2.80 for every dollar spent to install and maintain them, and three tickets are issued for every meter per month (Kuzemka 1997). Chicago issues about 4 million parking tickets a year and generates about $75 million from the violations (*The Parking Professional,* July 1997, 16). New electronic meters are beginning to offer a wide range of possible ways to manage curb parking. New York City, for example, has experimented with prepaid cards that allow delivery vehicles to pay for only the actual time they are parked.

However, traffic engineers have a long-standing canon against curb parking. In their 1957 book *Parking,* Burrage and Mogren wrote, "It has been stated as doctrine that the demands of traffic, together with safety considerations, have priority over parking in the use of street space" (1957, 83). Virtually every traffic engineering text since has restated this canon. Supporting arguments are as follows: From 10 to 20 percent of all nonhighway accidents are associated with curb parking; curb parking reduces the traffic capacity of a street; and curb parking can obstruct emergency vehicle access (Weant and Levinson 1990, 242).

The first of these arguments has been inadequately studied. Since we must park, the relevant question is, "Where is it safest to the general public to locate parking?" The data do not yet answer this question (Chapter 10). However, the location, design, and regulation of curb stalls can improve their safety, reduce their effects on traffic lanes, and minimize the conflict with emergency vehicle access.

In 1935, Oklahoma City planted the first parking meters. Meters are now a major revenue source and a significant tool for managing parking. Not only can we design for how long people may park, but we may regulate who parks and when, where, and how they park.

Who

The curb is valuable real estate. Trucks, buses, taxis, emergency vehicles, and private vehicles vie to use the curb. Emergency vehicles' priority is incontestable. Fire trucks must have unobstructed access to hydrants, and ambulances must have a clear way to the hospital. One indirect benefit of providing drop-off stalls is that they often make available extra space near building entrances for police, fire fighters, and ambulances beyond that which is normally reserved for emergency equipment.

After emergency access, curb space should be assigned to maximize pedestrian use of the sidewalk. Bus stops, for example, should usually have clear priority. Taxi stalls and private-car drop-offs should be given space where they are productive. Finally, meters should give priority to short-term parkers over all-day parking.

Truck loading and parking for the mobility-impaired clearly must be provided. However, in both cases the curb often does not provide adequate operating space and access. Alleys and service drives can provide for the delivery of goods, and off-street stalls often provide the best access for the mobility-impaired. However, if curb stalls are provided they must meet ADA standards (Chapter 13).

When

The value of the curb lane can be maximized through time-sharing or metering the space. There is no easy formula to determine how a curb lane should be apportioned. Traffic and parking studies can provide information about the characteristics of different uses (Chapter 12), but because it is a question of providing privileged use of public property, the question is fundamentally political. Merchants, for example, may depend on workers staying downtown an hour after work and demand the rush-hour use of the curb for parking rather than transit.

Some typical patterns of distributing curb time follow. Table 4.1 shows typical maximum meter times for different conditions. In 1997, 46 percent of meters in the United States were set for 2 hours and 33 percent for 1 hour, with an average fee of 50 cents per hour (Kuzemka 1997). There appears to be a trend toward reducing the public subsidy of parking by installing 8- and 10-hour meters where commuters had previously parked for free. During the morning and evening rush hour, downtown curb lanes may be cleared of parked cars to give buses a quick route. On weekend mornings, the curb lane may be converted to café or sidewalk-sale space (Figure 4.3).

Figure 4.3   Curb life—Pismo Beach, California, 1997.

When it is not possible to provide truck access elsewhere, the curb may be reserved in the early morning or other off-hours for deliveries. Delivery restrictions, however, require enforcement. In a 1998 pilot program aimed at reducing double and other illegal parking, New York City provided commercial drivers with prepaid electronic cards that allow them to pay for only the exact number of minutes they park at a meter.

Table 4.1   Meter Times

Category	Time	Location
Drop-offs	15 min	Banks, post offices
Drop-offs	15–30 min	Transit stations
Short	30–60 min	Near quick-service establishments—bakeries, cleaners
Medium	2–3 hr	Downtown fringe areas to discourage all-day parking
Commuters	8–10 hr	Where there are no significant short-term parking needs

SOURCE: Adapted from Weant and Levinson 1990, 250.

Where

Table 4.2 summarizes where parking is prohibited by the Uniform Vehicle Code and Model Traffic Ordinance (National Committee on Uniform Traffic Laws, 1987). Additionally, curb parking should be designed to allow drivers entering the street to see oncoming traffic.

How

Stall markings are essential to any complex regulation of curb space; additionally, they have been shown to reduce the average time it takes to park (Burrage 1957, 87). One critical feature of parallel parking is the maintenance of sufficient room between parked cars for parking and unparking maneuvers. One approach is to reserve space between pairs of cars for parking maneuvers (Figure 4.4). Table 13.12 shows stall dimensions for buses, trucks, and other vehicles.

Table 4.2 Curb Locations Where Parking Is Prohibited by Model Traffic Code

Distance	Location
In front	Driveway
Within	Intersection
Within	Bus stop
Along	Excavation or obstruction when parking would obstruct traffic
Along	Any highway bridge or within any highway tunnel
Along	Any controlled-access highway
Within	Any stall marked with an International Access Symbol without authorized display of the symbol
Within 20 ft (~6.1 m)	Crosswalk
Within 30 ft* (~9.2 m)	Safety zone
Within 15 ft (~4.6 m)	Fire hydrant
Within 30 ft approach side (~9.2 m)	Traffic sign or signal located at the side of a roadway
Within 20 ft (~6.1 m)	Fire station driveway
Within 75 ft (~22.9 m)	Fire station driveway on opposite side of street
Within 50 ft (~15.3 m)	Railroad crossing
As marked	Where official traffic-control devices prohibit parking

* May be modified by signs or markings.

Except when the street is a low-volume, low-speed street (Slow Streets, ensuing), parking should be parallel to the curb. Angle parking can provide double the number of stalls per curb length, but parallel and angle parking are similar in terms of square footage of land required per stall (Table 11.1). Furthermore, numerous studies have shown that angle parking on *busy* roads causes significantly more traffic accidents than does parallel parking.[1]

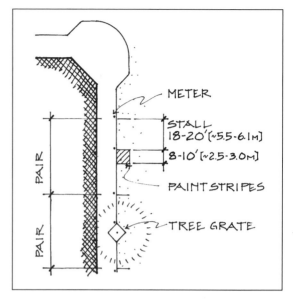

Figure 4.4 Paired curb parking. Either painted stripes or a tree planter may serve to retain space for maneuvering in and out.

METER FORM

Meters are typically planted 18 inches from the curb and 2 feet from the front of a stall (Weant and Levinson 1990, 253). Many cities color meters to indicate maximum time limits or that parking is prohibited during peak hours. However, it appears that the legibility and clarity of such time-limit indicators could be greatly improved by an innovative public art project.

Meters provide a secondary function of defining the sidewalk. They add a rhythm and provide an implied edge to the walking area. The zone between curb and meters is out of the flow of pedestrians and serves as a place for car passengers to disembark, people to stand, and street furniture to be placed.

STREET DESIGN

The United States Department of Transportation has conducted preliminary investigations of measures to reduce pedestrian accidents associated with curb parking (DOT HS-801, 346). Three designs appear promising: median barriers, adding midblock crosswalks, and diagonal parking on one-way streets.

Kiss and Walk

Drop-offs can encourage ride sharing, transit use, and remote parking. They can also complement pedestrian and bicycle access. Without giving the automobile a place to stay, drop-offs provide access for small children, people who have packages, and those who have difficulty walking. Whenever the driver may be expected to leave the car (e.g., hotels, schools, day care) off-street loops should be considered; otherwise curbside is the most time- and land-efficient location for drop-offs. (See Figure 4.5.)

We should jump at the opportunity to encourage a single car to do the work of two or more vehicles. Convenient drop-offs at commuter stations can discourage parking while increasing transit use. Drop-offs at offices can increase accessibility for the mobility-impaired. Whenever designated drop-offs are provided, at least one stall must be van-accessible. This van-accessible stall may be used by other vehicles (Chapter 13).

Figure 4.5   Hotel drop-off and porte cochere—Luxor Hotel, Las Vegas, Nevada, 1997.

Slow Streets

The appropriate balance of uses varies on different streets. The parking row, alley, and streetplaza are all streets in which traffic movement is not primary. Along busier streets, parking allées can support the sidewalk with on-street parking and reduce conflicts with traffic flow.

Since the invention of the automobile, streets have become increasingly single-purpose arteries, emphasizing through traffic over people and local uses (McShane 1994). Much of the social life of the street, from parade route to playground, has been driven off. Parking can be a significant component of "calm" streets.

Parking Rows

Short side streets in commercial areas with little through traffic are prime places to park. (See Figure 4.6.) Because these streets are not major traffic routes, the slow speeds and blocked traffic produced by angle parking are accept-

Figure 4.6   Parking row.
(Copyright 1998 Talbott Houk.)

able. If the street network allows efficient circulation, these streets may be one-way, allowing double-sided angle parking on a narrow street.

Alley

The alley deserves more respect and more care than it is typically given (Figure 4.7). In commercial districts, the alley can relieve the street of truck loading and garage entrances. In residential areas, garage shops, basketball hoops, gardening sheds, garage offices, and guest houses can all share space with parking and transform dark alleys into lively commons.

In both commercial and residential cases, care must be taken to compose the alley. Lighting must be adequate. Spaces off the alley should have angled sides allowing passersby to see all the way into them from more than 12 feet away so that they do not appear to offer hiding places

Figure 4.7 Residential alley on Capitol Hill, Seattle, 1997.
(Copyright 1997, Elaine Thomas.)

Figure 4.8 Streetplaza—Pike Place Market, Seattle showing pedestrians, vendors' stalls, and automobiles sharing use of the street.

for strangers, and as many activities as possible must fill and oversee the alley.

Alleys may serve a number of utilitarian functions, but they should not be treated as dumps. Garbage cans and dumpsters should be in fenced alcoves, and other utilities should be integrated into a pleasant space. Alleys should be paved to maintain their utility and good repute. However, alternative paving materials such as grass and concrete pavers, brick, or a pair of concrete wheelways may be helpful to differentiate the alley from the street and signal that cars should proceed slowly.

Streetplaza

The streetplaza is a street shared by automobiles and pedestrians in a commercial area (Figure 4.8). Streetplazas are similar to streetyards in residential areas, in that the pedestrian has the right-of-way over the entire street and the car is induced to slow down to the pace of the pedestrian. However, instead of playgrounds, cafés and places for vendors or musicians may be created in the right-of-way.

To provide as many spaces as possible and to help slow down traffic, parking is often at an angle to the traffic lanes. Curbs are not usually provided because they tend to restrict pedestrian movement. Rather, bollards, trees, and other devices prevent autos from encroaching into areas reserved exclusively for pedestrians. Entrances to streetplazas from traffic-dominated streets should be clearly marked. A clear change in pavement color and texture, gateways, overhead banners and lights, and a narrow passage may help form the entrance.

Parking Allée

Along classic boulevards such as the Champs-Élysées in Paris, parking is provided in access lanes called *contre-allées* (Figure 4.9). These consist of one or two parking lanes with a single aisle lane. Entrances and exits are limited, and parking is restricted along the center street. This reduces the conflict between parking cars and through traffic. It also allows a continuous sidewalk and building line. The grace of these streets, however, is the rows of trees planted between the main traffic lanes and the allée and along the sidewalk. These form a barrier between the arterial and the pedestrian world, provide shade and delight to the sidewalk and parking lanes, and help organize the street into a coherent place. This line of trees elaborates the threshold between traffic and sidewalk into a park.

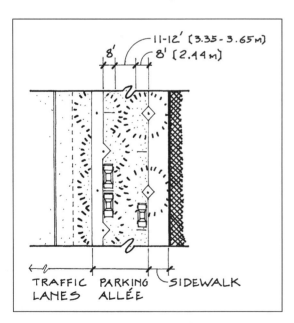

Figure 4.9 Parking allée with two rows of parallel parking.

Square and Courtyard

Build public spaces that allow some parking. Design these spaces primarily as outdoor rooms with a sense of enclosure, a comfortable microclimate, and sensory complexity. Provide parking that does not dominate the space. (See Figure 4.10.)

The traditions of urban public space design need not be abandoned because of the presence of automobiles. The medieval town square and the castle courtyard accommodated wagons, carts, and carriages and were outdoor living and meeting places. The descendants of these public spaces may allow parking.

The square is a public commons. Although a major public building such as a church or town hall may dominate the buildings around a square, many other buildings help define the common area. Squares typically are well connected to the street system and have multiple entrances.

On the other hand, the courtyard, according to the *Oxford English Dictionary,* is "an open area surrounded by walls or

Figure 4.10 Parking lot as square. Entry #5 by Karahan/Schwarting Architecture Co. in the Carscape competition.

(Used by permission. C. Miller. 1988. *Carscape: A Parking Handbook,* Irwin-Sweeney-Miller Foundation, Columbus, Indiana, p. 47.)

buildings within the precincts of a large house, castle, homestead, etc." The courtyard is the commons for a single institution and may have a single entranceway to the city.

This distinction in a space's inclusiveness is critical to the design of a public place regardless of legal ownership. A courtyard may be tailored to a select public and serve as the public face of an institution. A square must serve the general public. Issues of integration with the city, character, and control turn on this nicety.

Nevertheless, both courtyard and square serve as communal spaces. Parking can complement the communal use of a public space if it doesn't overwhelm it. The coming and going of vehicles and people, the delivery and pickup of goods, the edges and informal trunk and hood seats provided by parked cars can add life to a courtyard. For special events, cars can be banned and the field of parking space used for activities (Chapter 8).

The quality of both spaces also rests on a sense of gracious enclosure. Courtyards and squares must be designed as the primary room of its set of buildings, not as the space left over between buildings. The size of the space affects its intimacy. For example, beyond 65 feet it becomes difficult to read facial expressions. Thus, if a space is larger than this it includes people who are simply figures rather than people with whom you could potentially communicate. (Table 4.3 lists rough distances that alter relationships between people.)

Overall size, however, is mediated by the creation of subspaces. The well-used portions of plazas are places subtly subdivided from the whole by trees, seats, or other permeable edges, allowing multiple entries (Marcus and Francis 1990, 29). They must be small enough that a person sitting alone feels comfortable (roughly less than 40 feet [12 m] on a side). On the other hand, they must be large enough that people may enter without feeling they are intruding into a

Table 4.3 Perceptual Distances

	Notes	Reference
1.5–2.5 ft (.45–.76 m)	Close personal distance. People can easily touch each other.	Hall 1966, 119
2.5–4 ft (.76–1.22 m)	Arm's length. The viewer's 15° cone of *clear* vision covers the upper face of subject.	Hall 1966, 120
4–7 ft (1.22–2.13 m)	"Umbrella space." Close social distance. The viewer's 1° cone of *sharp* vision covers one of the subject's eyes.	Hall 1966, 121
7–12 ft (2.13–3.66 m)	Far social distance. The full figure of the subject is visible at a glance. This is the end of the "circle of involvement."	Hall 1966, 122
12–25 ft (3.66–7.6 m)	Public distance. A person can take evasive action to move away. The viewer's 1° of *sharp* vision covers subject's entire face.	Hall 1966, 123
45 ft (13.7 m)	Can see a face clearly.	Lynch 1971, 194
40–80 ft (12.2–24.4 m)	"Pleasant human scale" plaza.	Lynch 1971, 194
65–80 ft (19.8–24.4 m)	Maximum distance to read facial expressions and recognize a person.	Gehl 1987 / Lynch 1971, 194
230–330 ft (~70–100 m)	Maximum distance to follow events.	Gehl 1987
450 ft (~137 m)	Limit of successful historic enclosed squares.	Lynch 1971, 194
4000 ft (~1220 m)	Limit of detecting a person.	Lynch 1971, 194

private room (roughly allowing 12 feet [3.6 m] or more from an entry to an occupant), or so small that only four or five people will fit (a café table). Plazas that have large spaces for citywide events (e.g., Siena's Piazza del Campo) can feel alive and full of people even when a large space is empty if they are lined with subspaces. Parking areas can help form these subspaces.

Parking on the Side

As an alternative to the strip-mall practice of placing parking in front of a building, revive the older pattern and provide a parking courtyard to the side. Bring the building flush to the sidewalk and place the entrances on the sidewalk. Provide space for vendors, street furniture, automated teller machines, landscaping, and other uses to maintain the vitality of the sidewalk along the parking court. (See Figure 4.11.)

Figure 4.11   Parking on the side. Supermarket in Seattle, Washington. Note the active pedestrian frontage.

Prior to World War II, many car-oriented buildings retained a sidewalk frontage. Grocery stores and motels, for example, often had parking to the side and their main door on the corner facing the sidewalk and the parking. This pattern retains the visibility of parking provided by front-yard lots but supports the life of the sidewalk. It also allows the parking lot to become, at some later time, a building without obscuring the original structure.

The street edge of the parking court should be designed to work with the building facade to support the life of the sidewalk. If, for example, the building has a café on the sidewalk, seating and landscaping could be provided along the sidewalk in front of the parking. Vendors, street furniture, automated teller machines, landscaping, and other uses could also support the sidewalk. On occasion, the entire parking court can be transformed into a room for a festival, outdoor cinema, or other event (Chapter 8).

Hidden Parking

Preserve the connection between sidewalk and building by hiding off-street parking behind buildings. In this hidden parking, provide (1) pedestrian paths to the sidewalk instead of backdoor entrances to buildings; (2) windows in the surrounding buildings, vendors at the front of the lot, and/or café space to provide passive surveillance; and (3) legible automobile entrances and easy traffic flow. (See Figure 4.12.)

The pedestrian life of a street is sustained by buildings that engage the sidewalk. Entries, display windows, and sidewalk sales in commercial areas and front gardens and porches along residential streets bring life to the street. Streetside parking lots weaken or break this synergy between buildings and sidewalk. Hiding parking along alleys and behind buildings reduces its deadening effect.

In the design of hidden parking, care must be exercised to avoid three significant problems: the dark-alley syndrome, hidden pedestrians, and poor advertising.

By removing the parking lot from the street, we remove it from the view of passersby and cruising police. For the safety of drivers and vehicles, the hidden parking lot must not become a dark alley. Store and office windows that overlook the lot can add a sense of passive surveillance. A vendor booth or café seating that fronts the sidewalk but has views to the lot activates the street, hides the lot, and serves as a kind of gatekeeper or concierge for the lot (Majordomo, Chapter 10). Pedestrian shortcuts (see Paths and Shortcuts in Chapter 6) add another level of activity to the lot, and good lighting can prevent the dark-alley look. Hidden lots should be closed with gates at night when not in use.

Back lots can also drain pedestrian

Figure 4.12 Hidden parking. Archway into parking area for Chapman Market, Los Angeles, California.

(Copyright 1998, Talbott Houk.)

life from the street. People should enter and exit the lot from the street, not through back doors or skywalks; otherwise, the lot will hide not only the automobiles but the pedestrian activity they generate.

Finally, the visibility of streetside parking advertises easy access for drivers. Hidden parking must compete with this simple and direct display. A gateway facade along the street can provide architectural continuity to a sidewalk and advertise the presence of an otherwise hidden lot. Automobile circulation through the lot must be legible and simple, or it will quickly gain a reputation as a difficult maze. (See Figure 4.13.)

Hidden parking is strongly advocated by new urbanists as a prime method for mitigating the automobile's effects on the urban fabric and supporting the pedestrian realm (Calthorpe 1993, Sucher 1995). Strip-mall parking, Calthorpe claims, gives the message "arrive by car only"

Figure 4.13 A false front to a parking lot, Colorado Springs, Colorado. This design would have been more successful had the rooms of this structure served the pedestrian use of the sidewalk.

(1993, 55). Hidden parking supports multiple means of transportation.

Structured Parking

Parking structures should be a variation on hidden parking, with sidewalk-level shops and facades that grace the street. Particular care must be taken to make garages safe and secure and to connect pedestrians to the street. Garages should be considered buildings with doorways that one must have permission to be allowed through. (See Figure 4.14.)

Parking structures are complex buildings that cost 5 to 10 times more per stall than surface parking construction (*Parking,* March 1997, 31). Garages present a set of architectural design and technical issues not confronted in the design of surface parking, and they are not the focus of this book. However, as a matter of urban design, garages are similar to hidden parking lots and may be treated as particularly expensive and difficult hidden lots. Moreover, hidden surface lots may be, over time, replaced with structured parking, and thus the design of hidden lots should anticipate the added problems of structured parking.

Garages are related to hidden parking lots because they are separated from the public realm of the street. The tendency of structures to feel unsafe and their tendency to hide pedestrians surpasses that of the back lot. Extra care must be taken to overcome these problems. Garages, like hidden lots, also need legible entrances.

Figure 4.14 Structured parking, Santa Barbara, California. Pedestrians entering or exiting the parking structure use the pedestrian system and not hidden connections.

Parking structures are removed from the life of the street, and people use them only minimally as public space. It would be difficult to add a café to the third floor of a garage; a space two floors below the street will not function as well-used public space. (However, private space such as offices, sports clubs, or houses can readily sit above a parking deck.) Because it is difficult for parking garages to act as public space, they should whenever possible be private space, limited to a selected group who have permission to open a door and drive or walk in.

The sense of security can be increased by (1) controlled entrances that require cars and pedestrians to pass an attendant and/or shops, (2) good lighting, and (3) glassed-in elevators and windows into stairs and parking levels to allow people on the street and in adjacent buildings to see into the garage.

Additionally, the facades of garages should support the design of the street. Parking should not usurp space for sidewalk-level shops, lobbies, or offices.

In some cases, a site's topography allows cars to enter at grade from the alley or side street and park on the roof of a street-level building. These penthouse parking courts may provide the advantages of hidden parking and quiet courtyards. Stairs from the parking area should descend to the sidewalk and help add to the vitality of the street.

The engineering design of parking structures is a specialty. *Parking Structures* by Chrest, Smith, and Bhuyan (1996) is a strong technical reference on the planning and engineering of garages.

Cornerstone Parking

Design temporary parking lots as the framework for later construction. Establish patterns of circulation and a tradition of use through events such as food vendors, farmers' markets, or festivals. (See Figure 4.15.)

The usual practice in designing a temporary parking lot on a building site is to minimize expense and maximize future

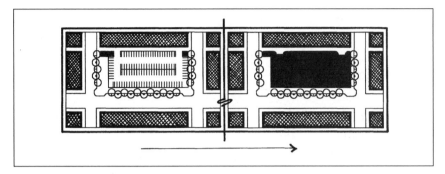

Figure 4.15 Diagram of parking lot configuration framing building footprint.

flexibility. This approach has much to recommend it. Why spend a penny more than is necessary on a utilitarian space that will soon be replaced, and why constrain future development?

An alternative approach is to view the parking lot as an initial investment that provides current income and yields dividends later. A temporary parking lot can lay the compositional foundation for future buildings if it is designed to anticipate the building's fit into the city. Requiring temporary lots to be pleasant parts of the city may be in a city's interest, simply because "temporary" can easily encompass a few decades.

Just as subdivision and platting play significant roles in the design of a city, the layout of a parking lot can provide the framework for later construction. The most literal application of this concept is to design the lot anticipating its use as a construction staging site. However, the lot may also serve as an initial sketch of the use of the site. For example, the location of curb cuts, pedestrian paths, bus shelters, and landscaping can establish a pattern of circulation. Facilities, such as plazas with vendors' booths, and events, such as farmers' markets or festivals (following chapters), can accustom people to using the site and help establish it as a destination.

This investment approach has additional benefits. First, the design of adjacent buildings and streets can respond to the site's patterns. Turn lanes may be established allowing easy automobile access; pedestrian paths can be connected though multiple sites; and buildings may be shaped to avoid shadowing plazas. Second, cornerstone parking reduces the disruption of change. Fewer off-site adjustments are required, and the public's sense of orientation and continuity is less threatened. Thus there are fewer grounds for objection to a project. Finally, the design of a temporary parking lot and an accompanying schematic building offers a low-budget means to test and develop the relationships between owner(s), architect, and regulators.

Calming the Seas

Where large parking lots exist or are necessary they should be civilized. Instead of hiding behind an undifferentiated sea of asphalt, buildings should retain pedestrian connections to the street and actively use the edge of the lot. The lot itself should be an orchard, forest, or garden composed of small bays connected by pedestrian paths. Bays that are used only at peak times should be designed for alternative uses.

At the other end of the spectrum from the small hidden parking lot is the vast parking landscape (Figure 4.16). As a rule, we should avoid creating these vast lots because they are disorienting, force pedestrians to walk great distances, separate the city into isolated bits, and are too big to use as comfortable social space. Wherever they exist—at airports, stadiums, big-box retail, or office parks—they indicate an opportunity for public transit. However, plenty of these asphalt seas presently exist and could benefit from remodeling, and new vast lots may be required in certain places. How, then, do we tame the vast lot?

Touch the Street

The fact that a large amount of access to a site is by automobile does not mean that pedestrians, bicyclists, and bus

Figure 4.16 A sea of asphalt, Anaheim, California. This hot asphalt expanse is unimaginative and disorienting.

riders should be abandoned. Shopping malls, stadiums, and other generators of large lots should bridge their asphalt moats at places that best support the pedestrian network. (See Figure 4.17.) These pedestrian entrances could serve as a prime habitat for cafés and other retail outlets.

Use the Edge

The shores of a parking sea should not be deserted. Stores should spill into the lot with sidewalk sales, hot-dog vendors, cafés, and so forth. (See Figure 4.18.) If the lot must front a city sidewalk, the edge should be designed to support the sidewalk. Gracious gestures might include bus stop shelters

Figure 4.17 Touch the street. Along a main street of Bellevue, Washington, the Bellevue Square Mall is connected to downtown by a major entrance aligned with a public pedestrian path. Although there are large parking lots on other sides of the mall, the buildings come to meet the street at critical points.

(Copyright 1997, Elaine Thomas.)

Figure 4.18   Use the building edge. The active use of the edge of this parking lot in Santa Barbara helps enliven the parking lot.

with nearby space for vendors, a linear park with chess tables or a skateboarding path, or simply a flowering hedge, shade trees, and proper lighting (Figure 4.19).

At many of these vast lots, new buildings with different uses can be added without increasing the demand for parking (Chapter 12). These new buildings can be sited to form lively pedestrian edges and/or break up the lot into courtyards.

Plant an Orchard, Forest, or Garden

Typical parking lot planting fails to have the density to reasonably shade the lot or to give the sense of being in a forest or orchard. Planting many large-canopied trees can give the charm of the old American elm street with its roof of branches to a lot (Chapter 7).

Another approach is to treat the lot as a vast formal garden. In *A Significance for A&P Parking Lots, or Learning from Las Vegas,* Venturi, Scott-Brown et al. (1972) suggest that the large parking lot is the evolutionary descendent of Versailles. They write, "The parking lot is the *parterre* of the asphalt landscape. . . . Grids of lamp posts substitute for obelisks, rows of urns and statues as points of identity and continuity in the vast space." Perhaps an aesthetic of the pure parking lot can be nurtured. One can imagine that in the hands of a master architect such as Luis Barragán the color, proportion, and sense of light in a parking lot could produce a profound place.

Figure 4.19 Create an active sidewalk edge. This parking lot in Santa Fe, New Mexico, provides a pleasant and active edge to the sidewalk.

Divide and Conquer

Divide the lot into bays no longer than 65 feet so that each bay has seven or eight cars per side.[2] This dimension allows someone entering the bay to recognize and read the expression of anyone in the space. These bay sizes also aid memory for parking location, particularly if the bays have distinct characteristics such as significantly different tree species to aid in mental mapping (Means et al. 1995).

Organize and design the bays according to their frequency of use. Spaces within 300 feet of building entrances should be allocated for the mobility-impaired, priority visitors, and other short-term parking; design these areas for heavy use, with durable surfaces and wide stalls. Midrange parking (between 300 and 600 feet of an entrance), serving long-term and busy-day needs, may use smaller stalls. The far reaches of a parking lot should provide peak-time parking capacity. These bays may be designed for alternative uses during nonpeak times. For shopping center lots, the peak activity time is primarily the four weekends before Christmas. Thus, during almost 11 months of the year these bays may house other uses, such as summer markets, fairs and circuses, and basketball courts or other sports facilities (Chapter 8).

CHAPTER 5

Parking at Home

We have within our natures tendencies toward both communality and individuality. A good house supports both kinds of experience: the intimacy of a private haven and our participation with a public world.

—CHRISTOPHER ALEXANDER, 1977*

A private car will usually be parked at or near the owner's residence for over half its life (Highway Research Board 1971). Where and how the car is parked in relationship to the house reflects and, to a degree, conditions our values and how we view the world.

Unless we have abandoned the ideal of a democratic society for a collection of fortified fiefdoms, a home should both provide a private haven *and* help build a neighborhood. The parking space is one place of transition between the private interior of home and the public realm. Too often, driveways and garages have been made into moats and bulwarks separating houses from the street and neighborhood. Neighborhood streets have become mazes to keep the public away, empty no-man's-lands instead of neighborhood commons. This may have its worst effect on children. To learn about and participate in society, children must cajole their parents into driving them somewhere else because they cannot watch the world passing their front porches, walk to the store for a soda, or even ride their bikes to school. Work is hidden away in another inaccessible part of the city, and neighbors are difficult to meet because they only emerge from their kingdoms clad in automobiles.

Driving also consumes a large portion of a household's time and budget. Americans spend an average of 32 hours a month driving (Durning 1996, 22), and automobile-related expenses account for 16 to 20 percent of American household expenditures, not including indirect costs such as the price of buying a three-car garage (Lincoln Institute 1995).

The following recipes suggest ways to accommodate the automobile at home and support the formation of a neighborhood.

Figure 5.1 Streetyard, Albuquerque, New Mexico. A curved curb, midstreet tree plantings, and textured paving help produce a slow street where pedestrians have the right-of-way.

Streetyards

Residential streets should be neighborhood commons in which pedestrians have the right-of-way and the driver is a guest. Parking can be located to help slow down traffic, to provide alcoves off the circulation route for play, and to replace off-street lots. (See Figure 5.1.)

Based on a 1959 British study, in 1969 the Dutch planner Niek De Boer developed residential street designs, called residential yards or woonerfs, that are public space shared by pedestrians and cars. Pedestrians have the right-of-way over the entire street, and car speed and movement is restricted by physical barriers and bends. Studies in multiple countries show that, compared with standard residential streets, there are over 20 percent fewer accidents and over 50 percent fewer severe accidents in shared streets (Southworth and Ben-Joseph 1997, 118). Parking is an integral part of shared street design.

On a streetyard, parking is placed to (1) provide access to front doors (rather than rear doors), (2) slow down traffic by causing traffic lanes to weave around the parking, and often (3) provide play area in unused parking places. Parking spaces are often unmarked but rather are formed by the placement of physical elements such as trees, planting beds, or play equipment. (See the appendix for works on the design and evaluation of shared streets.)

Apartment Closes

Arrange apartments around closes. Design the close as an entry court and common front yard. Place the main building entrances on the court, and line the close with porches, balconies, gardens, and playgrounds. (See Figure 5.2.)

Recently, the predominant model for apartment complexes has been the "building in the park." Unfortunately, as cars are added to this ideal, parking lots usurp the park, and the gardens and playgrounds are pushed into remote fragments of space. Three alternatives to this welter are (1) an apartment street (streetyards, discussed previously in this chapter), (2) an apartment campus (see Campus, Chapter 3), and (3) the close.

The close is a private courtyard serving a set of buildings with an entryway from a public street. A close serves as a commons and formal entry court for the residents. Cars may park in the close and garages or small lots may adjoin it, but the close must not

Figure 5.2 Residential close, Edinburgh, Scotland.

be simply a parking lot. The space must be primarily an outdoor parlor and common front yard, with sitting areas, gardens, and other amenities.

Place the main entries to buildings on the close, and surround the close with porches, balconies, kitchen windows, garden beds, playgrounds, and benches and chairs. Consider how the space could be used for festivities or gatherings as well as everyday civility.

Alley and Garage

Parking along the alley brings life to this casual right-of-way and preserves the street for guest parking, pedestrians, and social uses. Combine parking with workshops, offices, teenagers' cottages, basketball courts, and other uses. Provide screening for garbage cans, avoid creating hidden nooks, and provide adequate lighting.

Part of the pleasure of alleys is their informal character. However, if this informality degenerates into carelessness and neglect, then alleys become ugly and dangerous. In order to create pleasant residential alleys, they need to be integrated into the daily life of the neighborhood.

The alley garage provides a second, more informal, front to the world. Combining a garage with a guest house, teenager's cottage, office, potting shed, or artist's retreat can take natural advantage of this second front. Such uses can increase the security of the alley by supplying people who watch over and take care of the alley. A guest house or office separated from the main house also increases the privacy of both the main house and the secondary unit by providing each place with its own entrance.

Like porches, if garages are designed as rooms instead of just giant closets, then their role as part of the civic realm of the alley becomes clear. To provide for the use of the garage as a room, a human-sized door should offer access for people to the outside; ventilation, light, heating, insulation, electricity, and other facilities common to an inhabited room should be provided.

The garage is similar to the porch in another way: It mediates between outside and inside. Garage doors that open out can serve as awnings, and driveways, if they are not excessively sloped, may serve as extensions of the garage floor. Thus, shop work and yard sales can spill out onto driveway and alley.

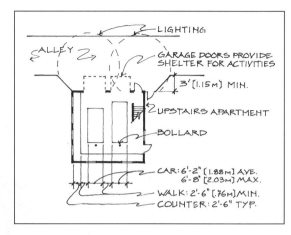

Figure 5.3 Dimensions for a garage.

This outdoor space should be carefully crafted. Driveways should be near level to allow multiple uses. Screened garbage can areas, adequate lighting, care to avoid creating hidden nooks, landscaping, windows overlooking the alley, and other defensible space design measures to show that people care and watch over the alley will dispel fear of the alley.

Alleys can be one-way lanes 12 feet (3.66 m) wide in 16 feet (4.88 m) of right-of-way. Garages should be set back 3 to 5 feet (.91 to 1.52 m) to allow turning area. Figure 5.3 shows dimensions for residential garages.

Shared Driveways and Parking Courts

When curb cuts are necessary, their disruption of the sidewalk and street can be minimized by sharing driveways. An 8- to 12-foot (2.43- to 3.65-m) access easement along lot lines can open onto a small parking courtyard serving two or more houses. The easement should specify agreements concerning maintenance and improvements. Make the courtyard a pleasant outdoor room that is a commons for the set of houses. Place mailboxes, seats, and other group facilities with this courtyard. (See Figure 5.4.)

Curb cuts and driveways are often hazardous obstacles. Cars backing out of residential driveways create a signifi-

Figure 5.4   Shared parking court, Santa Barbara, California. Note the mix of cars, bicycles, and seating.

cant risk, particularly to small children. Vehicles crossing the sidewalk are a danger and a hindrance to pedestrians, and driveway curb cuts often are a nuisance to walk over, present a tripping hazard, and are obstacles to such things as wheelchairs and baby carriages.

A driveway shared between two neighbors decreases the number of curb cuts by half, reduces paved surface area, and creates common ground. It does, however, require a modicum of civility, which is best backed by an easement or other standard legal agreement, and a design that minimizes potential conflict. For example, screened enclosures for garbage cans well back from the property line should be provided, the driveway surface should require minimal maintenance, and utility lines should not run under the length of driveway. Where shared property is not feasible, ganging driveways along property lines at least concentrates curb cuts (Figure 5.5).

Shared driveways for more than two houses should be designed as a commons. If ganged mailboxes are required, they can be placed under a shelter adjacent to the parking court. Perhaps a basketball hoop or a place to set up a barbecue can be provided. Kitchen windows, home offices, and/or alley houses should overlook the courtyard to provide casual surveillance.

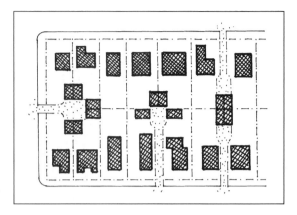

Figure 5.5 Diagram of parking courts for detached single-family houses.

Courtyard Housing in Los Angeles, by Stephanos Polyzoides, Roger Sherwood, and James Tice, documents some elegant examples of courtyard housing with off-street parking courts. These courts serve as one in a set of courtyards and are carefully designed as part of the overall composition of the compound.

Entry Courts and Backhouses

When curb cuts are necessary for a single house or a house with an accessory apartment, make an entry court. Both drivers and pedestrians come through this court to the front door, but the courtyard should be an outdoor room that may serve as work yard, garden, play space, parking area, and the place of arrival and departure. Separate entries for accessory apartments, home offices, workshops, or other backhouses from the entry court give both the main house and the backhouse more privacy.

When the car must leave the street or alley, a place of arrival should be created. An entry court provides a formal place of arrival and allows easy access between car and house (Figure 5.6). It also serves to organize a compound of buildings by providing a single place of arrival with separate doors for main house, guesthouse, workshop, backyard, and so forth.

Figure 5.6 Entry court, Santa Fe, New Mexico.

Figure 5.7 Driveway serving main house, garage, and accessory unit.

The entry court also allows a house to have a single front door serving both driver and pedestrian.

The courtyard should be a room or garden that hosts a number of uses, including parking. Not only is it the place where guests will be greeted and dates will be concluded, but it may serve as work yard, playground, and picnic court. If a garage is provided, it should open directly onto the courtyard. Thus the garage as workshop or play space may spill out onto the courtyard. Porches, arcades, and other half-enclosed rooms may also help enliven the courtyard. (See Figure 5.7.)

Shop-House

Houses that sit above streetfront garages should be designed and zoned to allow home offices and

shops in and adjacent to the garage. The garage should have light, ventilation, and the other features of a pleasant room. In addition to the house and garage doors there should be an office door.

Seeking ways to house the automobile in 1907, Marius C. Kraup advocated the French sixteenth-century urban row house with ground-floor stable and shop as a model (Figure 5.8). The street-dominating garages of current American suburbs could be rethought using this early model. Despite zoning codes to the contrary, current American garages do serve many of the same functions as the stable/shop in sixteenth-century French row houses. Garage sales, home offices, weekend workshops, art studios, garage bands, and lemonade stands all occupy garages.

If a garage must occupy this most precious space at street level along the sidewalk, then it should allow and support storefront uses. Zoning codes should be revised to allow commercial use of the garage. The driveway and the space within the garage should be designed as an extension of the street and sidewalk. Garage door(s) should be well-articulated facades, and the relationship between garage/shop and house should be carefully recrafted.

Porte Cochere

Make a room that supports the experience of coming and going. This covered outdoor room

Figure 5.8 Sixteenth-century French dwelling house with ground-floor stable.

(*Harper's Weekly* 20 November 1907, p. 1599. Discussed by Drummond Buckley in Wachs and Crawford 1992.)

shelters the parked car and the main entry to the house, but it is also a place in and of itself where people can wait and read a book, sit and talk, or lean against a column and say good-bye. It may be part of an entry court or replace the court. (See Figure 5.9.)

The threshold of a house is a critical place. Rather than creating separate entrances for arrival by car, bike and foot, the main entrance can serve all. This avoids confusion about where the "real" front door is.

This threshold should be a beautiful and significant place in its own right. It should be a room that shelters the car and where people can greet and say good-bye to friends, sit and watch the world go by, put on shoes or take off muddy boots, and perhaps even eat supper on a summer evening.

The porte cochere is a room combining front door, porch, and carport.

Figure 5.9   Porte cochere.
(Copyright 1998, Patrick Doherty. Used by permission.)

Figure 5.10   Game court. The surface of a driveway can double as a play space.

Game Court

Driveway basketball is an American icon. It transforms the driveway into a family and social space and makes a public declaration of this transformation. The driveway, whether along an alley or a street, should serve as a social forecourt to a house. Other uses such as large-scale chess, neighborhood picnics, outdoor movies, or alfresco recitals could similarly inhabit the driveway. (See Figure 5.10.)

Like the stork's nest on the chimney of a traditional northern European home, the basketball hoop over the garage door of an American home signifies child-oriented domesticity (Jackson 1980, 109). Other activities such as car washing have also traditionally occupied the driveway. However, because the basketball hoop permanently occupies the space and implies a reorganization of the ground, it transforms the driveway in a manner that car washing cannot.

Not all households wish to communicate child-centered

domesticity in this traditional manner or at all. The driveway, however, still offers the opportunity to engage the world. The driveway/courtyard could be designed, for example, for outdoor music performances, barbecues, or meetings of volunteer organizations. If these courts are along a streetyard, they can provide a set of alcoves off the common space.

Bicycle Garage

Provide bicycle garages either with or without car parking. Place the garage at street level near the main door. Use at least a 36-inch (.91-m)-wide door, provide a bench for putting on shoes, and supply storage places for helmets, pumps, and other equipment.

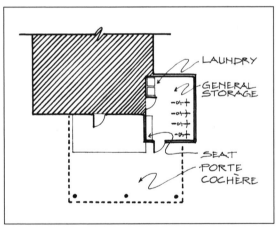

Figure 5.11 Bicycle garage off a porte cochere.

Bicycles are in more need of shelter and security than automobiles. One hundred square feet can provide a luxurious separate garage for four bikes and double as a mud room entrance (Figure 5.11). Bikes need roughly 2 ft 6 in × 6 ft (.76 × 1.83 m) for parking. Consideration should be given to adding space to house other street vehicles such as strollers and wheeled grocery carts.

Ideally, the bicycle garage should have easy access to both the house and the street. It could be to the side of a front porch or adjoin a porte cochere.

The City Afoot

It's on foot that you see people's faces and statures and that you meet and experience them. That is how public socializing and community enjoyment in daily life can most easily occur. And it's on foot that one can be most intimately involved with the urban environment; with stores, houses, the natural environment, and with people.

—ALLAN JACOBS, *GREAT STREETS*, 1993

Virtually everyone who arrives in a parking lot by car becomes a pedestrian. Walking decreases pollution and energy use, is inexpensive and land-efficient, and is good exercise. Moreover, it is as pedestrians (or in a wheelchair, on crutches, etc.)[1] that we do most of our talking, working, eating, shopping, and socializing. Thus parking places should be at least as safe, pleasant, and easy to use outside of the car as behind the wheel. The following patterns specifically address the pedestrian use of the parking lot.

Catchment

The critical element in locating a parking lot is not access to the lot by automobile but access to and egress from the lot by foot. Therefore, locate and design parking to promote pedestrian accessibility.

For short trips, walking is generally faster than driving. This is true for trips up to one-third to one-half mile (Figure 6.1), but obviously this is influenced by a number of conditions, such as the directness of the walking and driving routes,

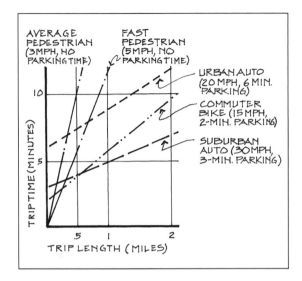

Figure 6.1   Modal travel time comparison.

(Redrawn from Federal Highway Administration 1978.)

traffic density, walking speed, and the time it takes to park.

The distance that people are willing to walk is influenced by their physique, their age and stamina, their cultural habits, the purpose of the trip, the microclimate, and the form of the path. The last three are within the purview of design. Weather protection, attractive shop windows, wide and direct paths, and mixed-use areas that allow one to combine trips will induce more walking. It is not unusual for shoppers to walk 2 miles during a visit to a regional mall (Untermann 1984, 1).

Average sustained walking speeds range from 2.5 to 6.0 feet per second (AASHTE 1990, 114). The common design standard is 4.0 ft/s but studies have shown that the mean speed of pedestrian traffic is 3.7 ft/s (Dewar 1992, 22). The elderly and small children have the slowest walking speeds. They are also at the greatest risk of injury if they are struck by an automobile. A speed of 2.2 ft/s was found to be the most comfortable speed for 85 percent of people over 70. Children's speeds vary considerably. Currently, Americans are willing to walk about 6 minutes for errands and other short trips. Walking distance is speed multiplied by time (of course, stoplights make a trip slower).

A walking catchment for a lot (that is, the area it serves) is a design judgment that integrates the demographics of the lot's clientele, their presumed destinations, and the quality of the pedestrian system. Generally, the radius of a catchment is the distance that only 5 to 15 percent of the population would exceed. That is, only 1 to 3 people out of 20 would walk farther than the catchment radius. Table 6.1 summarizes recommendations on catchment walking distances.

Table 6.1 Walking Catchment Distances

Distance	Activity	Source
300 ft (~91.5 m)	Close parking at shopping centers	Lynch 1971, 333
500 ft (~152.5 m)	70% of Americans willing to walk up to 500 ft for daily errands	Untermann 1984
600 ft (~183 m)	Peak parking for shopping centers	Lynch 1971, 333
900 ft (~274.5 m)	Average length of walk to plaza	Lieberman 1984
1000 ft (~305 m)	Parking for work	Lynch 1971, 341
1500–2000 ft (~457–610 m)	Max. walking distance in park-and-ride	*Traffic Engineering Handbook*
2000 ft (~610 m)	"Comfortable walking distance"	Calthorpe 1993, 56
½ mile (~805 m)	Walk to bus stop	Pushkarev and Zupan 1975
3000 ft (~915 m)	80% of trips less than 3000 ft	Pushkarev and Zupan 1975
1 mile (~1610 m)	Walk to work	Pushkarev and Zupan 1975

To make a judgment about the appropriate catchment of a particular project, the designer must have a sense of the general distances Americans will walk and how various factors influence walking distance (Table 6.2). The effect of city form and culture, and of the trip's purpose on walking distance, is shown in Figures 6.2, and 6.3, respectively.

The purpose of trips appears to affect the distance people

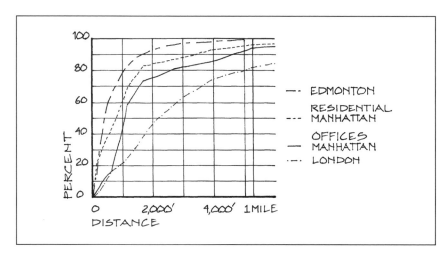

Figure 6.2 Cumulative walking distance distribution in selected cities.

(Redrawn from Boris Pushkarev and Jeffrey M. Zupan, *Urban Space for Pedestrians*. MIT Press. Copyright © 1975 by the Regional Plan Association. Used by permission of MIT Press.)

Table 6.2   Factors Influencing Walking Distance

Factor	Change	Source
Travel Mode	**$ paid to avoid walking 1000 ft**	
New York City parkers	.65 (1969)	Pushkarev and Zupan
Los Angeles parkers	.36–.45 (1972)	
New York city subway riders	.02–.35 (1972)	
Parking Type	**Walking distance**	
Free curb space	612 ft (~186.5 m)	Burrage, 50
Pay curb space	516 ft (~157.3 m)	Note: No data was
Free off-street	352 ft (~107.3 m)	supplied on length of
Pay off-street	799 ft (~243.6 m)	time or purpose of parking.
Parking Time	**Distance walked**	
Parked <15 min	392 ft (~119.5 m)	Burrage, 48
Parked 15–29 min	526 ft (~160.4 m)	Note: Data for cities
Parked 1–2 hr	688 ft (~210 m)	250,000 to 500,000
Parked 2–3 hr	768 ft (~234.2 m)	in population.
Parked 3–4 hr	801 ft (~244.2 m)	
Parked 7–8 hr	828 ft (~252.4 m)	
Path Impedances	**Walking speed**	
Stairs up (horiz. speed)	34% of normal	Report no.
7–8% slope ramp	91% of normal	FHWA-RD-79-47,
Escalators	34% of normal	figure 6-7
15 ft^2/person (~1.4 m^2/pers.)	85% of normal	
10 ft^2/person (~.93 m^2/pers.)	75% of normal	
7.5 ft^2/person (~.7 m^2/pers.)	66% of normal	
5 ft^2/person (~.47 m^2/pers.)	42% of normal	
Purpose	**Average distance walked**	
Work	571 ft (~174 m)	Burrage, 47
Business	435 ft (~132.6 m)	
Shopping	489 ft (~149 m)	
Culture	**Average distance walked**	
Holland	3000 ft (~915 m)/ 12 min to store	Untermann, 25
U.S. commuter	800 ft (~244 m)	
New York City Transit riders	1300 ft (~397 m)/ 4.5 min	
Suburban German shoppers	2400 ft (~732 m) to shopping center	

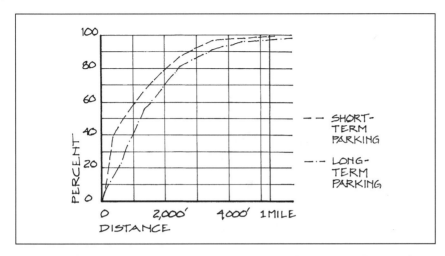

Figure 6.3 Cumulative walking distance distribution at parking lots and subway stations.
(Redrawn from Boris Pushkarev and Jeffrey M. Zupan, *Urban Space for Pedestrians.* MIT Press. Copyright ©
1975 by the Regional Plan Association. Used by permission of MIT Press.)

will walk in two ways. First, time equals money. People will
walk farther for free or low-cost parking. Second, the longer
one stays at a destination, the farther one is willing to walk.
Thus, people will take a long walk to work but are willing to
walk only a much shorter distance for errands. Observation
indicates there is a third factor not well reflected in the
data—the more people have to carry (including children),
the less willing they are to walk.

Paths and Shortcuts

**Walkways in and though parking lots can increase pedestrian safety, provide
surveillance of the lot, and increase the ease of access to the city. Therefore,
provide pleasant, safe, well-connected, and direct paths. (See Figure 6.4.)**

Americans' willingness to travel by walking has steadily
decreased, while our penchant for recreational walking and
jogging has increased. Perhaps this can be explained by the
money spent on improving automobile access and the con-
current decreasing quality of pedestrian facilities. Following
are aspects of physical design that may encourage walking.

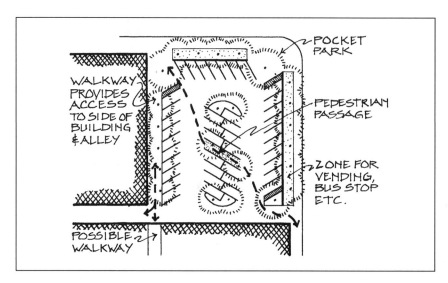

Figure 6.4   Diagram of pedestrian shortcut.

With or Without Cars

The traditional parking lot design where people walk in the driving lane has many strengths: it is compact; the presence of pedestrians reduces vehicle speeds; it legitimizes pedestrian use of the lot; and it provides wide walkways. However, it potentially puts pedestrians in harm's way. The most vulnerable pedestrians are wheelchair users and children because neither are easily seen in a rearview mirror. Methods to reduce the risk of accidents include the following:

- Protected paths from stalls for the mobility-impaired.

- Drop-off/loading zones, particularly where children's activities occur.

- One-way aisles with angled parking. This reduces the number of directions a pedestrian must monitor and increases the visibility of pedestrians by motorists.

- Pull-through stalls. These eliminate backing out of the stall, which is one of the most hazardous activities for drivers and pedestrians.

- Rumble strips, paving, and landscaping that differentiate the lot from the street. These should be designed to reduce vehicle speeds and communicate that this is a pedestrian space.

Separate pedestrian paths should be provided to stalls for the mobility-impaired and in the following lots:

- Those with a high turnover or long distances
- Lots that serve as a pedestrian short-cut
- Lots supporting additional activities such as vendors
- Those where pedestrians must cross roads or parking lot collector aisles to exit the lot

Route

To pedestrians, any detour is an annoyance and any short-cut a boon. People cut through parking lots, jaywalk, and climb barriers to shave a few feet off their route. Unless they are there to skate, people will not appreciate randomly curvy paths. When a corner is created by a building or other object it should be chamfered to the pedestrian turning radius of 6 to 10 feet.

Routes for the mobility-impaired should not pass behind parked cars, should be as direct and as short as possible, and should avoid crossing the vehicular aisles whenever possible. If the route crosses the vehicular aisle, it must be a marked crossing (ATBCB 1991 and 1994).

In addition to being direct, the route must be well connected. The world is full of examples of good walkways that stop at a property line well short of connecting to a sidewalk or adjacent walkway. A study for the advocacy group 1000 Friends of Oregon documented a correlation between the volume of walking trips and four factors: (1) the ease of street crossings (width, signals, and amount of traffic), (2) topography, (3) the continuity of the sidewalk system, and (4) network connectivity (e.g., lack of dead ends, frequency of cross paths) (PBQD 1993).

The perception of safety is also critical to route design. Visibility is the key. Lighting, clear sight distance, elimination of nooks, and passive surveillance increase the perception of safety (Chapter 10).

Walkways must offer a direct and complete route to entrances, sidewalks, and other destinations. Parking aisles should thus generally radiate from entrances, allowing paths to connect entrances to the city's pedestrian system.

Pathway Width

Ideally a walkway should be sized to its peak demand. One possible prescriptive method for matching walkway width to demand is to require additional sidewalk width according to the total square footage of a new building. This is an inexact method. However, sidewalk width is often determined before buildings are designed.

For pedestrians or wheelchair users to pass one another easily, each person should have about 30 inches (.76 m) of clear space. Shopping carts require from 18 to 36 inches (.45 to .91 m). For one-way aisles, wheelchairs require a clearance of 36 inches (.91 m). People avoid the area about 1.5 feet (.46 m) closest to the curb. Window-shoppers inhabit from 1.6 to 2.5 feet (.49 to .76 m) along buildings, and people standing at bus stops take up about 3.6 feet (1.1 m) (Pushkarev and Zupan 1975, 154). When measuring walkway width, area for car overhangs cannot be considered part of the walkway.

These spaces can overlap a bit. Thus, I recommend for any public walkway a *minimum* total width of 6 feet (1.83 m). Street furniture (parking meters, signs, etc.) or vehicle overhangs may not reduce the clear width below 5 feet (1.52 m), and the full 6 feet must be available at intervals for more than 50 percent of the length of the walk. This standard allows two wheelchairs to pass with ease and always allows two people to walk past each other without interference. (For short paths serving a minimal number of people and those for which alternative routes exist, the absolute minimum *unobstructed* width is 3 feet [.91 m].)

Wheelchair ramps cannot occupy the unloading space alongside the car (except along curb overhang space) and should arrive at a level part of the walkway that is a minimum of 3 feet (.91 m) wide.

The clear walkway area must be free of obstructions up to a minimum of 80 inches (2.03 m) above the sidewalk (ITE 5A-5 1995, 12). Since a significant number of people are taller than 80 inches, I recommend a minimum clearance of 90 inches (2.29 m); 102 inches (2.59 m) would add significant comfort.

The 6-foot (1.83-m) total width for public ways should be supplemented at intersections, along bus stops, at main building entrances, and around vendors. Street furniture and other activities require space beyond the clear width (see Zoning the Sidewalk, following). New York City zoning, for example, requires 4 ft^2 (.37 m^2) of off-sidewalk queuing space per seat for theaters.

Six feet is a minimum width for public passages; greater sizes are required for greater peak demand. Pushkarev and Zupan recommend, for example, a minimum dimension of 15 feet (4.57 m) for midblock walkways in Manhattan.

There are very limited data to help predict the number of pedestrians that will use a sidewalk or other pedestrian path. From their observations of downtown New York, Pushkarev and Zupan determined that the peak pedestrian density occurs around noon, and that during this time retail space attracts 2 to 7 times more pedestrians, and restaurants generate 13 to 25 times more pedestrians, than do offices per square foot of space (Pushkarev and Zupan 1975, 63). *The Pedestrian Planning Procedures Manual* published by the Federal Highway Administration provides a method of estimating pedestrian density, graphs of sidewalk pedestrian volume by time of day and type of uses along a street, and average pedestrian trip generation rates. This is an elaborate process and the authors caution, "The modeling effort output is not an end in itself; it is simply a means to (inform) . . . the pedestrian design plan. In some cases, simple counts or gross estimates may suffice" (1978, 27).

Finally, we should be careful not to treat pedestrianism as simply another means of travel. The social uses of the street—stopping and talking, laughing with a street performer, buying a cappuccino—cause "pedestrian traffic congestion" but are worth the price.

Grade and Surface

Trips and falls constitute the majority of liability claims in parking lots (Ellis 1996). Thus, the smooth, stable, and gently sloping pathways required to comply with the Americans with Disabilities Act (ADA) are also prudent general risk-reduction features. Concrete and asphalt are typical path materials, but other materials such as compacted rock fines, brick, rammed earth, and resin-stabilized soil can offer the necessary level, skid-resistant, and stable surface.

Table 6.3   Geometric Design for Walkways

	Dimension	Source
Cross slope	2% max.	*Design and Safety of Pedestrian Facilities*, 12
Grade	5% max.	*Traffic Engineering Handbook*, 4th edition, 24
	8% max. with level platforms every 30 ft (~9.15 m)	*Design and Safety of Pedestrian Facilities*, 12
Joints	¼ in. max. height (.64 cm)	*Design and Safety of Pedestrian Facilities*, 13
Width	6 ft min. with 5 ft min. clear. (1.83 m min. 1.53 m clr.)	
Clear height	80 in. min. 102 in. recommended (2.03 m min. 2.6 m typ.)	*Design and Safety of Pedestrian Facilities*, 12

Table 6.3 shows recommended geometrics for path design. Curb cut standards will be discussed subsequently.

Amenities

Pleasant pedestrian environments not only encourage walking[2] but improve the image of a parking area and its associated buildings. The subject of amenities is virtually unlimited in scope. However, three general categories of amenities are of particular significance.

First, control of the microclimate is critical. Heat, cold, rain, and snow reduce walking. Good drainage and slip-resistant surfaces are a necessity. Planting strips can help pedestrians avoid splashes from cars and provide a place to pile snow. Pavements colored to reflect rather than absorb heat, trees, drinking fountains, and even ice-cream vendors in hot climates can help produce a comfortable place to walk. But perhaps the most elegant response to all these climatic conditions is the arcade walkway. The arcade can be designed to offer shelter from rain and snow and/or sun and heat.

Second, support facilities make a path more amiable for strolling. Table 6.4 shows one study's ranking of support facilities. The final category is seating, which is discussed subsequently in its own section.

Care should be taken to make amenities accessible to all.

Table 6.4 Ranking of Walkway Amenities

Amenity	Work Trip	Social/Recreational	Shopping
Benches	5	4	3
Shade	3	1	4
Rest rooms	1	3	1
Newsstands	4	5	5
Water fountains	2	2	2

SOURCE: Adapted from Table 8-2 in *A Pedestrian Planning Procedures Manual,* Report No. FHWA-RD-79-47, Federal Highway Administration, 1978.
NOTE: 1 is most preferred.

Phone dials should be between 42 and 48 inches (1.07 to 1.22 m) above grade. Control panels for ATMs, crosswalks, and other devices should also be in this range and should be able to be activated with minimal hand strength and dexterity. Toe clearance 10 inches (.25 m) high and 7 inches (.18 m) deep at a minimum should be provided where wheelchairs may approach an amenity.

Zoning the Sidewalk

More does and should happen on walkways than walking, but a clear zone for walking is mandatory. Therefore, zone the sidewalk into a main walking aisle and areas for activities, street furniture, utility access, and so forth. Consider the design of adjacent uses such as parking stalls and storefronts as part of the design of the walkway.

In addition to a clear walking zone, parking lot walkways serve other purposes: Shopping carts are left near cars, street musicians play in commandeered parking stalls, and people queue up along the sidewalk to use an ATM. The zones of a walkway extend into the streets, parking lots, or buildings on both sides of it. As long as the walking aisle remains clear, the zones may overlap. Zones can be delineated by three-dimensional objects and, more subtly, by surface texture and level changes (curbs). Pedestrians totally ignore any color patterns on walkways (Pushkarev and Zupan 1975, 156). Typical zones include (Figure 6.5):

- *Street facade zone (exterior).*   An extension of the building into the sidewalk that houses cafés, sidewalk sales, window-shopping, front stoops, and/or display gardens. The zone ranges from 1.5 to about 20 feet (.46 to 6.1 m). In the French Quarter of New Orleans, multiple floors of balconies occupy this zone.

- *The walking aisle.*   This area was discussed previously under Paths and Shortcuts. In order to mark the edge of this zone for the visually impaired, the surfaces that

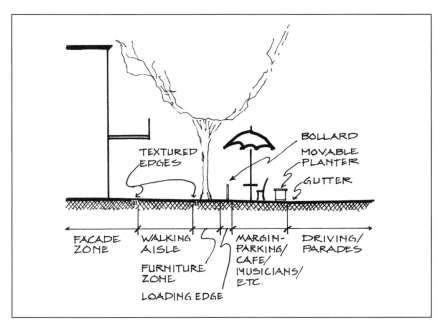

Figure 6.5 Diagram of sidewalk zones.

border on the walking aisle may be noticeably textured. Three-dimensional objects should not be closer than 6 inches (15.2 cm) from the edge of this zone and should be painted in high-contrast colors (ITE 5A-5 1995, 12).

- *The furniture zone.* A buffer along traffic or parking lanes that ranges from 6 inches for parking meters to many feet. This buffer may contain such things as street furniture, public sculpture, street trees, seating areas, and places for street musicians or other artists. Together with the following zones, it provides a buffer between pedestrians and moving traffic that allows for driveway and walkway curb cuts, provides a place to pile snow and park construction/repair equipment, and reduces exposure to noise, road spray, and the perception of hazard. (See Figure 6.6.)

- *The loading zone.* An 18- to 30-inch (.46- to .76-m) zone on the sidewalk along the curb that provides a

Figure 6.6 Sidewalk seating.

place for people getting into or out of cars. Along van-accessible curb parking there should be a clear space of 5 feet deep by 12 feet (1.52 by 3.66 m) centered on the parallel parking space (this space can overlap other zones as long as it is kept clear of obstructions).

Adjacent zones within the street, parking lot, and/or buildings should be incorporated in the design of the sidewalk. Typical zones include the following:

- *The street margin.* The curb parking lane can also provide for underground utilities, street cafés, and street performers.

- *Bike lane.* Bike lanes and curb parking are a difficult mix. Bike lanes may replace curb parking or be separated from curb parking by a planting strip.

- *Street facade zone (interior).* The street-level front of a building should support the sidewalk. It may be a storefront, display case, lobby, news and sundries store, or sheltered area for ATMs and street vendors.

Great Streets, by Allan Jacobs, analyzes many successful sidewalk designs in their full context.

Grade Crossings

Make it easy for people to use the safest route across vehicular lanes. Since people are more fragile and valuable than cars, use midblock crossings, raised crosswalks, sidewalk bulbs, roadway chatter strips, and simple traffic flows to give pedestrians the home-court advantage.

Crossings can be thought of as either pedestrians crossing a vehicular route or cars crossing a walkway. The viewpoint chosen is essentially a decision about which group has the right-of-way. However, in either case, crossings must be designed to accommodate both the driver's and the pedestrian's needs.

Mixed Traffic

Pedestrians and automobiles share the pavement in street-plazas, streetyards, and low-density parking lots. It is critical that the design of such places makes it clear to drivers that they do not have right-of-way. Landscaping, small curb radii, rumble pavement, and other features can help establish appropriate behavior.

Additionally, the volume of traffic should be limited. The Buchanan Report (Buchanan 1963) established a distinction between the crude capacity and the environmental capacity of a street. The *crude capacity* is a measure of the physical limits to the number of vehicles that may pass along a road in a given time. This is what traffic engineers usually refer to when they speak of a road's capacity. The *environmental capacity* is the number of vehicles that may travel along a street while maintaining the general comfort, convenience, and aesthetic quality of the physical surroundings for living. The environmental capacity of shared streets is set by the ability of pedestrians to freely cross the street, and this is clearly lower than the street's crude capacity.

The Design of Traffic Lanes

When vehicle density restricts the free flow of pedestrians, crosswalks are necessary. On streets, crosswalks occur mid-block or at intersections. Within parking lots, independent pedestrian paths are usually halfway between driving aisles ("midblock"). Even when paths are provided in parking lots, however, pedestrians will share space with cars along the aisles and intersections.

Midblock crossings are less complicated than intersection crossings because cars are approaching from only one or two directions and are not turning. Left-turning vehicles are involved in four times as many accidents and right-turning vehicles have twice as many accidents as vehicles going straight through an intersection (Dewar 1992, 19). However, it is important to warn drivers about midblock crossings. Within parking lots, the pedestrian path should take precedence over the driving lane because the efficiency of automobile movement is not critical. Stop signs, a raised crosswalk (Figure 6.7), chatter strips (lines of rough pave-

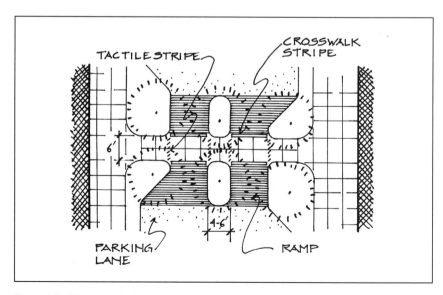

Figure 6.7   Diagram of raised crosswalk and midstream island.

ment) placed in advance of the crosswalk, and lighting can all give priority to the pedestrian.

Crosswalks at intersections require more care. How elaborate the design should be depends on pedestrian volumes, vehicular volumes, and vehicular speed. Four factors should be reviewed in the design of intersection crosswalks: vehicle speeds, the number of directions that cars can take within the intersection, visibility of cars and pedestrians, and the length of the crosswalk (Pietrucha and Plummer 1992). Slower vehicles have more time to see pedestrians and do less damage if they do hit them. Intersections of one-way streets have fewer pedestrian collisions than do two-way streets, and separate turn phases at signalized intersections reduce accidents. Lack of mutual visibility and the length of the crosswalk are directly related to a person's exposure to risk.

Sidewalk bulbs (Figure 6.8) increase the visibility of both pedestrians and vehicles, tend to slow turning traffic, and reduce crosswalk length. It is critical, however, not to put the curb edge too close to the driving lane. A buffer zone can be established by a wide gutter to provide a margin beyond the curb line that is not in the normal path of cars.

The curb radius is critical to a bulb's effectiveness. A 30-foot (9.15-m) curb radius creates 24 feet (7.32 m) more crosswalk than a 10-foot (3.05-m) radius. This equals about 10 seconds more crossing time for the elderly and 6 seconds more for the average pedestrian (Figure 6.9).

Pedestrian Crossing Design

Crossings are continuations of paths and should be as direct as possible. If you try to move people out of their natural path to a safe crossing, a good portion of them will simply continue on their route. Even barriers are not good substitutes for direct routes. "Barriers should be used with care, since most barriers have proven to be rather ineffective in stopping pedestrians" (ITE 5A-5 1995, 6). Instead of block-

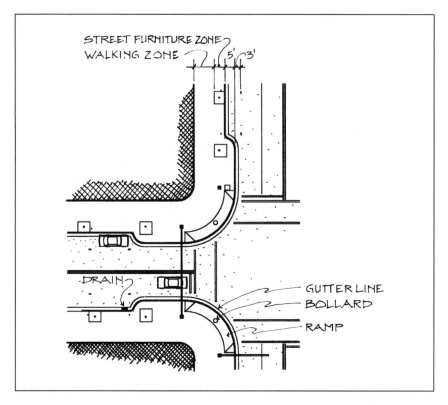

Figure 6.8   Sidewalk bulb.

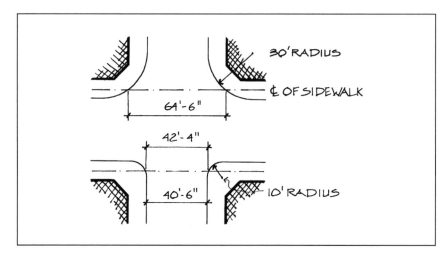

Figure 6.9   Comparison of crossing distance with different curb radii.

ing a path, improve the safety of the desired path. Crossings can be improved by the following means:

- A curb and/or a row of bollards marking the edge of the traffic zone.

- A 2- to 3-foot (.61- to .91-m) buffer zone just beyond this edge that appears as part of the driving lane but is not in the primary auto path.

- Grading to keep the crosswalk as flat as possible and as close to the level of the path as possible while draining water well away (1 to 2 percent cross grade).

- Midstream islands when there are more than two lanes to cross or very busy two-lane traffic. The islands must be accessible for people in wheelchairs. Islands should be as wide as the crossing, at least 4 feet (1.22 m) long and protected by curbs, bollards, or other barriers on either side (Figure 6.8).

- Any crosswalk controls must be no higher than 42 inches (1.07 m) and easily activated. Lighted crosswalk buttons would be beneficial.

- Solid white side strips a minimum of 6 inches (15.2 cm) wide, set a minimum of 6 feet (1.83 m) apart (*Manual of Uniform Traffic Control Devices*, section 3B-18).

- Chatter strips upstream from the crosswalk.

- Nighttime blue signs with flashing yellow beacons have been shown in the Netherlands to reduce nighttime accidents.

Over and Under

When the hazards of a crossing are high, and conditions can be created to induce pedestrians to use them, pedestrian bridges or tunnels may be necessary. Design bridges or tunnels to minimize the elevation change for

pedestrians, ensure that pedestrians are not hidden from passive surveillance, incorporate the crossing into the natural path, and keep the pedestrians associated with the buildings and the fabric of the city (Figure 6.10).

At parking lots surrounded by busy streets there may be a need for grade-separated street crossings. Pedestrian overpasses and underpasses should not be considered unless there is (1) a demand to cross a freeway or limited-access road of 100 pedestrians per hour in the peak 4 hours, (2) a demand of 300 pedestrians per hour in the peak 4 hours to cross a street with a vehicle volume of more than 7500 per hour during those same 4 hours, (3) a number of children or mobility-impaired people who must regularly cross a high-speed or high-volume road, (4) an extreme hazard for pedestrians, *or* (5) conditions where the roadway is significantly below or above the natural grade of the sidewalk (ITE 5A-5 1995, 42).

Grade-separated crossings will not be well used unless they are extensions of a major continuous level on which the pedestrians find themselves in the course of their natural itinerary and which involves no obvious vertical or horizontal detours (Pushkarev and Zupan 1975, 173). Ninety-five

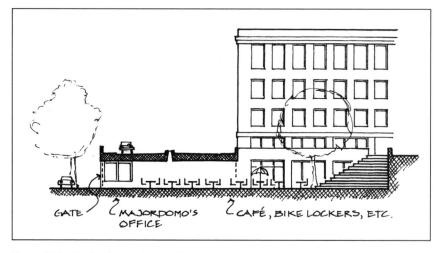

Figure 6.10   Pedestrian underpass diagram.

percent of people would use an underpass and 70 percent would use an overpass if the travel time is the same as that of an at-grade route. Passageways that require greater than 50 percent more travel time are virtually unused (Moore and Older 1965).

It should be pointed out that generally we assume the cars will remain at grade and the pedestrians will go over or under the street. However, in some cases the walkway may be kept at grade while the roadway changes grade, or the walkway and traffic lanes may share in creating the grade separation.

Pedestrian overpasses generally require a clearance of approximately 16 feet (4.87 m) and should be fenced to keep people from dropping things on cars. Pedestrian underpasses require a minimum clearance of 8 feet (2.44 m).

Tunnels should be well lit, wide, with a clear view to the other side, visible from nearby active areas, and, if at all possible, integrated with other uses such as cafés, parking attendants' offices, or the entrance to movie theaters. Policing the tunnel and providing gates to close it during off-hours will help with security.[3]

To Curb or Not to Curb

Curbs are overused. They cause tripping and wheelchair-access problems. On the other hand, curbs provide a sense of clarity and security. They can ease access to buses, help drain water, increase pedestrian visibility, and deter encroachment by cars onto sidewalks. Therefore, carefully consider the use of curbs. (See Figure 6.11.)

Parking lots are shared between motorists and pedestrians. In residential shared street design (streetyards), pedestrians have priority across the entire roadway. Therefore curbs are rarely used but the street is detailed to clearly communicate that cars are guests.

Curbs do provide a clear demarcation of areas off-limits

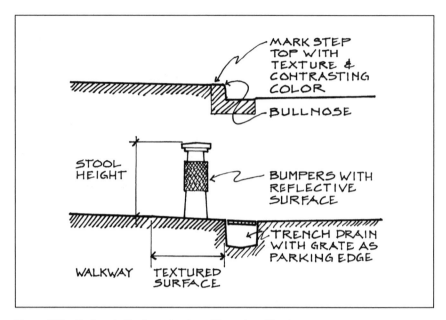

Figure 6.11 Curb or bollard as edge to traffic and parking lanes.

to cars, and thus provide a sense of security. The standard curb, however, can easily be mounted by an auto. Curbs should be designed as single steps. There is some disagreement in the engineering literature about appropriate curb height. Dewar (1992, 24) says 10 inches (25.4 cm) is about the maximum height. Reuter recommends an 11-inch (27.9-cm) curb to allow for a type of wheelchair-accessible bus (ITE 5A-5 1995, 14). A 6-inch (15.2-cm) curb approximates a normal stair step and presents less of a tripping hazard than higher curbs. Ideally, curbs should conform to good outdoor stair design, with a top (tread) at least 11 inches (~28 cm) wide, nosings with a maximum radius of ½ inch (1.27 cm), and colored indicator striping or edging to clearly show the leading edge of the curb.

No matter the height, curb cuts must be installed to provide access for the mobility-impaired (and for baby strollers, shopping carts, bikes, wheeled luggage, etc.). "The single most important feature of curb cuts is that they be flared [*sic*] into the street surface. Any sudden drop-off in a ramp descent by as little as ¼ inch (.635 cm) may cause a wheelchair to tip over" (ITE 5A-5 1995, 13).[4] Curb cuts must be a minimum of 36 inches (.91 m) wide excluding side slopes, must not exceed 8 percent in grade (or 16 percent for side slopes), have a grooved warning border, be slip-resistant, and should be in the direction of travel, not aimed to the center of an intersection. Finally, care must be taken to drain water away from the pathway (Figure 6.12).

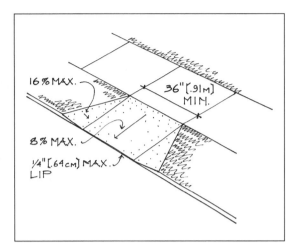

Figure 6.12 Curb cut.

Sitting and Leaning

Provide a generous amount of seating at least 18 inches (.46 m) deep. Formal and informal seating in a variety of orientations, groupings, shelter, and degrees of seclusion should be provided. Include places for leaning such as railings, bar-height ledges, and columns.

The term *pedestrian* is misleading. People are not simply another vehicular mode. We stroll; we wander; we lean and we sit (Figure 6.13). Places for pedestrians, whether they are meant to be places to hang out or pathways, must provide seating and leaning places. Allan Jacobs observes, "A remarkable number of the very best streets have benches. . . . Those same streets have other places for people to sit as well, notably at tables of streetside cafés" (1993, 300).

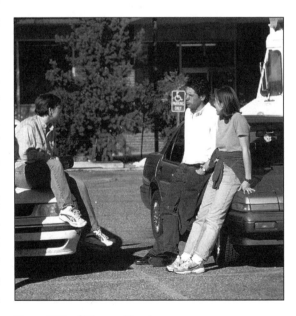

Figure 6.13 Sitting and leaning.

Table 6.5   Seating Recommendations

	Recommendation	Source
Depth	18 in. single-sided (~46 cm)	Interiors
	30–36 in. double-sided (~76–92 cm)	Whyte 1980, 31
	11 in. for stairs (~28 cm)	Whyte 1980, 33
Height	17 in. (~43 cm)	Interiors
	1–3 ft (ledges and steps) (~30–90 cm)	Whyte 1980, 31
Amount	1 lineal ft per lineal ft of plaza edge min.	1986 San Francisco Plan
	1 lineal ft per 30 ft^2 of plaza min.	Whyte 1980, 39
	(~1.1 lineal m per 10 m^2)	
	(Note: doesn't include steps or grass)	
Type	50% secondary seating—steps, grass, ledges	Marcus and Francis 1990, 33
	50% primary seating:	
	Chairs, movable benches	Whyte 1980, 34
	Tables with chairs for eating areas	Marcus and Francis 1990, 35
Orientation	Variety—toward people watching, toward city and landscape views, around play areas, inward focus for groups, etc.	Marcus and Francis 1990, 35
Place	People sit near circulation	Whyte 1980, 33
	Corners of planters, stairs, etc.	Marcus and Francis 1990, 35
	Along walkways at entrances and drop-offs, at the top and bottom of significant grades	
Materials	Responsive to temperature (e.g., wood)	Marcus and Francis 1990, 36
	Avoid materials that look like they might damage clothes (e.g., rough wood)	

Seats and places to lean are major props on the public stage and thus should be designed to enhance a variety of interpersonal interactions. "Ideally, sitting should be physically comfortable—benches with back rests, well-contoured chairs. It's more important, however, that it be socially comfortable" (Whyte 1980, 28). Table 6.5 summarizes recommendations for seating, but one point needs to be emphasized—flexibility. Provide chairs that the users can adjust, and plan to fine-tune the placement of benches, tables, and other seating areas after the opening of the place.

Seating along pathways should be provided for pedestrians who lack stamina or who have luggage, packages, or small children. Logical places include building entrances, pickups/drop-offs, and the tops and bottoms of significant grades.

Some people prefer to lean. It often signifies less of a commitment than sitting, and it engenders a different social relationship than sitting. A few people have back or other problems that make leaning more comfortable than sitting. The standard bar-counter height is 40 to 41 inches (1.04 m), and footrests are at about 4 to 6 inches (10.16 to 15.24 cm). Toe clearances for wheelchairs, however, are 10 inches (25.4 cm) high by 7 inches (17.78 cm) deep. A tilt to a railing of about 3° away from the leaner can add comfort.

A City of 10,000 Gardens

He that planteth a tree is the servant of God. He provideth a kindness for many generations. And faces that he hath not seen shall bless him.

—HENRY VAN DYKE, 1890

The term *lot* means simply a division of land. A lot is a legal entity whose geometry is not visible on the ground until it contains something. On the other hand, as Paul Groth points out in his essay "Parking Gardens," the term *garden* suggests a place actively made and cared for. A garden is a part of the living earth, shaped by stewardship, not simply by ownership.

A 1970 Harris poll reported that 95 percent of Americans listed "green grass and trees around me" as an important part of their environment (Miller 1997, 51). Gardens have been shown to lower stress levels, promote health and healing, and increase job satisfaction. Kaplan and Kaplan, for example, report on the effects of access to gardens and other "green spaces." The benefits of visual and physical access include "enjoyment, relaxation, and lowered stress levels. . . . People with access to nearby natural settings have been found to be healthier than other individuals . . . impacts also include increased levels of satisfaction with one's home, one's job and with life in general" (1989, 173).

The square enclosure and the "guardian" stone are, according to *The Poetics of Gardens* (Moore, Mitchell, and Turnbull 1988), the two "ur gardens," historic basic notions about how to compose gardens. The square enclosure is a world apart, a paradise. F. H. Burnett's children's story, *The Secret Garden,* is based on this archetype. The "guardian" stone, in the Japanese tradition, is the central point in a garden about which the garden and, by implication, the world is gathered. The courtyard of the Salk Institute, which opens to a view of the Pacific Ocean, rests on this gathering of the world about a place.

I believe there is a third historic theme, perhaps best illustrated by a fantasy of the future. *Star Trek*'s holodeck brings the wilds to the city so that citizens may play and conduct plays about their basic nature. Greek theaters were set in bowls in the landscape. Mayan temples are composed to evoke the presence of the volcanoes. And Lawrence Halprin's Lovejoy Plaza in Portland, Oregon, brings the waterfalls of the Cascade Mountains to the heart of the city. The third "ur garden" is the theater of the wilds.

Parking gardens may grow from any of these roots. Hidden parking, perhaps, is most easily composed as a secret garden. Public squares are by nature suited to gathering the world about them, and, perhaps, the large lot transformed into a forest can harbor a theater in the midst of its wilds.

"Most interesting, though, is the capacity gardens have to civilize . . ." Donlyn Lyndon writes (Lyndon and Moore 1994, 258). Gardens are portraits of the marriage of nature and culture, and thus they reflect, idealize, and refine the artist and his or her times.

Parking gardens are, in this sense, the subject of this entire book. Instead of creating a legally described parcel on which we may, for a time, abandon machines, I am suggesting that we make places that are valuable as part of the city and the living planet.

There are an uncountable number of ways to establish a

parking garden. Great cities should have 10,000 gardens, some of them incorporating cars, each speaking its own insight.

Depth and Coherence

Make parking gardens—outdoor rooms that provide an ideal habitat for public space. Give coherence and visible order to the garden, but provide a bit of mystery or depth, the sense that there is more to be seen. Frame and capture views from the parking garden of the city and landscape (Figure 7.1).

The Kaplans have conducted research into preferences for how gardens are composed (Kaplan and Kaplan 1989). The single aspect that most consistently predicts people's preference for a site is what they call "mystery." Mystery, or depth of place, they define as evidence that one could learn more—examples include a road bending out of sight or a bright clearing seen at a distance through the forest.

Figure 7.1 Arcade and parking. The columns provide a coherent rhythm, and the portals in both the arcade and parking court frame glimpses of spaces beyond.

Views from parking gardens can be composed as extensions of the garden, evoking the sense of adventure and depth of place. The Japanese gardening practice of *ikedori,* "capturing alive," provides a set of compositional techniques for incorporating a view into a garden. Capturing alive rests on a careful framing of the view, using middleground elements to knit the near garden and the far view and using elements in the garden that are associated with the far landscape (Itoh 1980).

Framing with a solid hedge or wall is often necessary to eliminate the clutter of nearby details that would otherwise come between the garden and the captured view. Care should be taken to ensure that this does not compromise security. Trees, lampposts, or other vertical elements placed on the edge of the garden both inside and outside the hedge help complete the framing and form a middle ground between the garden and the view. If these elements are somehow associated with the view, then they also provide a mental link. For example, the trees that forest a mountain may be planted to frame the view of the mountain, or the view of a boulevard may be framed by cars parked in the garden.

The Kaplans also identified the coherence of a garden as an element that people prefer. Coherence is the sense of order. Repeated elements, such as parking stalls, that measure and compose a site provide coherence.

Great Trees

Trees are the prime ingredient in parking gardens. Select trees that are compatible with the auto environment. (See Figure 7.2.)

Money doesn't grow on trees. It blooms in their shade. Trees increase the value of a house an average of 5 to 10 percent (in some cases up to 20 percent) and are widely believed to improve the value of many other building types (Kielbaso et

Figure 7.2 Tree garden.

al. 1988). Trees can reduce and retard stormwater runoff, diminish glare, act as windbreaks, and provide pleasant places. Trees and hedges moderate cooling and heating demands in their immediate vicinity, help cool cities, and are part of a strategy to reduce global warming and save energy (Akbari et al. 1992). One estimate done for Sacramento, California, places the value of all air-quality benefits from a healthy parking lot tree at about $25 to $35 annually (McPherson, Simpson and Scott 1997).

Trees are an ideal plant for parking gardens. They provide greenery without occupying a large part of the ground needed for parking. There are, of course, alternatives to trees. The SWA Group entry to the 1984 Carscape Competition, for example, suggested covering a lot with a wire network so that wisteria could form a fragrant and colorful ceiling (Figure 7.3).

Selecting the perfect trees for a site can be complex. In addition to general climate considerations, a parking garden

Figure 7.3 Ceiling created by wisteria vines. Entry #23, The SWA Group, Boston in the Carscape competition.

(Used by permission. C. Miller. 1988. *Carscape: A Parking Handbook,* Irwin-Sweeney-Miller Foundation, Columbus, Indiana, p. 80.)

tree must fit a difficult set of conditions to flourish among cars. The microclimate of a parking lot is usually more extreme than the general climate for an area. The pavement makes it hotter and dryer than an open field. There is both air- and waterborne pollution. The root zone for trees is restricted and the soil is often compacted. Unless protected, cars may run into or scrape trunks, and often there is minimal effort expended on maintenance.

Table 7.1 offers criteria to help select trees for parking gardens. Trees should be fit for the parking lot environment and not be apt to damage cars. Trees that shed gum and sap should be avoided, and species that produce air-pollution precursors should be not be planted in urban areas with air-pollution problems (Table 7.2). Trees must be able to be pruned up to about 7 to 10 feet (~2.2 to 3 m) above the pavement, and care must be taken to remove dead limbs and dying trees. A maintenance plan usually must include composting or disposal of the leaves and other detritus of the trees.

Additionally, it is advisable to plant a diversity of species both within the parking garden and in relation to the adjacent neighborhood. The International Society of

Table 7.1   Criteria for Parking Lot Trees

Requirements

High branching (leaving 7 ft min. above grade clear)
Strong wood (gives warning of branch dropping)
Clean tree—minimum litter
Tolerant to drought
Tolerant to pollution
Disease- and pest-resistant
Size of mature tree appropriate to available space
Tolerant of extreme microclimate (typically warmer and drier than general vicinity)
Deep roots or root barriers (limit disturbance to pavement)
Tolerant of soil compaction
Tolerant of salt/chemicals from snow removal
Ability to be upbranched (leaving 7 ft min. above grade clear)

Considerations

Design—size, shape, color, growth rate, foliage density, etc.
Limit smog precursor emissions (see Table 7.2)
Long-lived—50 to 100 years
Acceptable level of maintenance

Arboriculture has established the following diversification formula: No planting plan should contain more than 10 percent of one family or 5 percent of one species (Phillips 1993, 48). Diversification reduces the spread of tree diseases and reduces the effect of a disease on the overall tree cover. Diverse species with similar forms and habits can provide a unified design. See the appendix for sources of recommendations about urban trees suitable to your local environment.

Three Tree Classics

Three classic ways of organizing trees are particularly suited to parking gardens: the orchard, the hedgerow, and the clearing. In combination with adjacent buildings, they form the walls and ceiling of the parking area.

Many city zoning codes require a few trees. These required trees are, however, rarely sufficient to transform a lot into a

Table 7.2   Selected Trees with Low Air-Pollution Precursor Emissions

Latin Name	Common Name
Acer glabrum	Rocky Mountain maple
Acer macrophyllum	Bigleaf maple
Arbutus menziesii	Madrone
Calocedrus decurrens	Incense cedar
Cedrus atlantica	Atlas cedar
Cedrus deodara	Deodar cedar
Cercis canadensis	Redbud
Cercis occidentalis	Western redbud
Chamaecyparis lawsoniana	Port Orford cedar
Cinnamomum camphora	Camphor
Cupressocyparis leylandii	Leylandi cypress
Cupressus forbesii	Tecate cypress
Cupressus sempervirens	Italian cypress
Fraxinus latifolia	Oregon ash
Fraxinus pennsylvanica	Green ash
Fraxinus uhdei	Evergreen ash
Fraxinus velutina	Arizona ash
Fraxinus velutina coriacea	Montebello ash
Geijera parvifolia	Australian willow
Jacaranda mimosifolia	Jacaranda
Lagerstroemia indica	Crape myrtle
Malus sp.	Crabapple
Pinus halepensis	Aleppo pine
Pinus pinea	Italian stone pine
Pinus radiata	Monterey pine
Pinus sabiniana	Foothill pine
Pittosporum undulatum	Victorian box
Podocarpus macrophyllus	Yew pine
Prunus lusitanica	Portugal laurel
Pyrus calleryana Aristocrat	Aristocrat flowering pear
Pyrus calleryana Bradford	Bradford pear
Pyrus kawakamii	Evergreen pear
Sambucus neomexicana	Hairy blue elderberry
Thuja plicata	Western red cedar
Ulmus parvifolia	Chinese elm
Zelkova serrata	Sawleaf zelkova

Data selected from Michael T. Benjamin, Mark Sudol, Laura Bloch, and Arthur M. Winer, 1996, "Low-Emitting Urban Forests: A Taxonomic Methodology for Assigning Isoprene and Monoterpene Emission Rates" in *Atmospheric Environment,* vol. 30, no. 9, pp. 1437–1452. Copyright © 1996 Elsevier Science Ltd. Reprinted with kind permission from Elsevier Science Ltd., the Boulevard, Langford Lane, Kidlington OX5 1GB UK.

garden. With the addition of more trees, a lot may become an orchard, a field between hedges, or a clearing in the forest.

Orchard

The rows and columns of an orchard seem to offer a comfortable fit with rows of parking. Two factors, however, often lead to an unsatisfactory development of orchards in parking lots. First, we are often unwilling to plant a sufficient number of trees. Richard Untermann suggests planting three trees per parking stall (1984, 202). Zoning codes require far fewer. Second, the roughly 60-foot width necessary for parking bays is not well scaled to provide an orchard layout for any but the largest trees. Planting in the end islands of hard-paved lots can usually support only small trees unless extra space is incorporated into the design (see Figure 13.6 for minimal and large end-island dimensions).

Planting a "parking orchard" requires that the canopies of mature trees touch their neighbors to provide shade, cooling, and the sense of a ceiling. For this to occur either (1) trees with 60- to 70-foot (~18- to 21-m) canopies must be planted to span the typical double row of 90° parking; (2) angle parking or single-loaded aisles of parking are used to reduce the row width, and trees with 35- to 50-foot (~10.6- to 15-m) canopies are planted; or (3) trees are planted between stalls near the aisle (Figure 7.4).

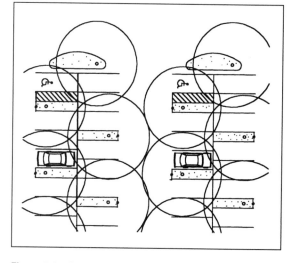

Figure 7.4 Parking orchard planting plan.

Hedgerow

A well-placed and tall hedge of trees can provide shade and serve as a windbreak. Hedgerows of trees and bushes are also often advocated to hide parking lots from the street. However, this creates safety concerns for parkers who can't be seen from the street and for pedestrians on the sidewalk who may fear that the hedge offers places for miscreants to hide. One survey of park-and-ride-lot users found that 70 percent prefer lots with landscaping but that safety and visibility were significantly more important than aesthetic preferences (Pfeiffer 1986). The same study noted that hedges are ineffective in directing pedestrians—people walk through them and destroy the plantings.

Hedgerows may, however, be successful along freeways or other places where a wall is appropriate. Note that a hedge of trees may help mask noise but will not significantly reduce it. Along a sidewalk or within a parking lot, the trunks of thickly planted trees with few low branches may provide a psychological screen, some shade, and a windbreak while allowing pedestrian passage and visual access.

Clearing

A clearing is the absence of trees amid a surrounding thickness of trees. Depending on the climate and the collection of functions in the parking garden, either of two patterns of clearings may be appropriate.

The first pattern is a set of clearings housing the bays of parking, separated by woods that shelter other uses. Meadow-edge species could border the lots, with deep-forest species forming the woods. The reverse pattern, in which the cars are in the shaded woods and pedestrian spaces are in the clearings, may be appropriate in some climates.

Elaborations

Orchard, hedgerow, and clearing are not the only possibilities. A single grand tree centered in a courtyard can be a powerful presence. Mixed patterns, such as an orchard bordered or crossed by hedgerows, may be appropriate. Furthermore, patterns derived from local ecosystems could be used.

Street Trees

The elegant American tradition of street trees should be continued. (See Figure 7.5.)

Street trees moderate the climate, potentially reduce motorists' exposure to glare from morning and evening sun, and provide a pleasant place for curb parking and sidewalk strolling. A good canopy of trees gives a sense of enclosure to a street, and it is believed that this sense of enclosure induces people to drive slower (Hass-Klau 1990, 212). Thus, trees may help reduce the number and severity of conflicts between curb parkers and through traffic. Street trees are typically planted between the sidewalk and curb, but they may also be planted at intervals in the parking lane, where they help define bays of parking.

The treelawn, or area of unpaved ground around a tree, is directly related to the size and health of the tree. Table

Figure 7.5   Street trees in downtown San Luis Obispo, California.

Table 7.3   Treelawn Widths by Tree Size

Treelawn Width	Trunk Diameter (30-yr.-old tree)	Tree Height (30-yr.-old tree)
>48 in. (>1.22 m)	>30 in. (>.76 m)	>40 ft (>12.2 m)
30–48 in. (.76–1.22 m)	15–30 in. (.38–.76 m)	Around 30 ft (~9.2 m)
<30 in. (<.76 m)	8–15 in. (.2–.38 m)	Around 18 ft (~5.5 m)

SOURCE: Adapted from New Jersey Federation of Shade Tree Commissions as reported in Schein, 1993.

7.3 shows recommended widths of continuous treelawns (also known as *planting strips* or *parking strips*) for three general sizes of trees.

A typical planting of street trees is a single age of a single species of trees placed at regular intervals. However, a mix of species means that a street is less apt to lose all its trees to a single disease, and it provides the opportunity for multiple events such as early- and late-spring blooms. A design based on trees of mixed age planted in loose patterns allows the replacement of individual trees without creating "missing teeth." The International Society of Arboriculture recommends that a planting plan contain no more than 10 percent from one family or 5 percent from one species.

Table 7.4 shows general recommendations for the spacing of trees. The exact species chosen, the density of shade desired, the quality of soil, the size of the treelawn, and many other factors may alter the spacing.

There are some potential hazards caused by street trees. They may block a driver's view around the corner of an

Table 7.4   Spacing of Street Trees

Mature Height	Planting Interval
<30 ft (~<9 m)	15–25 ft (~4.5–7.6 m)
30–45 ft (~9–14 m)	~40 ft (~12 m)
>45 ft (~>14 m)	50–70 ft (~15–21 m)

SOURCE: Adapted from Schein, *Street Trees,* 1993, 115.

intersection; dead tree limbs may fall on property or people; and street trees are sometimes considered a hazard to out-of-control vehicles because large trees do not give way when hit. All of these potential hazards can be minimized.

In order to maximize visibility at street corners, many municipalities have adopted regulations requiring clear-sight triangles at intersections within which trees or other obstructions should not be placed.

To minimize the hazards of falling branches, species such as *Eucalyptus cladocalyx* that shed limbs with little warning should be avoided, trees should be properly planted, and a regular inspection and maintenance program should be established. Often, residents and business owners can be enlisted to aid with inspection.

Finally, the hazard trees present to out-of-control vehicles can be minimized by avoiding planting trees with mature trunks in excess of 6 inches (~15 cm), calipered at locations with the highest probabilities of run-off-the-road accidents (Figure 7.6). Trees are not significant obstacles along streets with curb parking because the parked cars shield the trees (and pedestrians), and trees may be part of the traffic-calming scheme for streetyards and streetplazas. In these cases, bollards, raised planting beds, and other devices may be used to reduce the mutually harmful contact between cars and street trees.

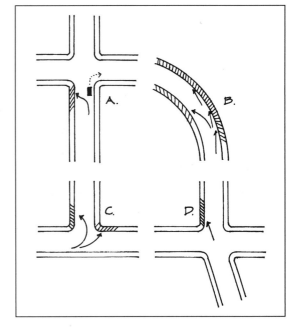

Figure 7.6 Typical run-off-the-road accident locations. (Adapted from O'Brien 1993.)

Community Forest

Parking gardens, particularly municipal lots, should be part of a community forest program. Consider each parking garden as one in a series of gardens within a district. Along a main street,

within a downtown, or around a campus, compose the gardens as variations on a theme (or charms on a necklace), so that they help give structure and character to the district. Consider developing a community forest program that includes private parking lot forests. (See Figure 7.7.)

Johnny Appleseed planted firmly in American soil the notion that trees are a public good. By 1637, Watertown, Massachusetts, was marking trees that the city deemed should be protected. The first public shade-tree planting in the United States occurred in 1646, when Bostonians replaced the forest they had cleared a decade earlier (Phillips 1993, 6). In 1700, Philadelphia, New Castle, Delaware, and Chester, Pennsylvania, required citizens to plant certain types of trees (Schein 1993, 13). In 1869, New York State rebated some of the highway taxes to communities for tree planting (Schein 1993, 24).

Today, community forest programs often manage the street trees of a city. In such a program, a city's trees are managed as a public asset. A municipal agency consults with the public, creates a master plan, and oversees the planting and maintenance of trees in public places such as streets and plazas. It would be a logical and efficient extension to include the trees of municipal parking lots.

In *Street Trees: A Manual for Municipalities,* Richard Schein discusses the benefits and requirements of a successful community forestry program for both large and small cities (1993). He suggests that municipalities adopt a community forestry ordinance that establishes an agency with a regular budget, regulates the planting and maintenance of public trees, and authorizes a master plan (including an inventory of existing trees and a list of appropriate trees for new plantings).

Each garden within the community forest can serve as a public resource in another way, by providing signs and/or artwork identifying plants, birds, or other animals likely to be found in the garden, the history or story of the garden, and other interpretive features. For example, Seattle, Wash-

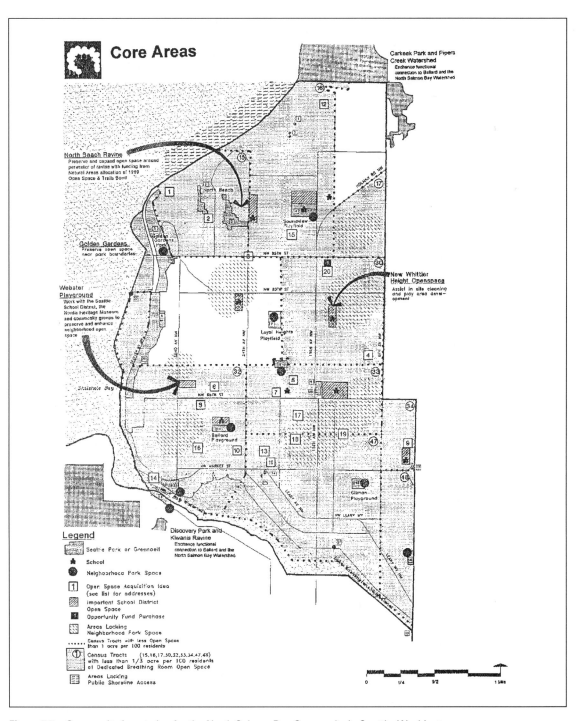

Figure 7.7 Community forest plan for the North Salmon Bay Community in Seattle, Washington.

(Courtesy Davidya Kasperzyk.)

ington has tree grates that identify and describe the trees within the grate.

Near the beginning of the automobile age, Frederick Law Olmstead promoted his parkways and parks as "emerald necklaces" for cities. The results from Boston, Massachusetts, to Seattle, Washington, are highly valued urban amenities. A community forest program can manage parking gardens to form new necklaces. Just as Olmstead elaborated the carriageway into a parkway, a series of parking lots can be transformed into a bouquet of gardens.

Municipal forestry programs could be expanded to include private parking lots. Zoning codes often address tree planting in parking lots, but frequently these ordinances are not effective. For example, a study of existing parking lots in Davis, California, found that none of the lots studied met the zoning requirement that 50 percent of paved surfaces be shaded by tree canopies within 15 years of construction (McPherson, Simpson, and Scott 1997). A municipal forestry program could help make more effective plantings.

Neighborhood and business associations could develop plans based on grants and voluntary actions. Municipalities could expand a park or urban forest program to include design and maintenance planning assistance, building-permit review, postoccupancy inspections of lots, and education programs. This expanded role could be financed from building-permit fees, air-pollution funds, energy-conservation funds, and urban beautification funds. Performance bonds could be required to ensure that plantings meet zoning requirements, and perhaps landscape architecture and forestry schools could support expanded programs that include student interns, research, and public seminars.

Planting Parking Lot Trees 101

Provide plenty of root area for each tree and plant in a group. Analyze the soil and select appropriate species. Loosen the soil; don't overplant

for instant effect; protect the trees from car bumpers; and plant trees that are free of most branches to a height of 7 feet (2.13 m) above the pavement. (See Figure 7.8.)

Parking lots and streets are difficult environments. In addition to selecting appropriate trees, proper sites must be prepared to keep trees healthy.

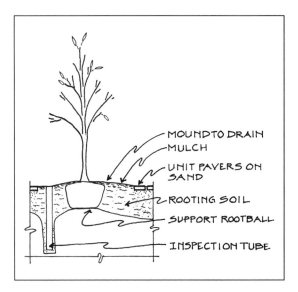

Figure 7.8   Tree-planting diagram.

The condition and preparation of the soil is critical. Tree species must be selected for the expected conditions. For example, if dry soils are likely, the trees must tolerate this condition. Perhaps the single most effective killer of parking lot trees is soil compaction. After the pavement has been placed, loosen at least the top foot of soil in the entire planting area. If soil toxicity, an extreme pH, or extensive rubble is suspected, test the soil and replace or amend it. Otherwise, native soil should be used to backfill around the planting. After planting, mulch around the tree to keep water in the soil and to reduce the growth of weeds and grass, and keep lawn mowers away from the trunk.

If tree grates are used, (1) plant the tree so that the top of the tree ball is at least 4 inches [~10 cm] below the underside of the grate to ensure the growth of roots will not move the grate, (2) use a grate whose surface area is at least 35 percent open, and (3) fill the grate with permeable soil so that gum, paper, and other trash does not fill the grate and strangle the root system.

Provide as much root area for each tree as possible (Table 7.3). The roots of most trees extend horizontally. The roots of most plants, including large trees, grow primarily in the top 3 feet of soil, and the majority of small, absorbing roots are in the upper 6 inches (~15 cm) (Schein 1993, 194). On small islands, plant small trees—20 to 30 feet (~6 to 7 m) tall. Along the sides or in medians, plant trees in groups so that they can share each others' root area. Group planting also moderates the temperatures to which each tree is exposed, increases humidity, and allows trees to serve as windbreaks for each other. However, do not overplant for instant effect, as this may cause diseases and increase maintenance.

Protect the trees from contact with the cars. Do not plant trees in the car overhang area. Place bollards with reflectors or tree guards around any tree that is potentially in harm's way. Trees are also subject to vandalism. One potential means of reducing the possibility of vandalism is to hire local youths to help plant the trees.

Trunk movement is necessary to build the strength of the trunk—thus trees should not be staked. If excessive wind is a problem, trees may be guyed, but the guys should either decompose or be removed with 12 to 18 months after planting (Phillips 1993, 73).

If a parking lot is constructed around existing trees, take care to cut as few roots as possible, retain as much treelawn as possible, and avoid compacting the soil within the treelawn. Trees that grew up within a grove should not be left as single trees. They have relied on their neighbors as windbreaks and often do not have the structural strength to survive a strong wind on their own. Choose trees that were already isolated or on the edge of a grove, or else save entire groves.

Prune and Weed

Design with maintenance in mind. Prepare a gardening plan and budget with the initial design. Include a description of the design intent, preventative maintenance plans, and regular care schedules for the garden and the pavement.

Trees require special care for 2 to 3 years after planting, including watering, light fertilization, pruning for proper shape, and mulch reapplication (Phillips 1993, 77). Additionally, parking areas often get heavy use. The design must anticipate this. For example, hedges and planting beds will not keep people from walking where they want to go, so a plan should allow easy access. Likewise, drivers occasionally jump curbs or pull into a stall until they hit something. Tree trunks must not be in the overhang space, and sprinklers should not be placed at curb edge where cars and pedestrians will break them.

Preparing a garden-care manual with the design helps ensure that the garden will have a long and healthy life. Regular maintenance keeps the landscape in better condition with less total effort and expense. Include a maintenance plan for the plants and the built features. Develop the plan with the assistance of the site manager, if there is one when the design is prepared, and work with a landscape maintenance firm to develop a budget for care. Anticipate the level of care that can be reasonably expected. Integrate the care of the flora with care of the pavement and other features. This will help to avoid conflicts in methods and materials (such as using salt to deice pavement that drains into planted areas).

Watering, fertilizing, weeding, and planting schedules should be included. Sketches of the intended mature conditions, documentation of hidden conditions, warranties, manufacturers' care instructions, a checklist of stress and disease symptoms, and suggestions for replacing diseased or damaged specimens are also helpful. Provide a means for the addition of information and notes by the gardener. The manual should be designed to help a maintenance person who may not be well versed in landscape maintenance keep the garden in good health.

Seven Gardeners

The components of a garden may be selected and composed based on many different ways of seeing. The traditions of various viewpoints are part of the

Figure 7.9 Artwork extends the Albuquerque Biological Park's theme of collection and display of species into the parking lot.

cultural material a designer may use to craft a garden. Establish a collector's garden, a painter's field of color, a dancer's succession of paths, a storyteller's stage set, a diplomat's meeting grounds, a philosopher's vision, or a child's kingdom. But have one clear, central idea. (See Figure 7.9.)

"Many of the pleasures of gardens come from sharing a point of view, from playing a game with agreed-upon pieces and rules and procedures. There is a collector's game, a painter's, a cinematographer's, a storyteller's, and a philosopher's, and of course there are many others, too," write Moore et al. in *The Poetics of Gardens* (1988, 23).

Each type of gardener sees different elements as the prime subject matter of the garden. The collector may breed exotic plants, compose rocks, or provide settings to display artifacts of the history of a site. The focus of the garden is in this case a set of objects and the garden is a gallery. The painter arrays pattern and color. Monet's water lilies are a prime example. The path and its setting is the main compositional element of the dancer's or stroller's garden. For the storyteller the garden is a world, or at least a stage, with a set of outdoor rooms and props. The diplomat's grove provides a variety of settings for discussion. The table and the walk in the woods provide different but well-used formats for negotiation. A Zen rock garden is a prime example of a philosopher's work. English hedge mazes also have cosmological underpinnings. A philosopher's or magician's garden provides a system for understanding the world. Finally, the child's garden offers props and places for play.

Any or all of these approaches could inform the design of a parking garden. The trappings of the diplomat's garden may be appropriate for research institutions, given that long debates often travel to and conclude in the parking lot. Perhaps university parking lots should be transformed into philosopher's gardens and libraries should have storyteller's gardens.

The following two chapters, "Time-Shares" and "Artpark," suggest various other activities that may be incorporated into a parking garden, and each may have its appropriate approach. An art gallery lot, for example, may best incorporate a collector's garden or perhaps a philosopher's garden. A demonstration garden may be an asset to a lot housing a farmers' market, and a large tree may provide the stage for poetry contests.

CHAPTER 8

Time-Shares

The City comes into existence, originating in the
bare needs of life, and continuing in existence for
the sake of a good life.

—ARISTOTLE, *POLITICS*

I n New Mexico," the *Albuquerque Journal* editorialized,
"fall is literally in the air these days—it's in the mouth-
watering scent of roasting green chili drifting on a breeze
from the propane-fueled roasters that have sprung up in grocery store parking lots" (August 31, 1997, B2). Perhaps the
most fundamental way to integrate the parking lot into a
town or city is to realize that they have multiple uses and to
make physical improvements to support these other uses.
Generally, parking lots have excess capacity that can be
shared. If a shopping center lot, for example, is designed to
have enough stalls to park all the cars that arrive on the
twentieth busiest hour of the year (a typical standard), then
there are vacant spaces more than 99 percent of the time,
and at least half the spaces are vacant 40 percent of the
time (ULI 1982, 12).

Haphazard occupations of parking lots by farmers' markets, roller skaters, and local festivals can and do occur. (See
Figures 8.1 and 8.2.) However, a little forethought can
improve the ease, safety and delight of such uses. The following patterns are not mutually exclusive but, rather, may

Figure 8.1   Parking lot in the Fremont district of Seattle, Washington.

(Copyright 1997, Elaine Thomas.)

Figure 8.2   Fremont parking lot with market.

(Copyright 1997, Elaine Thomas.)

benefit from being combined. Vending machines and a parking lot ice rink, for example, can support each other.

Provisions and Props

Provide the equipment for everyday life, such as toilets, telephones, bulletin boards, ATMs, soda vending machines, and mailboxes. Use this equipment to help make places where people would be comfortable socializing. (See Figure 8.3.)

An accidental meeting at the mailbox and the everyday public communications of the bulletin board allow strangers to become acquaintances and fellow citizens. Small amenities can increase the utility of a lot, show that it is intended as more than a storage place for vehicles, and give the excuse for people to socialize. If there are places to lean or sit and shade in the summer or sunny spots in winter, then people may be encouraged to chat more often and for longer periods than if the place is uncomfortable.

As adolescents, a friend and I would walk a mile to the

parking lot of the grocery store, nominally to buy a soda, but truly to experience the world, to be in public. Gum ball machines, newspaper racks, ATMs, weight-and-fortune scales, and other vending units provide further excuses for socialization, can activate what would otherwise be a blank wall, and generate a small income for the lot owner.

Care should be exercised to place the props to support social use of the space. A bench or chairs could be placed near newspaper racks. Bulletin boards may be near phones. A small writing shelf would be a pleasant amenity near mailboxes, as would a canopy sheltering the boxes from the rain. A set of small social places can be created around the props.

Each type of vending machine or collection box has its own specific requirements, and the proprietors of desired props should be contacted for current information. For example, the

Figure 8.3 Provisions and props, Nob Hill Shopping Center, Albuquerque, New Mexico. Note chairs, tables, mailbox, trash can, newspaper racks, and, in the distance, pay phone and bulletin board.

location of mail collection boxes is at the discretion of the local postmaster. Locations near post offices or other collection boxes are unlikely to receive a box. Mailboxes should allow for both pedestrian and driver deposits. This requires placing the box on the left-hand side of a lane and often means that the box is within the main parking area. The U.S. Postal Service requires that the end of the driver's mail chute be not less than 6 inches (15.2 cm) from the curb line and approximately 50 inches (127 cm) above the road surface. Type D-1 boxes are 28 inches (.71 m) on a side, and type D-2 boxes are 35 inches (.89 m) on a side. The box must be anchored by four legs to a concrete slab or to footings.

Look beyond the traditional amenities and see what may be useful to a community. Many lots have served as collection places for recycling. The old Bellevue Square Mall in Washington State was locally famous for its canine drinking fountain. Vending machines for duck food near a pond or sidewalk chalk and candy bars where children gather may bring moments of joy.

Vendors

Give cart vendors places to set up shop and engage them in the maintenance of the lot. Place them in the most visible locations so that they may be seen and so that they may monitor the lot. If at all possible, provide space for more than one vendor and concentrate them along a walkway so that they may look after each other. (See Figure 8.4.)

The novel *The Pushcart War,* by Jean Merrill, should be required reading for urban designers. With gentle humor it portrays a battle for the streets of New York eventually won by humane pushcart vendors over menacing truckers. Cart vendors have a direct interest in the civility of public space. They act as hosts and entertainers—initiating conversations, introducing customers to each other, bantering, and sometimes singing. They can watch over the space and may be engaged to clean lots, plant flowers, and maintain a place. The research of William H. Whyte (documented in *City: Rediscovering the Center and the Social Life of Small Urban Spaces*) and the observations of the Lennards (in *Livable Cities Observed*) confirm the insights of *The Pushcart War.*

Figure 8.4   Espresso vendor with reserved parking.

Vendors excel at finding and adapting to niches (Figure 8.5), but a small amount of planning can greatly increase their viability. Vendors' carts come in all sizes, but many commercially available portable shelters come in 10- by 10-foot (3.05 m on a side) and 12- by 12-foot (3.66 m on a side) sizes. Access to electricity and potable water increases the range of goods and services the vendors may offer. Do not isolate a vendor. Rather, provide space for two or three vendors and integrate them with adjacent stores. This increases their security and commercial viability.

Figure 8.5 Vendor at neighborhood market.

Most important, provide spaces for vendors in highly visible spots near pedestrian traffic but with sufficient room to allow people to linger just out of the flow of traffic. The balance between too far and too near the pedestrian route is delicate and dynamic. Thus, allow the vendor to adjust his or her exact location. Providing pleasant places to sit, lean, and stand is essential.

To Market, To Market

Design to allow the transformation of lots into weekend or evening markets. If possible, provide angled parking and allow trucks to pull through stalls. Include support facilities (rest rooms, potable water, shade) and permanent features such as signs or artwork to advertise the market and enable its spirit to "haunt" the lot on nonmarket days. (See Figure 8.6.)

Daniel Kemmis starts his book *The Good City and the Good Life: Reinventing the Sense of Community* at Missoula's public market because it is part of the essence of civil tradition

Figure 8.6 Santa Fe, New Mexico, Farmers Market. Note angled parking.

(1995). The public market is more than the selling of fruits and vegetables. It allows people to come together, exchange news, discuss the issues of the day, and share their lives. It provides a place for personal relationships between urban and rural people to form. It is a place where people can become a community, and a market can serve as an "incubator" for new businesses.

The Anchorage, Alaska, Parking Authority has run a Saturday market on one of its downtown lots since 1992. The approximately 150 booths draw close to 200,000 people each year. In 1997, the market was threatened with extinction because of the possible disbanding of the Parking Authority. Citizens objected to the closing of the market because it brought people and business to downtown and because, as participants said, "We like it . . . (we come) just to see everybody, run into friends," and "it brings a touch of (community) back" (*The Parking Professional,* July 1997, 11).

Parking lot markets can and do function without any physical improvements to the site. However, small things may help them flourish. To accommodate farmers' trucks and trailers, parking stalls should be large (10 by 20 feet) (~3 by 6 m), angled (45 to 60°), and allow vehicles to pull though. Homemade trailers vary in length, but the 40 feet (12.19 m) provided by pulling through two long stalls should accommodate most trailers. The sawtooth arrangement of farmers' booths produced by angled stalls has two advantages over a straight alignment: The booths can be seen from a distance, and the sawtooth provides places for customers to stand out of the flow of foot traffic.

Access to rest rooms is essential for a market. Electrical

outlets, a water supply, and garbage bins can also facilitate the running of a pleasant and fruitful market. Bicycle racks, a place to tie up dogs outside the market, a playground, and a pleasant place to wait for a companion to finish shopping are welcome additions.

A permanent on-site sign specifying the dates and times of the market gives the market a presence and sense of permanence. On market days, banners can be placed in permanent brackets to signal that the market is open. Site-based art or a permanent shade and rain shelter over the lot can help extend the spirit of the market into nonmarket days. Brass banana peels, cabbage leaves, and other leavings embedded in the street that hosts Boston's Haymarket celebrate the market's spirit all week long. The Project for Public Spaces (see appendix) has extensive experience in establishing farmers' markets.

Festival and Fair

Festivals and fairs are participatory stage sets. Thus, in addition to features one would design for a market, provide the equipment and services of a stage, and carefully consider the character of the props. (See Figure 8.7.)

Festivals are complex social events involving issues of local culture, politics, law, economics, tourism, and multicultural interaction. Festivals, however, are fundamentally rooted in urban and architectural expression. They are affirmations of community that rely on a conception of the place (e.g., "agricultural town," "historic center," or "Spanish homeland"), a "stage," and the architectural character of temporary structures (Childs 1995).

The character of the festival is

Figure 8.7 Festival. Vendor setting up for "Dickens on the Strand" Festival, Galveston, Texas.

Figure 8.8   Allocating space. Tent structure fits in parking stall. Note that angled stalls give two "facades" for the vendor and triangular areas out of the main pedestrian traffic.

accommodated and influenced by the design of the parking lot. For example, stage areas that are small and intimate set a different atmosphere than those that accommodate large crowds.

Vendors' booths are often the major component of the structures for a fair. A system for allocating space for stalls is necessary. Typical booth dimensions are 12 by 12 feet (3.66 m) and 10 by 10 feet (3.05 m). However, I recommend using the parking stalls to allocate space (Figure 8.8). This simplifies the process of counting, marking, locating, and adjudicating spaces and produces a sensible circulation pattern.

I also recommend that the design of the booths be gently regulated. In 1993, I conducted a survey of vendors at the *Dickens on the Strand* festival in Galveston, Texas.[1] Over 90 percent of the professional vendors preferred "theme" festivals. Reasons given for this preference were that themes draw larger crowds, are more fun, and provide the best environment for teaching about the vendors' crafts. The most important booth design considerations were ease of setup and image. The cost of construction and shelter from the weather were important for about half the respondents, and security was of only minor importance.

In addition to booth planning and design, other issues that should be considered by the designer of a parking lot/festival grounds include the local climate, locations for stages and backstage areas, power supply, lighting, and how to control entrance to the site. If large tents are to be used on a regular basis, lidded sockets in which tent poles may be set should be placed in the pavement.

See the appendix for recommended reading on festivals.

Shakespeare in the Parking Lot

Many parking lots are empty in the evenings and weekends. Reinhabit them with summer evening outdoor movies, Sunday matinee live theater, poetry slams, garage band competitions . . .

The parking lots of libraries, schools, and town halls could be ideal outdoor stages. Three elements are needed: (1) an admission system, (2) seating, and (3) a stage and makeup room or a screen and projection system.

Even if an event is free, I recommend that the organizers admit the audience through specified entries. This allows head counts, the exclusion of people who behave inappropriately, the solicitation of donations, and the option to charge admission at a later time. It also helps create a "house" for the theater by clearly separating people who are watching the show from people passing by or hanging out.

Seating is perhaps the most problematic issue. Low walls and planters within the parking lot can offer some seats, but to use the lot fully, chairs will be required. The Fremont District Outdoor Cinema in Seattle is a b.y.o.c. (bring your own chair) event and offers awards for the weirdest seats (Figure 8.9). Hay bales and blankets are used to convert asphalt to comfortable seating by the Albuquerque Little Theater.

A stuccoed back wall of a building can provide a movie screen. Projection equipment can be stored indoors and brought out to a sheltered and wired booth. Calculate projection distances and angles to provide good views for the audience, and place "set marks" in the pavement so that projectors can easily be correctly placed.

Live theater and concerts require

Figure 8.9 Fremont parking lot with concert before an evening movie.

(Copyright 1997, Elaine Thomas.)

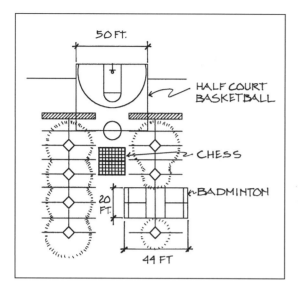

50 FT.

HALF COURT
BASKETBALL

CHESS

BADMINTON

20
FT.

44 FT

Figure 8.10 Diagram of various court games in parking lot.

both a backstage preparation area and a stage. However, the informality of the parking lot encourages innovative relationships between stage and house, and flexibility of stage design should be preserved.

Asphalt Sports

The hard, smooth surfaces and open area of parking lots are ideal for many sports. Find ways to allow and encourage parking lot hockey and other activities. (See Figure 8.10.)

For four nights during the summer, a municipal or private parking lot in Flagstaff, Arizona, is transformed into a sanctioned facility for skateboarders and stunt bicyclists. The Police Department and others offer these activities, competitions for car stereo performance, low-rider bike events, and basketball games. This official lot gives teenagers (who are the majority of the users) support for their activities, a central place to hang out, and a facility that can be adapted to their needs. It also reduces skateboarders' impact on the rest of downtown and may improve safety by removing them from general vehicular and pedestrian traffic.

A 1994 study by the Trust for Public Land provides evidence that programs such as this can also significantly reduce juvenile crime. For example, when Phoenix's recreational facilities such as basketball courts are kept open until 2 A.M., police calls reporting juvenile crime drop by as much as 55 percent (Trust for Public Lands 1994). In many areas, finding land and/or money to purchase land for sports facilities is difficult. Parking lots are a vast resource waiting to be fully used.

Sports such as basketball, ice skating, tennis, or others

using hard, flat surfaces may also time-share a lot with parking if (1) their specific requirements are incorporated into the design, (2) a reasonable schedule can be established, and (3) liability issues are resolved. An entry to the 1984 Carscape Competition provides an illustration. Studio C designed a fenced lot with swinging gates to transform parking stalls into tennis courts (Miller 1988, 43).

Perhaps a local parking-lot hockey or basketball league could be formed as part of a parks department program. This league could approach developers and parking lot owners to incorporate sports facilities, lease lots on weekends, set schedules for pickup and team games, and provide liability coverage. A corporation could design its lot as a practice court for its company team. Likewise, sports and activities for children, such as tricycle races, bubble-making festivals, and hopscotch rallies could be held in church or school lots.

In *People Places,* along with many other informed and wise recommendations, Clare Cooper Marcus and Carolyn Francis suggest that a place to hang out be provided in conjunction with sports facilities (Marcus and Francis 1990, 102). Placing seating close to the entrance of a parking lot and facing the lot creates a place where teenagers may see and be seen.

Play Lots

The parking lots of neighborhood schools and office buildings near residential neighborhoods should be physically closed to cars on weekends and holidays and given over to playgrounds. If possible, equipment for a range of ages, including parents, should be incorporated. Any adjacent permanent playground should be fenced off from the parking lot to clearly define when the parking lot may and may not be used for play. (See Figure 8.11.)

Kids play in empty parking lots, particularly ones that are in "their" territory, such as the lots of neighborhood schools.

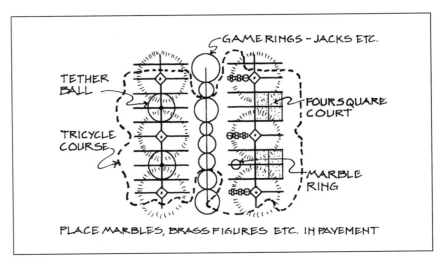

Figure 8.11   Diagram of various games for children in parking lot.

We should improve both the play value and the safety of these places.

According to Professor David Driskill, AIA, Director of the Children's Resource Lab for Architecture at Texas Technical University, the most important issues for playground design are (1) developmentally appropriate spaces and equipment, (2) safety, and (3) accessibility. Designing "rooms" or zones for specific purposes (e.g., a nature/wildlife preserve, tricycle paths, dramatic play, sand and water play, ball games, and an area for making stuff) helps increase the play value and reduce the conflicts and injuries that result from conflicting uses of a space (e.g., swings and running after a ball). Climbing equipment or swings that require a fall surface should not be placed on asphalt or concrete.[2]

One significant difficulty is the issue of liability. It may be possible for a municipality to lease lots on weekends for a minimal dollar amount, thereby providing liability coverage. If the provision of such a parking/play lot removes games from the street, overall public risk may decrease.

Provide facilities for parents and teenagers as part of the play lot. Place benches, chairs, and informal seating (stairs,

planter edges) to overlook the play area and to allow socializing. Provide tables to allow caretakers to picnic, read,
write, or simply repack the baby bag. Perimeter jogging
trails and/or exercise stations are a welcome addition.

It is important to be clear about how the lot is shared. If
there is an adjacent permanent playground, separate it from
the lot with fencing and gates to make clear when the lot can
be used for play and when it cannot. Likewise, use bollards or
gates to close entrances for automobiles when it is playtime.
Select appropriate games for pavement, and top the pavement with a smooth but not slick finish (e.g., broom-finished
concrete or asphalt with a tennis slurry coat). Involve the
children in the design and construction. Have fun.

See the appendix for recommended reading about playgrounds.

Tailgating

**The tradition of tailgate parties is well established. At least parts of stadium
parking lots should be designed to support this public celebration. Rest
rooms and first-aid stations equipped with fire equipment should be provided. Perhaps a lot with concession stands, a music stage, movie-size TV
screens, and grills could double as a hangout on non–game days.**

The tailgate party is a prime example of the occupation of
the parking lot for public space. Tailgate parties in parking
lots near stadiums can run from the simple sharing of food
and drink to a bacchanalian festival.

On January 31, 1989, *USA Today* reported that fans of
the University of South Carolina football team were paying
up to $8500 for parking spaces next to the stadium. One
170-space lot is equipped with bathrooms and an open-air
clubhouse where bands play, beer flows, and a pig is roasted
on a spit on game day.

Clearly, stadium parking lots can be designed to better
support these community festivals. Improvements could

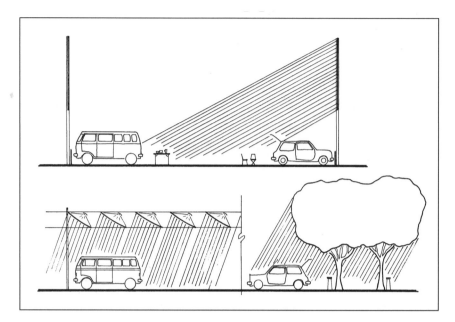

Figure 8.12 Three alternatives for shade. Top: afternoon shade from vertical banners along end of stalls. Bottom left: horizontal cloth shades can allow in morning light, block afternoon sun, and diffuse nighttime illumination. Bottom right: trees along a pedestrian path can also provide a comfortable place for tailgate parties.

include crafting the microclimate of the lot with the provision of shade, windbreaks, and pleasant lighting (Figure 8.12). Stalls in lots or portions of lots that are used only for games and are in wet climates may be paved, with grass planted between a concrete or plastic gridwork. Grass pavement provides a cooler and more pleasant environment for parties. More elaborate designs could aim to transform the parking lot of stadiums into public plazas or forecourts to the public arena.

The Vehicles of Memory

Places become fundamental constituents of the city when they are integrated into private and public memories. Retain artifacts of the site's previous inhabitations. Make places for public display and celebration, and provide places for memorials yet to be made. (See Figure 8.13.)

Figure 8.13   Sidewalk memorial to a vendor at Pike Place Market, Seattle, Washington.

Memory is not only the evocation of the past in the present, but speaks to the possibility of the present living into the future. Thus, for a place to be rich in mnemonic power it should display artifacts of its past, provide for the public display and the commemoration of individual citizens' arts and deeds, and display the potential for future commemorations.

We have developed formal and informal vehicles of public memory. Monuments and memorials formally honor particular people and events. The collection or retention of local artifacts such as the ruins of a former building make manifest the general history of the city and speak to the value of anonymous and humble acts of building.

Parking lots often occupy former building sites. Evidence of these buildings can enrich the parking lot and display the continuity of history. The evidence can be bold or subtle—parts of facades may be left to provide a face to the street; bricks, stones, or terra-cotta figures from the previous building may be incorporated into paving or walls; or an outline of the building's foundations may be left in the pavement.

The leaving of marks and objects provides deep ties of memory between a place and its people. Murals created by local children, bricks chiseled with donors' names, community gardens, even pennies tossed in wishing wells and comments scribbled on chalkboards provide notes of memory. If a place holds memorials from the past and places for memorials yet to come, then it speaks to the possibility that our own history can be honored and that we can be part of tradition.

Art Park

Our artists . . . have to become something more than merely mirrors of violence and disintegration; they, through their own efforts, will have to regain the initiative for the human person and the forces of life, chaining up the demons we have allowed to run loose, and releasing the angels and ministers of grace we have shamefacedly—and shamefully— incarcerated.

—LEWIS MUMFORD, 1954

Public art can enrich the bare utility of a parking lot with the vitality of a public art park. The parking lots of corporations, public institutions, and some retail enterprises could serve naturally as an art park.

Simply putting art in public places does not make it public art. Taking a place in the public realm brings the responsibility to speak eloquently and civilly. Excellent public art will not be addressed only to the cognoscenti but will speak to many different kinds of people. It will not take the simple path of reflecting social disintegration but rather will seek to reweave the fragments of community, express values that help civilize us, and provide meaning to everyday life.[1]

Public art has a long and dignified history as an integral part of public space. The fifth-century B.C. colossus of Zeus at Olympia, the 1500s' equestrian statue of Marcus Aurelius on the Capitoline hill in Rome, and the Fremont Troll under a bridge of U.S. 99 in Seattle (Figure 9.1) are all works poetically bound to their place. This poetic relation-

Figure 9.1   Car-eating troll, Fremont district of Seattle, Washington.
(Artists: Steve Badanes, Will Martin, Donna Walter, and Ross Whitehead.)

ship between a work of public art and its site is subtle and multivalent. Paris's Arc de Triomphe serves as a focal point for Baron Haussmann's boulevards and the surrounding city. The Vietnam Veterans' Memorial relationship to Washington D.C.'s mall is a more subtle matter, and some work, such as Rodin's *The Thinker,* is at home in many places. However, as a tool for thought, categories of association can be characterized. The following recipes present types of relationships between public art and parking lots. Any actual design may partake of any or all of these approaches.

In all these patterns, the character of the junctions between lot, street, sidewalk, and buildings should inform the artwork. Public art may serve to represent a building to the public. Artwork in the parking lot of a newspaper office could, for example, be a collection of old presses or could provide chalkboards for letters to the editor. A lot that is not a building's forecourt but is more of a public plaza may be the place for works that speak to local history, traditions, or festivals.

The success of any of these approaches also rests on the relationship between artist, architect, and the public. Since they are generally on private property, parking lots do not face the full set of issues that confront the (re)designer of publicly owned space such as a street. However, to the degree that the lot is presented as an extension of the public realm, it is prudent and helpful to consult the public.[2]

Public art may be a public joy.

Museum Parking Court

A courtyard, square, or open parking lot may serve as an outdoor art gallery. The design of the gallery (1) establishes the audience's means of observation and contemplation and (2) crafts the general climate and light into a specific context for outdoor artwork. (See Figure 9.2.)

A single work or a collection of art may be housed and displayed in a parking court. This outdoor gallery may stand alone or be part of a set of galleries and support services to form a small museum.

A good museum is made of simple rooms but is much more than simply rooms. The architecture of a museum should not call attention to itself but rather serve to focus attention on the art. Bruno Molajoli writes of museums in *Time Savers Standards for Building Types,* "A museum in which the works of art were relegated to the background and used to 'complete' a pretentious

Figure 9.2 The Mirage Sculpture Park in Albuquerque. This commercial gallery displays work in the parking lot. Proprietor Greg Reiche strongly believes the benefits to him, the artists, and the public far outweigh the one theft and one tagging he has had in seven years. Artwork by George Manus.

architectural scheme could not be regarded as successful; but neither could a museum which went to the other extreme, where the construction was subordinated to cold, mechanically functional considerations so that no spatial relationship could be created between the works of art and other exhibits—a museum with a completely impersonal atmosphere" (1990).[3]

If a collection of art is to transform a parking lot into a compelling public space, it is critical that the designers and curators heed this injunction to gracefully consider the relationship between the collection and the character of the place (the salient features of which may go well beyond the limits of the parking area).

First, architect, artist, curator, and client must agree on the intended ties between site and art.[4] Some work may require simply to be under the sky. On the other hand, work conceived for the lot may be inseparable from its site.

Second, the degree of publicness of the parking gallery must also be clear. The civic responsibilities of a collectively used lot are clearly greater than those of a lot that is legibly a forecourt of a private institution. Truly public art is primarily for the benefit of the public. It should engage the public as actors. Low poolside benches or water jets emerging from the pavement could, for example, encourage children to play with a fountain. The work should represent the community memory through myth, story, local history, or work and serve as a catalyst for conversation between citizens (providing what urban researcher William H. Whyte calls *triangulation*).

Unless these two relationships, the ties between site and artwork and the degree of publicness, are settled, one may be left with an artifact torn from its dwelling or a bunch of unappreciated sculptures cluttering a parking lot.

For an indoor art gallery, central issues are orienting the visitor to the collection, providing a variety of means of observation and contemplation, creating legible but flexible circulation to adjoining galleries and supporting space, and crafting the qualities of light, noise, and enclosure. A public outdoor gallery must gracefully resolve all of these issues and contend with the vagaries of climate.

The set sequence of entry to a parking lot—turning in from the street, parking in a stall, emerging from the car and stepping onto a sidewalk—provides a choreography to orient patrons and a narrative of viewpoints from which to regard the artwork. The nuances of a view through a windshield structure this story of arrival and thus must be contemplated.

For example, Figure 9.3 shows one possible placement of art to take advantage of this succession of views. Patrons approaching the lot circle the central piece. When they park on the inner ring their windshields present a static framed view which, particularly if the sculpture is tall, may focus on

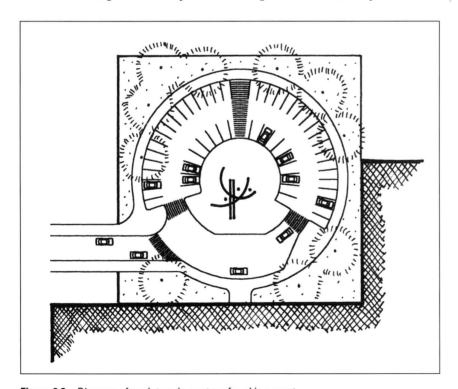

Figure 9.3 Diagram of sculpture in center of parking court.

a fragment of the piece. Finally, as pedestrians they may come together and examine the work from multiple viewpoints.

To choreograph such a set of views, the designer must be aware of the different perspectives of the driver and pedestrian. Not only is a driver limited by the driving lanes, but the car windows frame views. Cars vary greatly, but as a rule of thumb a driver's head is about 8 feet (2.44 m) from the front of a car, and the eye height of a driver is about 3.25 to 3.5 feet (.99 to 1.06 m) above the pavement.

Crafting the light and climate of an outdoor public room requires not only accepting events that would be unacceptable indoors but designing to delight in them. The maturation and death of trees, the noises of a city, adjacent construction that could block a view or alter the pattern of sunlight, and the energy of the elements should be anticipated as part of the life of the space. Artwork animated by the wind, fountains iced in the night, and sculpture that invites children's play may be examples of work best suited to a courtyard collection.

Drive-in Art

The view from the car—moving past, through, or under, and parking among objects of art—may be made a prime means of contemplating artwork. The size, scale, and character of the work must address the contained view of the audience. (See Figure 9.4.)

The drive-in museum is culturally more problematic than the museum court. The drive-in is created by a change of emphasis that plays more on the relationship between art, car, and driver than on the symbiosis between art, courtyard, and unencased patrons. The public in attendance becomes less a congregation contemplating a civic statement than a series of individual spectators taking a ride. If we are aiming to increase the civic use of public space, the museum

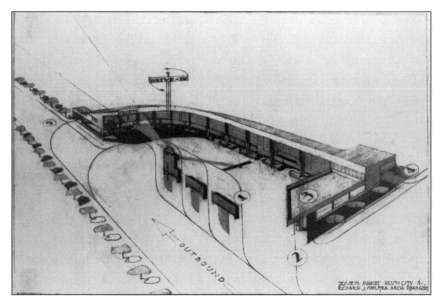

Figure 9.4 Photograph of drive-in market for Rush City Reformed by Richard Neutra.

(Drawing: Neutra Archive, UCLA Special Collections. Photograph of drawing: Collection of Thomas S. Hines, used by permission.)

court, which culminates with people out of their cars and possibly in dialogue, may be preferable to the drive-in. However, for drive-through banks, car washes, and other places built around the car as client, the parking and waiting areas may benefit from architectural and sculptural attention. (See Figure 9.5.)

The drive-in may be the prime milieu of some works. In fact, a significant body of commercial and vernacular drive-in sculpture exists: the early twentieth century freeway architecture of windmill restaurants, tepee-shaped motor courts, gas stations topped by sombreros and magpie-nest curio shops.

Figure 9.5 Garage door art, Seattle, Washington.

Artwork here is meant to be experienced primarily from the seat of the car. Moving past, through, or under and parking among works is the intended mode of contemplation. The play of headlights over surfaces, the rattle of the suspension on rough pavement, the acoustic semi-isolation and social distance created by an auto's enclosure could be significant parts of the dialogue between artist and audience.

Because the work of art, in this approach, aims to manipulate the experience of driving and parking, a careful traffic safety review should be part and parcel of each installation. For example, clear-sight triangles, adequate clearances, and legible circulation patterns with minimal conflicts should not be compromised. The parking lot must continue to serve as a safe and gracious, if a bit more fun, place.

Both the design and curatorship of a drive-in museum, I believe, will require a witty but judicious hand. Steering between short-lived kitsch and overbearing social criticism could be worse than parallel parking a semi. However, the potential for pithy delight is abundant.

The Poetry of Parking

The character of the parking lot as a social place is ripe for artistic commentary. Choreographing how we park, use of narrative sculpture and graffiti, and gracious and witty furnishings may help us imaginatively inhabit this public space. (See Figure 9.6.)

The parking lot is not yet a mythic place. We have not inhabited it with creatures like the dim-witted troll under the bridge, the gargoyle of the wall, the spirit of the well, or even the UFOs of cornfields. Occasionally in movies, a menace will lurk in a lot's dark shadows, but generally these specters prefer the isolated depths of a parking garage. In order to civilize the carpark and make it a valued part of the city fabric, we need to develop a poetic narrative of the parking lot. Important parts of our lives take place in parking lots—welcomed arrivals, quiet interludes, informal meetings, awkward farewells. The lot itself is ripe for artistic commentary.

Artist Heath Schenker has orchestrated drivers in auto-horn music and arranged patterns of parked cars. In his article "Parking Gardens," Paul Groth suggests using automobile-scaled mazes to bring humor into the search for a parking space, and lots that are maps of the region (Francis and Hester 1995, 135–137).

Perhaps the parking lots of airports, ski resorts, and skyscrapers could be designed as sculpture to be seen from above. Lighting could be used to transform the lot's daytime pattern into another form. On another scale, the pavement could be patterned with the prints from various tires, either in an

Figure 9.6 "Cruising San Mateo," 1991. Barbara Grygutis, artist.

abstract pattern or realistically, to look like a parking lot after a light snow. In 1978, Site Projects Incorporated draped the asphalt pavement of a parking lot over 20 cars to create a "ghost parking lot." Sculpture of neighbors conversing over their shopping carts could speak to the informal connections of community. Likewise, local history can be embodied. Visitors to the street that houses Boston's Haymarket discover a bronzed lettuce leaf and other market refuse littered across the pavement. Perhaps even the car itself, as driverless demon or friendly family member, can be captured by art.

Narrative sculpture is not the only means to inhabit the parking lot. Well-crafted furnishings make a place more fit to be inhabited (Square and Courtyard, Chapter 4). Etched poetry, mosaics, and performances (Shakespeare in the Parking Lot, Chapter 8) may, like sculpture, build on this foundation.

Parking lots are often inhabited with art in another manner. The display of automobiles is a significant social activity. The parking lot is the packaging or framework for this display.

Whether they are low-riders, bugs, Bentleys, or rebuilt Model Ts, cars can be emblems to be displayed. Car dealerships, auto rallies, and homeowners all rely on parking lots to provide a landscape for this display.

The fictional landscapes of automobile ads are effervescent but always carefully distilled. The brick driveways of upscale ads or the rugged wilderness landscapes of sports-utility vehicle ads could inspire auto dealerships to move beyond the traditional asphalt, balloon, and searchlight decor. I am not advocating the continual restaging of auto lots to keep pace with the electronic fluidity of marketing, but rather a quieter and more stable attention to the ambiance of the landscape. Brick pavers and graceful landscaping may be appropriate for some dealerships, and perhaps the ambiance of the racetrack could be used for others. Dealerships' lots should be a significant market for urban landscape architects.

Likewise, a convocation of individually recrafted cars, a car rally, can benefit from a well-designed lot. Perhaps the parking lots of fairgrounds or malls could be designed to host annual rallies. Utilities such as water and electricity should be provided, the lot should be planned for pedestrian entry and circulation, and the lot's maximum capacity determined by a space plan for car display, support (e.g., bathrooms, security, information), and vendors. Lighting can be added to highlight the sparkle and gleam of the cars.

Asphalt Canvas

The materials of a lot—pavement, bumpers, stripes—may compose an artwork, or the pavement may be a canvas for applied works in temporary chalk or more permanent paint. (See Figure 9.7.)

Pavement can be a canvas in at least three ways.

First, the artifacts of the lot can be redesigned to compose its appearance. Industrial designers and artists have delightfully and fruitfully played with trifles such as the soda straw and the paper clip and have begun to play with the artifacts of the street. For example, Seattle, Washington, has manhole covers graced with a street map of the city (for other examples, see Melnick and Melnick 1994), as well as tree grates labeled with the name of the tree species and composed of the appropriate metal leaves. Design opportunities await in parking stall wheel stops, lot striping and lane lines, drains and oil traps, street reflectors, and bumps. (See Figure 9.8.)

Perhaps a palette of colored or patterned stall striping could provide clarity for stall assignments or landmarks for locating one's car. In Europe and England, colors other than white and yellow are used for roadway and parking lot markings without any apparent decrease in safety. Lane bumps that double as electrical outlets for festivals and a variety of numbered reflectors could also prove useful. The wheel stop, too, is in need of atten-

Figure 9.7 The *I Madonnari* Italian Street Painting Festivals take place at the historic California Missions during May in Santa Barbara and during April in San Luis Obispo. In 1987, the Children's Creative Project, a nonprofit arts education program of the Santa Barbara County Education Office, created and produced the first street-painting festival in the western hemisphere to benefit the organization. Street painting by architects Tim Steele, Pat Pouler, and Lori Kari.

(Image used by permission. Copyright 1998, Nell Campbell.)

tion. Colored concrete, molds lined with tire treads, or forms more expressive of its function may be worth exploring.

Second, the pavement may serve literally as a canvas for street painting (with chalk), street stencils, or more permanent murals. Children dominate this genre but are not the sole practitioners. In Seattle's Pike Place Market a cobblestone street is decorated by the public during summer festivals. On the sidewalks and piazzas of Italy, master artists create chalk artworks for the delight and spare change of the public. New York City has a rich tradition of street artists whose talents could enliven a parking lot. A steel-troweled concrete lot with drawing area allotments and aisles established by the stall stripes could provide the perfect canvas for a chalk party.

Finally, the pavement itself may be patterned, and the design of car parks can draw from the history of plaza pavements.

Figure 9.8 Detail of bollard.

CHAPTER 10

Safety and Security

The desire for safety stands against every great and noble enterprise.

—TACITUS, *ANNALS*

According to the U.S. Department of Justice, in 1994, approximately 757,000 violent crimes (such as robbery, assault, and rape) occurred in U.S. parking garages and lots (Kangas 1996). These amount to approximately 40 percent of all violent crimes reported that year in the United States (U.S. Department of Justice 1995). About one out of six urban automobile accidents occur in parking facilities (Box 1981), and an uncounted number of people tripped and fell in parking lots.

Risk

Every activity entails an amount of risk. That is, there is always the possibility that something we consider undesirable may happen as a result of our actions. It is, of course, desirable to reduce the chance that a problem will occur, and it is a designer's and an owner's duty to avoid creating intemperate risks. However, when we seek to eliminate risk we often unduly restrict the possibilities for fun and profit. There are, for example, risks for the parking lot owner, clients, and vendors when a farmers' market inhabits a car commons. The only way to totally eliminate these additional risks is to eliminate the market. The argument that safety trumps any other consideration is misleading. Risk is inherent in activity, and without assuming some risk we could do nothing.

This observation, however, belies the complexities of considering risk. What we wish to do, and the standard that liability law generally holds us to do, is to avoid undue or unreasonable risk. The general concept of negligence is defined in *The Emanuel Law Outlines* as imposing "an *unreasonable risk* [emphasis in original] upon another which results in injury to that other" (Emanuel 1994, c-12).

Defining the exact meaning of *unreasonable* is one of the things that keeps lawyers busy (Calabresi and Klevorick 1984). Risk and legal liability depend on the particulars of the site, peoples' actions, the culture's propensity to tolerate risk, current legislation, and tort law. The following general outline of issues and approaches to reducing risk should be taken as a broad overview. Professional judgment must be used to determine applicability to any particular problem. Important details not presented in this overview may bear on a particular case. Consult a lawyer about specific instances. A discussion with insurance professionals can help designers and owners develop good liability-reduction practices. (For a discussion of risk, see Adams 1995.)

Standard of Care

The duty to avoid creating unreasonable risks does not mean that the designers of car commons must be perfect, but rather that they act with the skill and learning commonly possessed by members of their profession in good standing (Emanuel 1994, c-14 and c-15). For example, ignorance of the importance of avoiding tripping hazards in a car commons could lead to negligence. Violation of a statute (and in some cases ordinances and regulations) can conclusively establish negligence (Emanuel 1994, c-15).

Business owners additionally have a legal, as well as an ethical, duty to give assistance to people in need of help on their property, and they must make a reasonable inspection of their property to find hidden dangers. A business owner cannot delegate his or her duty to keep the premises safe for business visitors (Emanuel 1994, c-44).

Viewpoint

Risk is a slippery concept that depends on one's purpose and perspective. Consider, for example, ice in a parking lot. To the elderly, getting out of a car and slipping on ice may present a significant risk—one that they would take considerable action to avoid. On the other hand, teenagers may *seek* the opportunity to walk on ice and consider a sudden fall part of the fun. If you add a music system and ice the entire lot, people of all ages may pay you to allow them to go ice-skating.

Risk Compensation

Risk becomes even more complicated to pin down when we realize that once people identify a risk they may act to avoid it. An old pothole in an employee parking lot may, for example, cause fewer problems than a new one, because drivers and pedestrians know to steer clear of it. Likewise, relatively few pedestrians are hit by cars in parking lots (approximately 1 percent of parking lot accidents), despite the fact that pedestrians regularly walk in the driving lane, partially because drivers expect to share the lane with pedestrians and adjust their driving style accordingly.

Risk Thermostat

People have certain propensities to take risks, and there is evidence that design changes (e.g., snow tires) that reduce risk without changing people's risk-taking behavior simply allow people to do things (e.g., go faster) that reestablish the level of risk with which they are comfortable (Adams 1995).

On the other hand, design changes that increase the *perception* of risk and/or decrease the rewards for risky behavior may reduce collisions. For example, drivers of small cars apparently reduce their risk taking compared to the drivers of large cars and thus have significantly fewer accidents (Evans 1985). This may be another reason why shared streets and parking lots have few pedestrian accidents—the environment makes it clear that there is a risk of hitting pedestrians and at the same time makes it difficult to speed.

Imposed versus Accepted Risks

Yet another factor in the complicated calculus of risk is the degree to which the risk is imposed. An ice-skater has chosen to take the risk of falling on ice, whereas employees walking across an icy walkway may feel resentful that they had no viable choice but to take the risk of falling.

Risks can also be displaced from one person or place to another. John Adams illustrates this shifting: "The larger your vehicle relative to everyone else on the road, the less likely you are to injure yourself and the more likely you are to injure someone else" (Adams 1995, 155). Similarly, banning curb parking may shift collisions from the public realm of the street where they are recorded in police statistics to the private world of the parking lot where accident record keeping is not as systematic.

Measurement?

The measurement of risk rests on the balancing of benefits and costs. But what counts as a benefit or cost? Whose benefits matter? The effect of these questions can be seen in the following example.

Traffic engineering literature often suggests that curb parking should not be allowed. Two reasons are frequently given: Curb parking restricts traffic flow, and it presents a safety hazard.

Clearly, however, traffic engineers do not mean to suggest that parking should not be provided in cities. They just don't want it on the streets. To determine whether curb parking should be banned because it is unduly hazardous, we should compare the hazards associated with curb parking to the hazards of parking in garages and lots. Moreover, we must compare the full set of hazards associated with each parking type. Are there more rapes per parked car in a garage, a parking lot, or in cars parked at the curb? Curb parking slows down traffic. Might this reduced speed actually decrease the number and severity of roadway accidents? Eighteen percent of street accidents involve driveways (Box 1981), and cars backing up on residential driveways are considered a significant hazard to children; eliminating curb parking may increase the use of driveways and thus the number of driveway accidents. Additionally, the research to support a safety claim must control all relevant variables. Otherwise, it is at best only suggestive that there may be a problem. One of the major accident types traffic engineers have identified as associated with curb parking is pedestrians entering the street midblock (dart-outs). To know to what extent and under what conditions curb parking contributes to the frequency and severity of these accidents, we must compare sites with similar pedestrian and vehicular densities, number of lanes, posted and actual speeds, land uses, and quality of formal crosswalks. Some data suggest that most dart-outs occur in residential areas. Thus citywide dart-out data should not be used to justify a ban on curb parking in commercial areas.

I have been unable to find a well-controlled comparative analysis of curb parking and off-street parking. The claim that curb parking is an undue safety hazard may be accurate. However, without a solid analysis it appears colored by the stated goal of increasing traffic flow.

The costs to traffic flow should be included in an analysis of the risks of parking. To decide a matter of policy such as banning curb parking, we must weigh the costs against the benefits. However, as I hope this book has suggested, the costs and benefits of various types of parking extend beyond automobile traffic flow to include the quality of the pedestrian system, the amount of land and money consumed by parking, and the quality of life in the public realm.

What to Do?

The complexity of risk can make it difficult to judge what constitutes reasonable design. It is often not possible to collect data on all the significant costs and benefits, much less to judge what constitutes a reasonable balance. How best to balance risks and benefits remains a matter of informed judgment based on the totality of each design. A conservative approach is to base designs on well-known and thoroughly studied examples. This helps ensure that the public has previous experience with the balance of risks and that the designer can learn from previous mistakes. The conservative approach may, however, miss significant opportunities for innovation.

Another approach is to be risk-efficient—that is, to search for actions that help minimize risk without undue cost. First, pursue actions that are of significant value in their own right and that also help reduce a known risk. Increasing the public use of a space and practicing good maintenance fall into this category. Second, seek to reduce risk taking and the consequences of accidents. Slowing down traffic fits into this approach. Third, design to minimize conditions that lead to the most frequent types of accidents, such as tripping and backing-out collisions. Next, where possible, provide the users of a car commons with options so that they may adapt to specific conditions. Last but not least, organize the stewardship of the car commons so that due care is well orchestrated.

Majordomo

Hire a steward whose role is the overall care of the car commons. This steward, or majordomo, may be a full-time employee, but may also be a vendor, a gardener, or something similar. Provide an office for the majordomo in the car commons.

A majordomo is a steward entrusted with the overall care of a place. The majordomo coordinates and participates in the maintenance and daily management of a place.

Not every parking lot can afford to have a full-time on-site manager, but the majordomo may be a parking attendant, the janitor for a corporate building, or a vendor. However, to be the majordomo, he or she must be given responsibility for the overall character of the place, not simply presented with a list of tasks.

Benefits of a majordomo's presence include improved public service and image, regular preventive maintenance, increased security, and day-to-day management. All of these require that the majordomo's office not be hidden away but rather have a clear presence in the space and that the majordomo be able and willing to circulate throughout the space. (See Figure 10.1.)

To provide public service, the majordomo's office should be equipped with a telephone, car battery starter, fire extinguishers, and first-aid equipment. CPR training for the majordomo and other staff, regular contacts with building security and municipal police, and plans for emergency management could prove vital.

A person who is responsible for the overall character of a place and is in daily contact with its clients is in a better position to assess maintenance needs than someone who merely performs assigned tasks. Interactions between different tasks can be observed and managed. For example, salt used for deicing can poison landscaping; if landscape maintenance and parking lot safety are performed by separate

Figure 10.1 "Majordomo's office." (In all fairness to the gentleman in the picture, I had to wait a long time to catch him reading the newspaper.)

organizations, resolution of this conflict can be slow and difficult. A majordomo has a direct interest in avoiding such conflicts. Additionally, since the majordomo's charge is the overall quality of the place, new and unanticipated issues can be addressed without the owner rewriting and renegotiating a set of prescribed tasks.

Security may be increased by two aspects of the majordomo's role. First, the actual presence of the majordomo, combined with the overview and implied presence of a visible majordomo's office, provides the effect of surveillance. Second, a high level of general maintenance and quick response to vandalism are strongly believed to deter crime (Kelling and Moore 1988). Trash, weeds, and an uncared-for appearance give the message to hooligans that the place is an easy mark. If no one cares, what's a little vandalism? If no one is there, won't this be an easy place to steal a car?

Finally, a majordomo is in position to see opportunities and needs and to suggest fine-tuning to the management of the place. For example, *The Parking Professional* magazine publishes good ideas gleaned from participants at the International Parking Institute's annual conference. In 1997, over 50 suggestions from parking facility operators included the following:

- Instituting a part-time parker program in undersubscribed monthly parking facilities

- Providing bicycle-taxi service at night from lots to campus locations

- Converting parking spaces to "park and dine" areas to handle overflow from convention dinners

- At the beginning of the school year, setting up a temporary office in campus parking lots to sell parking decals

- Selling advertising space on the back of parking stubs

These suggestions came from people who were obviously involved and thinking about the management of their parking facility, not from people who were confined to a narrow task.

When a parking lot is combined with other uses as suggested in previous chapters, then the role of majordomo becomes both more necessary and more interesting. A vendor, for example, may provide all the roles described here and also coordinate functions with other vendors.

Majordomo's Office

The majordomo needs an office, but this office should be strategically placed so that it is integrated with the public space. The office may serve as a landmark, a gateway, and as a minor focus. Care should be taken, however, to make certain that it does not dominate the space, obstruct entry, or otherwise intimidate people. The office should be visible and easily accessible, but off to the side so that other uses may take center stage.

If the office also serves as a landmark, then clocks, local

maps, bus stop benches, and such should be integrated into the structure. ATMs and the entrance to toilets could be made more secure by being placed adjacent to and within the direct line of sight of the majordomo's office. Controls for lighting, safety and service equipment, and other accessories should be housed in the office. If, for example, the parking lot is also an outdoor movie theater, then the projector booth may be integrated with the office.

The mobility-impaired must be able to get to the office and maneuver within the structure. This is true whether the office is a separate structure for a full-time majordomo or an elaborate ticket-taking booth. The space should be simple and flexible. One majordomo may use it primarily as a storage shed; another may use it to sell ice cream.

Inhabit!

There is safety in numbers. Induce people to use and hang out in car commons, and consider closing the car commons when it is unused.

Although crime certainly does happen in well-inhabited places, the presence of people serves as a deterrent to assault, rape, auto theft, and vandalism. Even the frail who could not bodily intervene to stop a crime provide deterrence, because they can offer rebuke, call the police, and act as witnesses. On the other hand, the more people use a place the more likely that the absolute number of accidents and crimes will increase. The presence of people may reduce the *rate* of aggressive crime but *could* increase the *number* of incidents occurring at a given place.

The presence of undesirables such as street people, while not necessarily a source of crime, is threatening to some. Again, the presence of many people reduces this perception. If a lot is inhabited by a single drunk, his or her presence dominates the place. If the drunk shares the car commons with 20 espresso drinkers, then the ambiance is not dominated by the drunk. William Whyte points out that measures such as spikes on ledges that attempt to discourage undesirables usually discourage the general public and, ironically, lead to a place dominated by one or two unsavory characters (Whyte 1980, 60–63).

In particularly difficult areas such as rest rooms or entire car commons in high-crime areas, consider closing facilities at night and at other times of low use. This can help reduce the possibility that a criminal atmosphere will infect the site and kill off public use.

Surveillance

Ensure that it is readily apparent to anyone in a car commons that he or she can be seen. Create a web of joint oversight so that employees can literally look out for each other and observe critical areas such as the entrance to rest rooms, ATM machines, and entry to the car commons. Provide adjacent buildings with windows overlooking the car commons. Use technology to reinforce but not to replace the presence of people. Most important, encourage the majordomo to help set a tone of civility and to defuse situations before they become problems. (See Figure 10.2.)

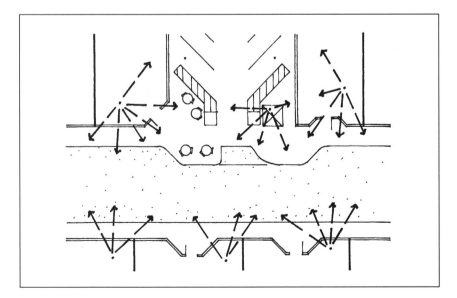

Figure 10.2 Web of surveillance.

There will not always be an assemblage of people when a car commons is in operation. However, employees and neighbors can watch over a site. To provide a sense of security, surveillance works best when it is itself most visible. People in the car commons are a more effective deterrent than people behind windows. Overlooking windows are, in turn, more effective than cameras.

Maintain a presence of people in the car commons. Have employees walk through the car commons at times of low occupancy to retrieve grocery carts, pick up trash, or perform other duties. Schedule maintenance, deliveries, and other work activities for slow hours. Encourage street performers to play in the early evenings to entice people to hang out after work. Most important, train the majordomo and other employees to help set a tone of civility and to gently defuse situations before they become problems.

Design to create a web of joint oversight. Employees at their regular stations (e.g., cash registers, lobby desk) should be able to see the car commons and as many other employee stations in other buildings as possible. Make it easy for the police and other passersby on the street to see into the car commons.

Areas that are frequent sites of crime (rest-room entrances, ATMs, and public telephones) should be under close surveillance. Rest rooms, if possible, should be within a building. Doorless, "maze" entrances should be used, and they should be in the direct view of employees. Maze entrances are not only more sanitary, but prevent assailants from trapping victims between doorways or within the lavatory. ATMs should be adjacent to and overlooked by one or more storefronts. They should not be in nooks in which people could be trapped. Enclosed bike lockers should be inspected to guard against their use as staging places for crimes. Consideration should be given to closing rest rooms and ATMs during the hours that no employees are on-site. To reduce the chance that public telephones will be used for drug deals, place them in locations in which they are observed by employees and customers and in which it seems possible that conversations could be overheard.

If the car commons is a pleasant space—a garden, courtyard, or plaza—then neighboring buildings will not automatically turn their backs to it. Thus, the car commons in turn becomes a more enjoyable and secure place. Windows, decks, and storefronts that overlook a car commons deter crime because they suggest to criminals that their actions will be observed.

Finally, place closed-circuit television, motion detectors, alarms, and other technological props to support but not replace human surveillance. These devices are counterproductive if they are not backed by the quick response of people. Alarms and motion detectors are perhaps most useful in rest rooms, elevators, and other locations that are shielded from general view.

Surveillance should be a by-product of other activities, not an aggressive or overly defensive stance.

Maintain Visibility

Visibility is critical for passive surveillance and to minimize collisions and tripping. Install and maintain adequate lighting. Avoid creating hidden nooks. Minimize vegetation and other obstructions between 30 inches and 7 feet (.76 to 2.13 m) above grade. (See Figure 10.3.)

Without good visibility throughout a car commons, neither general inhabitation nor employee-based surveillance is effective. Visibility is also critical to the safe parking of cars and to minimize the potential for tripping.

Lighting is a key component of visi-

Figure 10.3 Zone of visibility.

bility. The National Parking Association's 1987 recommendations for general parking areas call for lighting levels at 6 foot-candles as measured 30 inches from grade, although other recommendations range as low as 2 foot-candles (Box 1994). The illumination should be uniform to avoid creating shadows, which may cause tripping and which can give the sense that there are places for criminals to hide. A regular maintenance plan should include washing light fixtures and replacing lightbulbs before the end of their life expectancy. (However, use the removed bulbs in easily accessible fixtures rather than wastefully discarding them.) Additionally, sources of daytime glare such as reflective glass should be minimized. Lights that contrast in color with the general lighting may be used to highlight exits, building entrances, seating areas, and so forth. For example, when the yellow light of high-pressure sodium is used for general illumination, the white light of metal halide fixtures could be used to mark automobile exits, and incandescent bulbs could fill in a café.

Vegetation, artwork, and other obstacles should not create hidden nooks or obstruct drivers' views. Generally, keep the zone between 30 inches and 7 feet (.76 to 2.13 m) above grade clear of significant obstructions.

Maintenance Plans

Show that the car commons is actively cared for. Regularly pick up trash; immediately repair vandalism; maintain landscaping and lighting. If possible, include the neighborhood in decorating the car commons for celebrations and in cleanup afterward. Prepare a maintenance plan in conjunction with the design documents. Include a description of the design intent, care and maintenance instructions, and drawings or photographs of critical hidden conditions. Pay particular attention to maintenance to avoid tripping hazards and to ensure the vitality of plantings.

In addition to sustaining the character of a car commons, maintenance is critical to safety. It is believed that maintenance reduces crime and vandalism because it shows that the place is well cared for and monitored. Additionally, regular maintenance can catch an emerging tripping hazard before it is a problem and help spot unanticipated problems.

The design of a car commons should include a maintenance plan. Preparing the maintenance plan at the same time as the design and construction documents helps ensure that the designers and owners are cognizant of the maintenance requirements of the proposed design. Document the design intent, hidden conditions, warranties, and manufacturers' or suppliers' care instructions. Provide a means for the addition of information and notes by the majordomo.

Each parking area will, of course, have its own specific set of maintenance issues. However, two issues are almost universally important: avoiding tripping hazards and care of landscaping.

Uneven settling can create tripping hazards, either by fracturing pavement and making uneven joints or by producing dips where water can collect and freeze. Good construction practices can help avoid undue settling but cannot absolutely ensure against it. A regular maintenance schedule should prescribe inspecting for emerging settlement problems and should also suggest that the majordomo inspect for other unanticipated tripping hazards.

Regular replacement of lightbulbs near, but *before,* the end of their life expectancy and annual cleaning of light fixtures will reduce the potential for tripping. Light maintenance will also preserve the atmosphere of safety that strong and even lighting produces.

Care for special conditions such as artwork, large-scale chess pieces, movie projectors, or stage lighting should also be included in the maintenance plan, even if it is anticipated that people other than the majordomo will have prime responsibility. The majordomo must have this information to understand how his or her actions could affect the special items. For example, metal sculptures should not be exposed to prolonged contact with road salt.

As described in Chapter 7, "A City of 10,000 Gardens," a landscape maintenance plan is critical to the long-term success of parking gardens. Watering, fertilizing, weeding, and planting schedules should be included. Sketches of the intended mature conditions, a checklist of stress and disease symptoms, and suggestions for replacing diseased or damaged specimens are also helpful. The manual should be designed to help a majordomo who may not be well versed in landscape maintenance keep the garden in good health.

Maintenance does not have to be done entirely by employees, and there can be important benefits to including others. Flower beds, for example, may be "adopted" by a neighboring home for the elderly. The art class of a middle school may be delighted to provide holiday decorations. This help may not directly reduce the maintenance budget, but has significant benefits, including increasing the number of people who watch over the commons and adjoining buildings.

Slow Down

Design the car commons to make it clear that pedestrians have the right-of-way over cars. Particularly at driveway entrances, use rumble strips, landscaping, curved driving lanes, small turning radii, and so on to induce drivers to slow down and pay attention to the immediate environment.

When a car strikes a pedestrian at 43.5 mph (70 kph), the accident is fatal to the pedestrian 83 percent of the time. At approximately 31 mph (50 kph), 37 percent of the collisions are fatal, and at about 15 mph (25 kph), only 3.5 percent are fatal (Hass-Klau 1990, 5). The damage to auto bodies and occupants also significantly decreases with speed. This may be why parking lot accidents tend to be less severe than those on the street and highway (Box 1981).

Parking lots are inherently environments shared by drivers and pedestrians. However, available studies suggest that car-pedestrian collisions make up only about 1 percent of parking lot accidents (Box 1981). Nevertheless, the pedestrian is at a distinct disadvantage to the driver in terms of the consequences of collisions, and the general level of perceived threat to pedestrians is a critical ingredient in the character of a car commons. Therefore, the design of the environment should seek to give priority to the pedestrian.

The message that drivers must slow down and pay close attention to the environment and that pedestrians have the right-of-way may be communicated by the design of the space. The character of automobile entrances is critical in giving clues to drivers that they have left the road and that the car is no longer king. The narrowest turning radius that will not cause undue problems on the road should be used. This will cause cars to slow down and will minimize the driveway-crossing distance for pedestrians on the sidewalk (Figure 6.10). Rough paving blocks and rumble strips will give drivers audible and kinesthetic clues to slow down. Trees, patterned pavements, and other landscaping features can indicate that the facility is a car commons designed for pedestrians. Trees can be placed to curve the driving path and restrict the speed of vehicles, but be sure to take measures to protect the tree and driver (see Chapter 7).

Speed bumps are problematic because they may cause automobile damage and represent a possible tripping hazard. However, in locations where other features have failed to reduce problems of excess speed, the risks associated with bumps may be outweighed by the risks associated with speeding vehicles. Where there is sufficient room, speed platforms (Figure 10.4) should be used instead of speed bumps. Speed platforms may be less likely to damage cars and cause tripping than the classic bump.

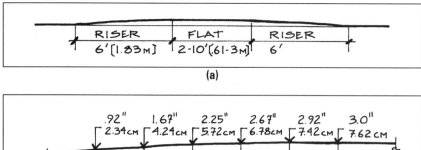

Figure 10.4   Speed platform. (a) Profile of platform. (b) Riser detail.
(Adapted from City of Albuquerque standards.)

Tripping

Avoid creating tripping hazards such as iced puddles, wheel stops in the walking aisle, and uneven joints in pavement. Provide adequate and even illumination. Design stairs with low risers and wide treads. Consider using bollards instead of curbs to provide an edge to walkways.

Trips and falls account for almost 75 percent of liability claims in parking lots (Ellis 1996). One tripping hazard can be easily removed: wheel stops that cross a walking aisle. Except at the edges of lots where walls and other objects must be protected, wheel stops are often unnecessary. The traditional white line or a change in pavement is usually sufficient to indicate the end of a stall, and it allows easy snow removal. Curbs or bollards can often be used at the edge of lots and around islands. Where wheel stops are necessary, use 6-foot or shorter stops, centered on the stall to keep the walking aisle clear.

Care in the initial design, along with regular maintenance, can reduce the occurrence of ice puddles. In asphalt lots, use a 1 to 2 percent slope instead of the AASHTE's recommended minimum of .5 percent, and place drains in areas away from pedestrian circulation. Avoid slick paving materials such as polished stone. Broom-finish concrete to provide traction in slippery conditions, and consider rolling a layer of small aggregate into the top of asphalt paving.

Curbs and stairs are also likely places for trips and falls. Bollards, a line of street furniture, and changes in pavement type can substitute for curbs in many cases, thus eliminating a place to trip. When curbs are used, the *Traffic Engineering Manual* suggests a maximum curb height of 10 inches, but the height of a step, about 6 inches, is preferable. Consideration should be given to the details of curbs and stairs. Contrasting colors and textures can be used to sharpen the visibility of the nose of steps. A rounded stair nose should be used so that feet do not catch on the tread.

Finally, provide even lighting. Ensure that lighting does not cast shadows that look like curb edges, and make certain that stairs are well lighted.

Offer Options

Wherever possible, provide options. Provide some stalls adjacent to walkways; construct both ramps and stairs; have more than one pedestrian exit.

In order to allow people to adapt their behavior to their personal circumstances, to the climate, and to other environmental conditions, there must be more than one way to conduct an activity. Many able-bodied adults prefer to walk in the driving aisle even when a direct walkway is available. However, when accompanied by small children or sporting a leg cast, these same adults may well prefer the walkway. A person using a cane may consider it safer to walk a shorter distance using a handrail and steps than to take the longer route often required by a ramp, particularly after a light dusting of snow. Multiple exits from a car commons allow pedestrians to avoid people or situations they consider dangerous.

Providing options allows users to act on their judgment of risks and benefits. Multiple options on the same site (and subject to similar conditions) also provide the best conditions under which to observe and collect data about behavior and risk.

A Note on Stall Design

According to a study by Paul C. Box (1981), the vast majority of vehicular accidents in parking lots involve cars hitting other cars. Backing out of stalls appears to be associated with the most collisions. His data suggest that there are fewer accidents at lots with stalls 90° to the aisle than at lots with angled parking, but more study is needed. The relationship of stall width to accident rate is unclear. Where possible, allow drivers to pull through stalls, eliminating the necessity for backing up.

There are no conclusive data to suggest that we should significantly alter the design standards for stall layout. However, the designer should beware of any features that will make backing up more difficult.

CHAPTER 11

Paving the Planet

We stand today poised on a pinnacle of wealth and power, yet we live in a land of vanishing beauty, of increasing ugliness, of shrinking open space, and an overall environment that is diminished daily by pollution and noise and blight.

—STEWART UDALL*

Parking lots cover a significant portion of the land in our cities, and consequently have important effects on the quality of our environments. The acres of pavement in a city's parking lots can increase the severity of flooding, destabilize streambeds, reduce groundwater recharge, degrade water quality, raise summer air temperatures, fragment natural habitat, segregate the city into islands of separate activities, and increase car use and thus air pollution. Proper design of lots can help reduce this harm.

The following is an overview of possible environmental harms due to parking lots and of ways to ameliorate those harms through good design practices. It is not intended as a full environmental impact statement, which could include the effects of mining gravel, asphalt, cement, and other paving materials, habitat loss, crime, noise, and nuisance light caused by parking lots. The degree and range of important environmental effects is dependent on local conditions,

---

* As quoted by Raj Barr-Kumar in "From the President's Office: Shades of Green" *AIA Architect,* August 1997, 24.

and, as always, the developers, designers, builders, and operators of a car commons must exercise their judgment to minimize environmental harm.

Water

Reduce the total amount, limit the intensity, and filter the pollutants of rainwater runoff from a parking lot. Plant trees, allow infiltration in areas unlikely to pollute groundwater, provide mechanical and biological filters for the most polluted water, and design the detention and release system to reducing flooding and mimic natural stream flows.

The amount and intensity of water running off parking lots often produce significant environmental problems. For example, coho salmon are rarely found in the streams of the Pacific Northwest in areas where the impervious surface from buildings and parking lots exceeds 15 percent of the land (During 1996, 26). The oil, grease, hydrocarbons, and heavy metals left by the normal operation of automobiles can have a significant cumulative impact on the quality of downstream waters. A hydrologist should be consulted for large projects, and municipalities should develop jurisdiction-wide runoff management plans. However, the designer of a parking lot should be familiar with the general issues in order to integrate techniques that will minimize harm into initial designs rather than trying to add solutions after completing the design.

Floods and Stream Shaping

When a field is paved, the amount of water that runs off the land increases in amount and is more concentrated in time (flash flooding). Pavement doesn't allow water to soak into the ground, and in a paved lot there is no grass or other ground cover to which rain may cling. In light and medium rains a field may produce little or no runoff, whereas a paved lot will shed a large portion of the rainfall.

Minimizing the area devoted to parking is the primary means to reduce runoff. Second, if instead of a few small scattered trees, the parking lot is redesigned to be covered with a thick canopy, then the trees can capture a light rain and slow down the impact of a stronger rain (Xiao et al. 1997). If rainstorms are typically driven by the wind from a consistent compass direction, buildings or trees can serve as sheltering wind (and rain) breaks. In some places, pocket wetlands can be designed to absorb the runoff from small storms and allow it to evaporate (Figure 11.1).

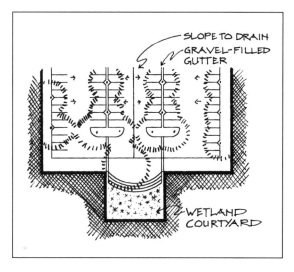

Figure 11.1 Pocket wetland.

Storm drainage regulations are intended to reduce or eliminate the increase in stormwater runoff associated with development that contributes to increased peak stream flow and local flooding problems. The regulations typically specify a maximum allowable increase in peak runoff rate, compared to the existing condition, for a particular storm size, usually the 100-year storm. Detention ponds are a traditional means of reducing peak runoff rates. They accomplish this by limiting the maximum rate of outflow from the pond, and storing, or detaining, the inflow that exceeds this maximum allowed outflow. The maximum outflow rate is limited, but the time over which it occurs is lengthened. This approach does not address a number of significant problems.

Rather than limiting flooding, the outflow of this detained water could actually *add* to flooding if it is released as the peak from upstream events passes the facility. In this case, water that could have flowed downstream before the peak is detained and added to the peak.

Streams have a characteristic shape that is determined by

their hydrology, sediment, and vegetation. Over time, the frequent, smaller storms play a more important role in determining this characteristic shape than the less frequent storms that produce floods (Leopold 1994). Changes in land use that increase the amount of runoff produced by a given storm intensity (e.g., increasing the amount of impervious surface) change the hydrology and the sediment characteristics of the stream. The increased amount and intensity of runoff from parking lots changes the stream's water flow, and soon downstream trees are undercut, banks collapse, fish spawning beds are swept away, the concentration of soil in the stream increases, and adjoining property is eroded. Additionally, because these flash floods recede rapidly, saturated embankments do not have time to drain and are left exposed and heavy with water, causing more slumping and erosion. Typical parking lot detention basins are designed to limit out-of-channel flooding and do little to control runoff from frequent, smaller squalls.

Parking lots should be designed to mimic as closely as possible the undeveloped field's infiltration rates and timing of runoff during typical storms. Some possible techniques include the following:

- Instead of being raised above the pavement, planting beds can be placed to receive stormwater. These mini-infiltration basins can handle up to about 20 percent of a lot's runoff (Prey 1994).

- Rain falling on tree canopies is both detained and evaporated, reducing the peak and total amount of runoff. A study of the Sacramento, California, area calculated an annual interception loss of 11.1 percent for the area covered by tree canopy (Xiao et al. 1997). This rate varies by type of tree, time of year (leaves on or off and air temperature), and the duration and intensity of rainfall. Higher interception rates occur for broadleaf evergreens, warm summer storms, and short, light rains.

For example, the aforementioned study calculated a 36 percent interception loss for a broadleaf evergreen and conifer urban forest during Sacramento summers and a 2.4 percent interception loss for a broadleaf deciduous and medium-size conifer canopy during a wintertime 200-year storm.

- The main outlet pipes can have caps to release water at the field's natural rate but be otherwise oversized to provide detention capacity without using surface area that could be put to other uses. These pipes may be perforated and wrapped in root-barrier fiber. Tree roots will thus have access to this water without clogging the pipe.

- The bottom of detention areas can be constructed as a labyrinthine swale to slow down the release of nonflood waters, and other strategies to hold back the excess runoff of normal storms can be employed.

Pollutants

Greases and oils, hydrocarbons, phosphorus, heavy metals, suspended solids, and trash are washed off our pavements by rain. The full range of pollutants and their impact is not known, and thus it would be prudent to limit their dispersal into the environment.

Annually cleaned catch basins and oil separators provide a first line of defense against the release of pollutants. However, second stages of control are usually necessary. Table 11.1 shows the reported efficiencies of various systems. A promising system not included in Table 11.1 is a biological filter using cartridges of composted leaves within modified catch basins. Barring a major spill in the parking lot, the leaves can be recomposted after three years and used to mulch around trees in the car commons. These biological filter systems can be placed in underground catch basins and thus do not take up the room that a pond or swale system

Table 11.1 Reported Removal Efficiencies for Runoff Treatment Systems[2]

Removal Rate for Stormwater Pollutants (%)[1]	Ponds	Wetlands	Filters[3]	Channels	Swales
Total suspended solids	67%	78%	87%	0%	81%
Total phosphorus	48%	51%	51%	−14%	29%
Soluble phosphorus	52%	39%	−31%	−15%	34%
Total nitrogen	31%	21%	44%	0%	No data
Bacteria	65%	77%	55%	0%	−50%
Hydrocarbons	83%	90%	81%	No data	62%
Copper	57%	39%	34%	14%	51%
Lead	73%	63%	71%	30%	67%
Zinc	26%	54%	80%	29%	71%

SOURCE: *Watershed Protection Techniques,* vol. 2, no. 4, June 1997, p. 519.
[1] Data is median removal rate, except for bacteria, which is mean removal rate.
[2] This data summarizes multiple studies. Individual types of any of these systems may perform significantly differently than the median reported here.
[3] Filters exclude vertical sand filters and vegetated filter strips.

would. This system appears to have a high pollutant removal rate compared to other alternatives.[1]

Not all the water from a site is significantly polluted. In a residential or commercial development, the vast majority of stormwater pollutants come from the parking lots and streets. To avoid the expense of unneeded filtering, runoff from buildings and grounds should not be dumped onto a parking lot. Low-flow bypasses are sometimes installed to allow continuous inflows caused by groundwater seepage to bypass the filters, because this water usually does not require treatment. Likewise, filters are not sized to treat all the water from a 100-year storm, but are designed to treat the majority (often 95 percent) of the polluted water. The first water to run off a lot carries the highest concentration of pollutants; the later runoff from large storms is relatively clean. The characteristic frequency, duration, and size of storms in an area, as well as the roughness of the pavement, will determine the size of a treatment facility. For example, in King County, Washington, parking lot filtering devices are typically sized to handle the runoff from a two-year storm.

Land

Concentrate development and distribute parking throughout the district to (1) shorten walking distances, (2) avoid fragmenting natural habitat, and (3) minimize the amount of land devoted to parking. Find uses for unused or underused parking lots, particularly along sidewalks.

Parking lots cover from 6 to 40 percent of the land in our communities. Many of these lots are oversized and/or inefficiently used, resulting in unnecessarily long walking distances, increased construction costs, and environmental harms.

Parking lots are the transfer point between driving and walking. If there is a choice between making access to the lot easier for cars or for pedestrians, the pedestrian should be favored. A hundred feet of extra walking distance or a rise of 10 feet will discourage a significant number of people from walking but will be insignificant for drivers. This is particularly true for people carrying packages or who are otherwise mobility-impaired.

Another consequence of diffuse development is the fragmentation of natural habitats. The theory of living lightly on the land has often been misapplied to support sprawling, low-density land development. Unfortunately, parking lots are not environmentally light. They have been described as "killing fields" for amphibians and other small creatures. Even a two-lane driveway separating fields can be an impenetrably hot and dry barrier for native species. Additionally, the edges of roads and parking lots often create microhabitats that differ from the native habitat. Roadside species from across the country spread along the road margins and can invade local ecosystems. The small islands of natural habitat left amid diffuse development rapidly become unstable and may lose many of their native species. (For a discussion of biological "islands" see MacArthur and Wilson 1967 or Pielou 1979.)

Less land is needed for parking per person in concentrated settlements than in the typical suburban development. This is due to two factors. First, in a concentrated town, shared parking is feasible. Office workers, for example, can walk to lunch or shopping. Second, the amount of land used for roads, driveways, and access aisles decreases as a settlement becomes more compact. Even in suburban areas, however, current requirements tend to require excessive parking and can be reduced (Willson 1995 and Chapter 12). Table 11.2 shows the relationship between parking requirements and building density.

Compared to on-street parking, off-street parking has the same problems as diffuse development. Frequently, off-street parking creates long walking distances and interrupts walkways. Curb parking and parking streets are inherently

Table 11.2   Effect of Parking Requirements on Floor Area Ratio

NOTES: A number of simplifying assumptions were made to generate this chart.
No uses other than building and parking were included.
Parking stalls were assumed to require 370 square feet of surface area.
FORMULA: Floor area ratio = building area/ land area; building area = footprint × floors; footprint = land area − parking area; parking area = 370 × required rate × building area.

shared parking. Off-street lots are more difficult to share than curb parking because they are frequently privately owned and because they typically have direct pedestrian access to only one or two buildings. Finally, Table 11.3 shows that curb parking is more land-efficient than the typical off-street lot.

As with unused buildings, unused or underused parking lots can have a detrimental effect on the vitality of a district. The community should find uses for at least the sidewalk edges of these lots. (See Chapter 8 for activities that may occupy the underused portions of a lot.)

Air

Reduce air pollution in three ways: (1) use parking to support pedestrian and transit mobility; (2) shade parking lots to reduce "sitting" emissions and heat-island smog formation; and (3) in areas with critical air pollution problems, consider using pavements other than asphalt, or use asphalt types and application methods that limit emissions.

Parking lots affect air quality in at least four ways. First, they support the use of automobiles. Second, the high temperatures of unshaded parking lots cause evaporation of gasoline from cracked hoses and other parts of cars' fuel systems. Third, they contribute to urban heat islands and

Table 11.3 Land Area per Parking Stall

	Curb Parking	Lot Parking
Stall size	8 × 22 ft (2.4 × 6.7 m)	8.25 × 18.4 ft (2.5 × 5.6 m)
Stall area	176 ft^2 (15.8 m^2)	151.8 ft^2 (13.7 m^2)
Aisle width	None	24.03 ft (7.33 m)
Aisle area per stall	None	99 ft^2 (8.9 m^2)
Subtotal area	176 ft^2 (15.8 m^2)	250.8 ft^2 (22.57 m^2)
Cross aisles, driveways, etc.	None	~120 ft^2 (~11.2 m^2)
Total area	176 ft^2 (15.8 m^2)	~370 ft^2 (~34.3 m^2)

NOTE: Calculation for cross aisles, driveways, etc., varies by configuration; 120 ft^2 is the average of five sites surveyed by author.

thus the formation of smog. Finally, the materials used for paving can contribute to air pollution.

Automobile Use

Other portions of this book discuss supporting pedestrian environments and public transit, promoting shared parking, and otherwise managing the demand for parking spaces. To the extent that they are successful, those actions may also reduce air pollution. In particular, replacing short hops made by car with walking trips has a number of benefits. Not only is the number of vehicle miles reduced, but the number of parking spaces required and urban street congestion are reduced. Additionally, the disproportionately high level of pollution emitted when a car first starts is avoided. Table 11.4 shows emission factors for starting cars.

Hot Lots

A study in Sacramento, California, shows that parked cars produce about 20 percent of the hydrocarbon emissions from vehicles (McPherson, Simpson, and Scott 1997). This is due to gasoline vapors leaking from cars' fuel systems. Using light-colored pavements and shading cars in parking

Table 11.4   Emission Factors for Vehicles with Gross Weight of 6000 Pounds or Less

| | Air Pollutants | | | | |
| | CO (grams) | ROG (grams) | NOx (grams) | PM10 (grams) | |
				Exhaust	Tire Wear
1 mile @ 15 mph	10.46	0.72	0.77	0.01	0.1
Cold start	82.00	4.37	2.52		
Hot start	10.92	0.96	1.31		
Hot soak		1.11			

SOURCE: Table A9-5-J-3, CEQA *Air Quality Handbook,* SCAQMD.
NOTES: *Cold start* refers to starting a cold engine or one that has been off for more than an hour. *Hot start* refers to starting a hot or warm engine. *Hot soak* refers to the emissions from an engine as it cools off. CO is carbon monoxide. ROG is reactive compounds. NOx is oxides of nitrogen. PM10 is particulate matter.

lots can decrease these emissions because the rate of gasoline evaporation is lower at cooler temperatures.

Hot parking lots also contribute to the heating of urban areas; the formation of photochemical smog increases as air temperature rises. One estimate done for Sacramento, California, places the value of all air-quality benefits from a healthy parking lot tree at about $25 to $35 annually (McPherson, Simpson, and Scott 1997).

Pavement

A smaller contribution to air-quality problems is the creation and installation of pavement materials. The United States is a major consumer of paving asphalt, with a production rate of about 678,000 barrels per day (A. Cantrell 1984). Asphalts are complex mixtures of different types of hydrocarbons and have been shown to have adverse health effects on workers exposed to their fumes (Chase et al. 1994, Chiazze et al. 1991). The application of asphalt can contribute to smog. The emissions from hot asphalt mixes vary according to the source of asphalt, the temperature of the mix, and outdoor temperatures. Continuing research is aimed at finding the conditions under which asphalt may be installed with the least air pollution. At a minimum, in critical air pollution areas, paving should be scheduled during cooler months to reduce its contribution to smog. Contact California's South Coast Air Quality Management District or the Asphalt Institute for recommendations on current best practices (see appendix).

The production of concrete is an energy-intensive activity that, depending on the location and source of energy, may also contribute to producing critical air pollution problems. Brick production also uses significant amounts of energy. Unfortunately, beyond avoiding profligate uses of materials and properly maintaining them, there are no simple guides to the best practices regarding air pollution caused by pavements.

Climate

Plant shade trees and use light-colored pavements. Use a light-colored aggregate in asphalt and a light-colored slurry or chip seal when resurfacing. Initiate a program to identify local sources of high-albedo (light-colored) aggregate, and develop municipal programs to moderate city climates. (See Figure 11.2.)

Parking lots have a direct effect on microclimates and city climates. The dark surfaces of parking lots significantly increase the local summer air temperature, and the open expanses of large lots increase wind speed in comparison to forested lots.

Since the advent of widespread use of the automobile in the United States, the difference between summer temperatures in urban areas and adjacent rural areas has been in-

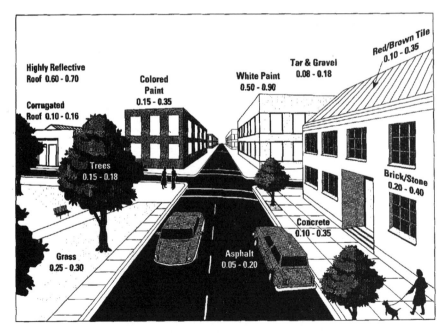

Figure 11.2 Surface albedo values. Surfaces with high albedo values reflect more solar radiation and are generally cooler.

(Courtesy of Joe Huang, staff scientist, Lawrence Berkeley Labs.)

creasing by about .67°F (.37°C) per decade. Summer temperatures in urban areas are presently about 2 to 8°F (1.1 to 4.4°C) higher than in their rural surroundings, increasing electricity demand, smog, and discomfort (Akbari et al. 1992, figure 1-15, 16). A rough estimate by the EPA concludes that up to $1 billion a year in cooling costs could be saved nationally by reducing urban air temperatures (Akbari et al., ed., 1992, xix), and that violations of air-quality standards could be reduced 10 percent by a 5°F (2.78°C) reduction in air temperature. The EPA recommends two simple actions to achieve these benefits: planting trees and using light-colored (high-albedo) materials for pavements and roofs.

Temperatures can drop up to 9°F (5°C) in the immediate vicinity of trees, and one to three trees strategically placed around a house can reduce the demand for air-conditioning by 10 to 50 percent. Computer simulations suggest that replacing dark asphalt pavement and roofs with lighter-colored surfaces could reduce a sunny city's summer air temperature by up to 5°F (2.78°C) and reduce the use of energy for cooling from 30 to 50 percent (Akbari et al. 1992, xxii–xxiv). The top coat of asphalt can include light-colored large aggregate and/or fines to increase albedo. Rolling a light-colored aggregate onto the top of asphalt pavement can significantly increase its albedo and create an attractive surface. Slurry seal, an aggregate of fine particles mixed with asphalt, is often used as a top coat on asphalt pavement. Light-colored slurry seals are manufactured in Europe and have been used on parking lots, plazas, and tennis courts. These seals have the added benefit of being developed as sports surfaces with good traction and a reduction in rough asphalt's tendency to skin one's knees.

The summer energy savings from light-colored pavements is not wiped off the books by a winter increase in demand for heating. In many climates, winter clouds limit the heating effects of sunlight on pavement. Second, particularly in the cooler (more northerly) parts of the United States, the sun is lower in the sky in winter than in the summer. Thus, in the summer, pavements and roofs receive the most sunlight, while walls can be shaded. In the winter, walls receive direct sunlight and pavements receive light at an angle. Dark walls can absorb winter sun but be shaded from summer sun. Light pavements reduce summer heat gain and reflect any winter sunlight to adjacent walls. Trees can act as buffers to winter winds, allowing buildings to retain their heat, and deciduous trees shed their leaves, allowing in winter sunlight. Obviously, design for the microclimate must be tailored to the site.

Parking lots can also play a critical role in reducing excessive winds in cities. Parking lot orchards can serve as windbreaks at the edge of cities, and courtyard trees may help diminish gusts at building entrances. In *The Granite Garden,* Anne Spirn discusses a proposal to decrease winds in Dayton, Ohio, by planting parking lots (1984, 77–80).

Although the climatic effects of any single parking lot may appear minor, because parking lots cover a good portion of our settlements their cumulative effect on a city's climate is significant. It is clearly in the public interest for municipalities to develop programs and ordinances to improve their microclimates.

Materials

Reduce, reuse, and recycle parking lot materials. Consider the total life-cycle costs when selecting pavement material. Don't pave more land than is necessary; use on-site materials when possible; maintain and repair pavements; and consider using recycled asphalt or pavements mixed with recycled materials such as used asphalt roofing, ground tires, or petroleum-contaminated soil. (See Figure 11.3.)

There are approximately 250 billion tons of asphalt on roads in the United States (Shulman 1995). Roughly 95

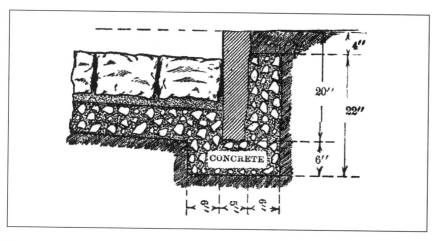

Figure 11.3 Detail of granite curb and stone pavement.

(From George W. Tillson, 1912. *Street Pavements and Paving Materials,* figure 83.)

percent of asphalt and 75 percent of concrete is sand and gravel. Thus it should not be surprising that the second largest mining business in the United States is the quarrying of sand and gravel (Spirn 1984, 101).

Depending on site conditions, pavements other than asphalt and concrete may be appropriate. Compacted pea gravel, crusher fines, and sand are often used. Care must be taken to provide a surface on which the mobility-impaired can safely and conveniently negotiate; the benefits of lower runoff from these loose pavements must be balanced against the infiltration of parking lot contaminants into the soil and possibly the groundwater. Another pavement option is the transformation of local soil materials into a pavement by the addition of a resin emulsion or other soil stabilizer. Last but not least, traditional and extremely durable pavements such as brick, a carefully made cobble, or stone blocks may be the most appropriate. At the turn of the century, various species of wood were made into pavers. Sydney, Australia, for example, boasted mahogany streets (Tillson 1912, 364). When selecting a pavement material, one should consider the total life cycle of the alternatives. Pavers, for example, may have a longer life than asphalt and can be easily and cleanly rein-stalled after underground utility work.

The most direct means to reduce the effects of mining, transportation, and use of any material is to reduce the amount of parking space. Oversizing lots not only costs more initially but increases maintenance costs and the impact of the lot on the environment. This does not mean that one should install a substandard thickness or skimp on the quality of the pavement. Repair and replacement also have monetary and environmental costs. Parking areas may be zoned, with heavy pavement used in the busiest parts of the lot, lighter materials in less-used zones, and perhaps grass in areas used only occasionally.

Regular preventative maintenance can extend the lifetime of pavements and reduce the environmental impacts of replacement. Light-colored materials may show stains from dripping oil more readily than black surfaces. Although a mottled surface may reduce the visibility of small stains, it may require regular washing.

After considering measures to reduce the overall area and extend the useful life of a pavement, three approaches to recycling should be investigated. First, on-site materials such as concrete and brick rubble from an old building can be used for decorative pavements, short retaining walls, and, in some cases, pavement undercourses. Second, there are well-established methods for recycling both on-site and off-site asphalt into new pavement. Third, various waste materials can be added to asphalt or concrete or may be used as a base course. Recycled asphalt roofing material was used successfully in the parking lots at Disney World, and there has been extensive experimentation with adding rubber from used car tires, glass, petroleum-contaminated soils, polyethylene waste, and various ashes and slags from industrial processes (Waller and May 1993). Research in Canada showed that asphalt with 12 to 15 percent crumb rubber from recycled tires can outperform the standard mix. The rubber asphalt demonstrated markedly superior performance in moisture-damage testing and repetitive uniaxial compression (Svec 1996). Chipped tires have been used as a base course under gravel roads to reduce road wetness and as an insulator to reduce the depth of frost penetration. Ongoing research examines ways to incorporate waste materials into pavements without compromising (perhaps even improving) durability. Contact local suppliers, the Asphalt Institute, or the Portland Cement Association for specific applications (see the appendix).

Demands, Demands, Demands

If you ever find a place to park your car in New York, don't move it. Leave that car there for parking purposes and buy another one for driving around.

—WILL ROGERS*

How Much Parking?

How many parking spots should be built? For the architect of a project, the answer is usually frustratingly simple—the highest number that either the client, the client's bank, or the city demands. These demands are often inflexible, despite the fact that, for municipalities, banks, and building owners, they represent a balance of complex and competing interests. Money and land spent on parking could be invested elsewhere. Professor Donald Shoup calculated that the maintenance and amortized construction costs of parking spaces at UCLA were at least $124 (1994 dollars) per stall per month and that providing the required parking for office space in Los Angeles (four stalls per 1000 square feet) accounts for roughly 39 percent of construction costs (Shoup 1997). There are also secondary costs of excessive parking, such as erosion of the quality of the pedestrian system, demand on the road network, water and air pollution,

* As quoted by David R. Levin in *Transportation Quarterly,* vol. 2, no. 2, April 1948.

and ugly cities. In 1983, the Federal Highway Administration estimated that a local highway agency would save up to $200 (1982 dollars) annually per peak-hour vehicle eliminated (Federal Highway Administration 1983). Managing the parking supply may be a significant way to reduce the number of cars on the road during rush hour.

This chapter outlines the current methods of determining how much parking should be supplied, and then presents alternative approaches.

Current Methods

In the mid-twentieth century, streets became clogged by the rising tide of automobiles. American cities saw it to be in the public interest to require more off-site parking than building owners would willingly provide. This same rising tide gave new commercial establishments with large parking lots a competitive advantage over downtown establishments with little parking and congested streets (Longstreth 1997).

In response to these conditions, a set of parking requirements arose. Municipalities generally require a minimum number of parking spaces according to the square footage and uses of a proposed building. Banks, the Federal Housing Authority, and other lenders often have their own minimum parking standards that must be met in order to receive a loan, and as a rule, business owners firmly believe that more parking space equals more profit. The standards used by municipalities and lenders are often derived from national studies.

National Studies

To determine parking demand and set standards, both cities and business owners have relied on national parking-demand studies. The International Traffic Institute's (ITE) *Parking Generation Manual* and the Urban Land Institute's (ULI) *Shared Parking Manual* are the major references for estimating demand. These two works provide the best general data available. Unfortunately, they have significant limitations.

First, the data are limited in number, detail, and scope. Approximately half of the reported parking-generation rates in the 1987 *Parking Generation Manual* are based on four or fewer case studies, and 22 are based on only a single case study. The number of types of buildings studied is limited, and assumptions or data about average automobile occupancy, transit ridership, and the amount of other modes of travel are often not given.

Second, change over time is not well accounted for by the studies. The typical demand for parking spaces changes over time. For example, recommendations for stalls per square foot of shopping center have been decreasing for about two decades. Building uses change over time (for discussion, see Brand 1994), and typical occupancy rates for any one type of use change over time. For example, the square footage of office space per employee has been increasing. Thus, the number of parking spaces needed for a given office building should be decreasing.

Third, the interaction between buildings, alternative transit systems, and the economy is not well addressed. The attractiveness and the time and monetary costs of parking affect the demand for parking, as do the availability and quality of alternative travel modes and the socioeconomic characteristics of the expected users.[1] None of these factors are well documented in these national studies.

These difficulties could possibly be remedied with more study. There are, however, three methodological difficulties with the current procedures for estimating the demand for parking.

The first problem is determining how to respond to peak demand. The number of stalls necessary to meet the peak demand for parking may greatly exceed those necessary for a typical day. Moreover, there may be very few hours in a year during which the peak demand is approached. It is clearly unreasonable to build a facility that will be underutilized 99 percent of the year. Most studies recognize this and, instead of designing for the absolute peak of demand, choose a "design hour" to set demand. Typically, for parking lots the design hour has been set as the tenth busiest hour of the year, but major highway facilities that serve them are often designed for the thirtieth busiest hour of the year. Clearly determining the appropriate design hour is a judgment balancing the costs and benefits of parking. Striking this balance is not a simple engineering exercise, but rather requires determining *whose* costs and benefits should be counted.

Furthermore, these costs and benefits evolve. Individuals and communities adapt to what is supplied. If there is virtually unlimited free parking, people will drive more often than if there is a fee to park. If, on the other hand, it is well known that it is difficult to park downtown during the week before Christmas, people will share rides, take the bus, shop after work, or shop earlier in the year. They may also shop elsewhere. Fearing the loss of customers, downtown stores may hand out bus tokens and support downtown festivities. A study specific to local conditions would be needed to know if the benefit to a store of building and maintaining stalls for the Christmas rush is more or less than the cost of festivities and bus passes. Determining the appropriate design hour is a complex, local, political-economic judgment that is currently too often made by applying a rule of thumb.

Second, the bulk of demand data is based on isolated suburban development. The instructions for submitting data for use in the ITE *Parking Generation Manual* state that the ideal site is a freestanding, single-land-use type with ample convenient parking facilities for the exclusive use of traffic generated by the site and free of any unique characteristics. Moreover, the introduction notes that only a small minority of the sites measured had any transit ridership.

There are no data on the quality of pedestrian or bicycle access to the sites.

This suburban sample bias means that the unit of analysis is the single building or isolated complex. The introduction notes that "the analyst should also use discretion when studying a multi-use project" and "variations may also exist because of the geographic location." It is a complete leap of faith to believe that these data are applicable to sets of buildings in complex urban conditions. For instance, one case study in downtown Oakland, California, showed that the amount of parking within 1000 feet of a subway station was less than predicted by national studies—by 40 percent for offices, 58 percent for residential, and 72 percent for retail and hotels (ITE 6F-52 1996, 49). The use of these suburb-based data to establish requirements has helped create disjointed suburban development where denser, more mixed, and more pedestrian neighborhoods could have been built, and this has helped erode once viable pedestrian downtowns.

Finally, by observing conditions in which there is "ample" convenient parking, what is being measured is the use of parking when it has no significant cost to the user and there is no competition between users—that is, *free* parking. Eighty-five percent of the subsidies that autos receive are external costs, incurred, for example, by congestion, parking, accidents, and pollution (Miller and Moffat 1991). There are very few goods in this country that we provide free to the user, particularly when it costs the provider a significant amount to provide the good. We don't provide food, clothing, shelter, or health care on this basis. Why, then, do we require buildings to provide free parking?

It is an economic maxim that the lower the monetary and time costs of the user for any good, the higher the demand for that good will be. Zoning requirements for off-street parking were instituted to relieve congestion. They have failed. With our ever increasing supply of parking and road capacity, the cost of driving and parking goes down, so more cars are driven until the system is again congested. The time cost of congestion is, under this model, the only significant cost of parking that drivers perceive. The average cost for a new car's gasoline, oil, maintenance, and tires was 9.2 cents per mile in 1994 (AAMA 1994, 56). If we spread the cost of building and maintaining a parking space at work across the average miles driven to work, the parking space is worth about 27 cents per mile driven—triple the vehicle operating costs for driving to work (Shoup 1997). However this cost, hidden in higher mortgages and rents, is not identified as part of the cost of "free" parking.

The current standards thus have four significant hidden assumptions. The first assumption is that unhindered free parking is a public good, on which a significant amount of public and private funds should be spent. Second, the standards assume that the amount of parking supplied should be based on current driving habits such as automobile occupancy rates. The third supposition is that sites have no other feasible means of access, and finally, the standards, blindly applied, presume that all proposed development consists of isolated single-function buildings.

Alternative Methods

The supply of parking and its effects on the city is a public concern, and it is well established that a municipality may use its powers to regulate parking. Many other parties share in the costs and benefits of parking. The character of the district affects the municipal and private interests in parking. The costs and benefits of a parking lot for a store on the outskirts of Houston, for example, are very different than those for a store in downtown Chicago. The current zoning-based requirements for a minimum amount of off-street parking supplied by each building may not be the best way to provide parking.

Alternative methods for determining how much parking to provide should rest on reexamining the public and private motives for supplying parking spaces and looking more closely at local conditions.

A Building Owner's Demand for Parking

There are generally five forces affecting a building owner's desire for parking: the characteristics of the clients, the actions of competitors, the nature of the business's operations, the cost of providing parking, and the public interest (as expressed by municipal regulations).

The desires and actions of employees, shoppers, and other clients of a building are the basis for measurements of demand. However, human behavior is complex. What percentage of employees would take transit if they could be guaranteed a ride home if they worked late? What percentage of a new restaurant's patronage can be expected from local walk-in customers? How many people avoid a particular parking lot because it is dark and isolated? How do these and other factors interact? Research can give clues to assist in the design of demand-management programs. However, judgment and flexibility will always be required.

The actions of competitors frame a business owner's response to clients' desires. Downtown stores often oppose parking restrictions because suburban malls have virtually unlimited parking. Mimicry is not, however, the only possible or necessarily best response to competitors. A downtown store, for example, instead of building expensive parking, may more profitably spend its money and political capital by catering to office workers with free downtown transit, lunchtime events, and evening hours.

The third factor influencing a building owner's desire for parking is the nature and working requirements of the business. It would be extremely difficult to convince a car dealership to have its employees bike to work. Likewise, employees who must frequently inspect sites or attend distant meetings will have a strong need for a parking space. Conversely, a business that promotes itself as environmentally conscious could buy goodwill and publicity by investing in alternatives to car parking.

The fourth factor is the cost of providing parking. There is no such thing as a free lunch or free parking. Building and maintaining parking is too often considered part of the cost of doing business and not explicitly examined. The effect of excessive parking regulations can be clearly seen when we compare the cost of parking regulations to other impact fees. Cities in California have a well-developed set of impact fees covering a broad range of public services such as roads and sewer systems. For various California cities, Professor Donald Shoup calculated the cost of required parking at 6 to 12 times the impact fee for all other public services combined.

Finally, municipal regulations may alter the amount of parking an owner would otherwise construct. The regulations often require more stalls than even the national suburban-based studies suggest. Surveys of 33 cities in the southeast (Polanis and Price 1991, 32) and 117 cities in California (Shoup 1995, 18) found parking requirements for office space to be 32 and 36 percent higher, respectively, than the ITE study rate. A number of studies have shown that these required stalls are not necessary (Willson 1995, Gruen Associates 1986).

In addition to explicit parking requirements, other municipal codes and actions may encourage excessive parking in subtle ways. For example, many codes include various setback requirements. Often the choice of what to do with the land in the setback comes down to providing more landscaping or more parking. Parking is often cheaper to maintain; thus, parking usually wins. Cities also tend to make a significant effort to ease the flow of automobile traffic, but pay scant attention to the pedestrian system. In many cities, up-to-date vehicle traffic counts are available for every major street, but pedestrian or bicycle counts have never been conducted. With little public investment in pedestrian or other nonauto systems, it is difficult for a business relying on these alternative modes to get customers or employees to its building.

Parking as a Public Good

The city as a whole has an interest in the character of the city, the economic viability of its buildings, the congestion of its streets, the viability and quality of pedestrian, bicycle, and bus systems, traffic-related deaths and injuries, and the noise, air, and land pollution caused by automobiles. Municipalities also wish to provide for the vitality of their businesses and to improve the quality of life for their citizens. Balancing the health, safety, and welfare implications of parking is not a simple matter of requiring more parking. For example, a study in Oakland, California, before and after Oakland began requiring parking for apartment buildings, found that the construction cost per dwelling increased by 18 percent and housing density fell by 33 percent, making housing less affordable and transit less feasible (Bertha 1964).

Recommendations for Local Studies

Many of the deficiencies of national studies can be rectified with local information. Furthermore, local studies can be tailored to local policy and conditions. There are as many types of parking studies as there are parking questions. As previously outlined, it is not sufficient to determine the demand for parking without qualifying the conditions under which demand is to be measured (e.g., paid parking, metered parking, special-event parking). Parking is always a local issue dependent on the character and form of the district. Finally, the cost of obtaining the information must be weighed against its expected value. Sizing an underground garage, for example, calls for formal research, while locating a vendor in an underused parking lot may be informed by a simple survey.

The typical ingredients in a parking study are (1) a clear description of the purposes, assumptions, and methods of the study, (2) a parking facility map that indicates the number, location, cost(s), access restrictions, and/or ownership of stalls, (3) parking use data such as the time, location, and duration of parking, automobile occupancy rates, and the purpose(s) of current and historical use of the system, (4) descriptions of the district and of nonautomobile means of access, and (5) an estimate of how the system will react to any proposed changes (e.g., adding a building, closing a lane of curb parking, or adding a trolley from remote parking) based on information from the study and studies of previous similar changes. The first and last steps require the most judgment.

A tutorial on the art of survey design is beyond the scope of this book. The more elaborate studies should be planned by experts in survey design. However, the car commons designer or owner may conduct quick-and-dirty surveys and should be aware of the general methods, assumptions, and approaches of complex studies. Following is a brief outline of complex studies, along with descriptions of a few quick-and-dirty surveys.

DEMAND PREDICTIONS

Studies designed to elucidate the number of parking stalls provided by new construction are conducted to establish zoning requirements, to challenge minimum zoning requirements, to establish requirements for special conditions not covered by zoning, or to examine an owner's belief that parking in excess of requirements is needed. In all these cases, an expert in survey design should be consulted. Typically, these studies begin with national data (see preceding) and modify them for local conditions.

Ideally, these studies determine the point at which adding

another stall would cost more than it is worth. Remember, however, that costs and benefits change according to whose cost the study is addressing. Relevant costs are very different for a building owner than for a city.

Often, the national data are modified by examining the parking characteristics of the immediate neighborhood and/ or similar projects. For example, a study might show that the majority of the neighboring buildings provide significantly less parking than the national data suggest and that this has not created a major problem (or perhaps that it has helped create some benefit such as high bus occupancy or a dense and lively pedestrian street).

A demand study could also investigate the opportunity to share parking with existing on-street and off-street facilities. This requires an analysis of the components and duration of parking (e.g., commuters parking all day use X percent of the stalls). A time sequence of photographs of the parking areas, along with a survey of parkers, is often used to obtain these data.

ELASTICITY STUDIES

Perhaps the most useful but also most involved studies are econometric studies that attempt to determine the elasticity of demand for parking. This type of study seeks to answer the following types of questions: "How much farther will commuters walk to save one dollar for a day's parking?" "How many more people will use a carpool if the spaces next to the door are reserved for carpools?"

To conduct these elasticity studies, conditions must be found where the variable of interest changes between one measurement and another. All other significant factors must stay the same or their effects must be removed (mathematically) from the study. In the real life of cities it is difficult to find perfect sites.

Before-and-after studies of changing situations (a remodeled lot, a lot that has raised its prices, or the addition of a building to a street) offer the best opportunities for elasticity research. Unfortunately, the vast majority of demand-prediction investigations are simply "before" studies. Demand-prediction studies rarely include a postconstruction review, nor are they often collected in a central public place for future use. A city's traffic or planning department should archive parking studies done for individual buildings and select useful ones for postconstruction review.

COST CONTOURS

A relatively quick method to estimate the value of parking stalls is to construct a cost contour map (Figure 12.1). To make a cost contour map, parking lots and/or garages that charge the market rate (i.e., are not subsidized) are located

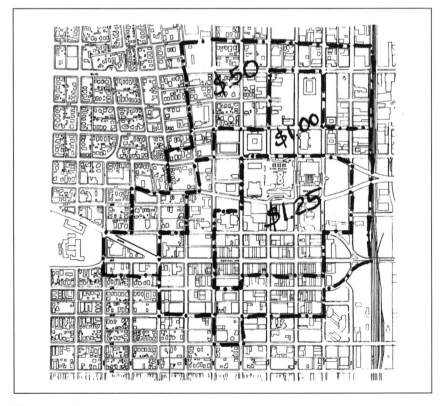

Figure 12.1   Cost contour map.

on a map of the district surrounding the site of study. Next, the monthly, daily, special-event, and/or hourly parking fees of these facilities are determined and placed on the map. Finally, circles are drawn to include all the sites charging a fee within a certain range (e.g., 25 to 49 cents an hour).

OCCUPANCY MAPS

To locate places and times for shared parking or multiple uses of a parking lot, a set of occupancy maps can easily be assembled (Figure 12.2). Assume, for example, that you would like to determine when and where there is space in an existing lot for vendors. Make a booklet containing multiple copies of a simple map of the lot.[2] Over a period of visits to the site, record on the maps the stalls that are unoccupied (or occupied, whichever is easier, but be consistent). Record the time, date, weather, notes of unusual conditions, and name of observer on each map. After you have recorded enough observations to establish trends (always a judgment, and more is always better), overlay the maps for each time of day to see if there are places that are consistently under-used.

Methods of Sizing the Supply of Parking

The following four alternative approaches to determining the supply of parking may be more responsive to local conditions and goals, reduce excess parking, make the costs of parking more visible, and improve the quality of our cities and towns.

TINKERING

The incremental approach is to slowly modify current practices. A number of possible steps are outlined below.

Shared parking: There are two different methods of sharing parking. Individual parking requirements can

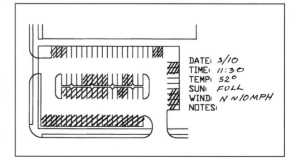

Figure 12.2 Occupancy record.

be reduced if, for two or more adjacent uses, each use's greatest demand for parking occurs at different times of the day or week. This is the time-share approach to shared parking; each building uses the parking spaces in shifts. Table 12.1 lists uses that can readily share parking.

Parking is also shared if, instead of driving, people park once and walk to various destinations. ITE's 1995 *Shared Parking Planning Guidelines* should be used in conjunction with ULI's *Shared Parking* as an initial basis to compute demand when parking is shared. Significant reductions to the ULI's shared parking standards can be achieved with ITE's information. In reviewing a study of shared parking in Mountain View, California, ITE concludes, "Even in a suburban CBD (central business district), simply using the ULI default demand rates and time-of-day adjustments will significantly overstate the actual demand (by a factor of two in this case)." As experience and local data are gained, they should replace the national standards.

I recommend that municipalities allow shared parking reductions by both prescriptive and performance means. That is, the required parking for a project that meets shared parking criteria may be reduced either by a standard formula or by submission of an approved parking-demand analysis. The legal requirements to approve a shared parking plan should be as simple as possible. Criteria for transit service, maximum walking distances, and minimum quality

Table 12.1   Shared Parking Companions

Main Use	Companion Uses
Daytime employment (e.g., office)	Weekend and nighttime uses (e.g., church, theater) and residential
Park-and-rides	Weekend and nighttime uses
Restaurant and retail	Large employment centers
Primary and secondary schools	Weekend and summer uses (e.g., camps)

SOURCES: ITE 6F-52, and Weant and Levinson 1990.

of the pedestrian system should be incorporated into shared parking regulations (Chapter 6). Curb parking, parking streets, and parking squares are well fit for shared parking strategies.

Ride-sharing promotion: The need for parking spaces decreases as the occupancy of vehicles increases. Promotion of carpooling and vanpooling can substantially reduce parking requirements. Table 12.2 shows an example of parking lot size reductions and cost savings produced by increasing the average number of people per car arriving at work.

Model Parking Code Provisions, a 1983 report by the Federal Highway Administration, estimates that parking requirements (i.e., number of parking spaces) can be reduced in the following ways:

- Providing a coordinator and matching service for ride sharing for a large employee pool can typically save 5 to 10 percent, and strong programs can reduce parking needs by 30 to 35 percent.

Table 12.2 Sample Cost Savings from Increased Automobile Occupancy

Persons per Car	Percent Reduction in Stalls Needed	Construction Cost Savings	Land Cost Savings	Annualized Construct. and Maintenance Cost Savings
1.2	4	$24,000	$79,000	$2,600
1.3	12	$72,000	$238,000	$7,900
1.4	18	$108,000	$356,000	$11,900
1.6	28	$168,000	$554,000	$15,000
1.8	36	$216,000	$713,000	$23,800
2	42	$252,000	$832,000	$27,700
2.5	54	$324,000	$1,090,000	$35,700
Assumptions				
1.15 typ.	600 total stalls	$1,000 per stall	$10 per square foot	

SOURCE: *Model Parking Code Provisions to Encourage Ridesharing and Transit Use,* Table 2

- Placing parking for carpools near the building entrance can result in a 1 to 3 percent reduction.

- Reducing the parking costs for carpools can shave another 5 percent off the necessary parking.

- Subsidizing or operating vanpools can eliminate up to 40 to 50 percent of the parking demand.

Land released from parking: Land should be easily available for other uses once it is clear that it is not needed for parking. A simple system to release land occupied by excessive parking should be part of a city's zoning code. This system could include both permanent and seasonal or periodic releases. If, for example, except during November and December, only 60 percent of the required stalls in a lot are used, then the remaining 40 percent should be available for temporary uses during the remaining 10 months of the year.

If possible, building and site plans submitted for city approval should identify suspected areas of excess parking and indicate alternative uses for this land. If the city will not modify its requirements, it may agree to allow temporary uses or future conversion of the land based on the submitted plans and future proof that the parking requirements were indeed excessive.

Phased-in parking: A more trusting municipality could allow a development to provide a first phase of parking with only the parking that the developer considers necessary. The city could require a bond or other assurance that a second phase of parking will be constructed a year after the project is occupied if a city review deems it necessary. If the review finds the additional parking unnecessary, then the requirement is waived.

Standard waivers: Many jurisdictions reduce parking requirements by a set percentage if certain conditions are met (e.g., providing a sheltered transit stop or bicycle lockers and showers for employees).

Cash-outs: Since 1993, the State of California requires

employers who have 50 or more employees[3] and who subsidize parking to offer employees a choice: either a subsidized parking place or the money equivalent to the subsidy of the space. This policy makes it clear to the driver that parking is not free and allows a choice. Studies suggest that changing from employer-paid parking to driver-paid parking results in about a 19 percent decrease in employee parking demand (Shoup 1995).

Matching: This is a more indirect and uncertain method of reducing parking, but its benefits make it worth considering. Environmental consultant Gene Mullins has developed a method to allow employees of companies with many branches in a city (such as banks and grocery stores) to relocate to a branch closer to their home in order to minimize their commute. In a trial of the method funded by the Washington State Transportation Department, the average commute distance for all workers at Key Bank in the Seattle region dropped 17 percent (*Technology Review,* July 1997, 16). These shorter commutes may make bicycling, busing, or walking feasible.

Competitive alternatives: Municipalities may seek to reduce the demand for parking and road capacity by investing in the infrastructure for other means of travel and by eliminating or reducing subsidies and requirements for parking. This approach works by reducing the costs of alternative travel modes and by increasing the cost of auto travel. Bus ridership levels have been shown to be related to the cost of parking at work (Messenger and Ewing 1996), and the number of trips made by walking is related to the quality of the sidewalk system (PBQD 1993).

This may be a relatively economical approach. Excellent sidewalks, bike paths (and parking), and bus shelters are inexpensive compared to roads and parking lots. In addition to direct municipal funding, cities could develop zoning regulations and impact fees that allow a development to provide high-quality pedestrian, bicycle, and transit facilities in lieu of some of the requirements to support the automobile (e.g., parking facilities, road improvements). For the price of constructing two automobile stalls in a garage, for example, one could buy 10 or more bikes, lockers, helmets, and stalls. Perhaps, corporations could reduce the number of employees driving to work if a corporate fleet of bicycles were available for local trips during the day. Boeing has for decades had a fleet of bicycles for employees to travel around its giant production facilities.

On a grander scale, various European cities have municipal bikes that the public may use to travel through the city, and they have made significant investments in bike lanes, racks, and traffic signals. Portland, Oregon, and Victoria, British Columbia, have recently begun similar programs. The University of Washington, in cooperation with the local bus system, initiated a low-cost student bus pass in lieu of undertaking significant roadway and parking improvements.

A significant and sustained investment in nonautomobile facilities, I believe, will have a greater return than the sum of individual small actions would suggest. There are thresholds at which social practices change, and it may become feasible, perhaps fashionable, to buy a yearly bus pass, a bicycle for commuting, or a cart for walking home with groceries.

DISTRICT PARKING

In the first part of the twentieth century there was considerable debate about the appropriateness, proper scope, and effects of zoning. An article in the April 1948 issue of *Transportation Quarterly* argues that since a big city concentrates a supply and demand for parking, it is a civic responsibility to make this concentration efficient, and that the piecemeal requirements of zoning are maladroit.

One approach is to supply parking, not to individual buildings, but to commercial streets, campuses, downtowns, or other districts. District parking maximizes the potential for shared parking.

The municipalities of Santa Monica and Los Gatos in California have district parking programs. In 1977, Boulder, Colorado, revitalized its downtown with a district parking program. The city waived on-site parking requirements and formed a general improvement district organization with the goal, among other things, of supplying parking facilities. The elimination of on-site parking requirements allowed new developments to use more of their sites for buildings, thus maximizing the potential return on the investment in the land and producing a pedestrian-supportive environment. The success of this approach resulted in a tight parking supply, but this problem is preferable to high vacancy rates and a decaying downtown. As *Shared Parking Planning Guidelines* (ITE 6F-52, 48) notes, "Requiring new uses to provide parking on a stand-alone basis may completely discourage new development or redevelopment in an economically strapped area."

Because curb and public lot stalls are inherently shared parking for facilities within walking distance, a smaller number of stalls are needed than under current conditions. In essence, district parking is a return to the concept of containing traffic to public streets and facilities.

I would suggest that the concept of district parking be taken a step further. Access management districts (similar to traffic-demand management areas) could be formed to manage and/or coordinate improvements to the streets, sidewalks, parking lots, carpooling facilities, bus stops, bicycle lanes and lockers, and other means of access to a district. People should be able to walk from one location to another within the district, which should generally be no larger than 4000 to 5000 feet in diameter. Parking facilites should include curb parking, parking streets, and publicly accessible hidden parking or structured parking. Pedestrians exiting a hidden or structured parking facility should arrive in a public space connected to the public pedestrian system.

A combination of property taxes, fees in lieu of zoning-required on-site parking, air-quality funds, traffic-generation taxes, and parking fees could fund operation of the parking district. A district could direct funds to balance various means of access. Goals for the percentage of trips by transit, carpooling, and so forth, combined with determining the maximum amount of ground space to be set aside for parking, could be used to establish the number of parking stalls built.

Collecting more complete data about the effects of various amounts of parking on economic, urban, and social viability of districts would help the management of traffic districts. Modeling these more urban conditions is significantly more complex than measuring the unfettered demand for parking at stand-alone suburban buildings. However, even without a rigorous modeling system, these plans may be initiated as long as they allow for involvement of the affected parties, regular measurements of capacity, incremental adaptations, and unexpected solutions (i.e., the conditions necessary to let an ecosystem adaptively evolve). When a parking district is created, measures should be taken to keep parking demand from spilling over into adjacent districts (such as residential parking zones). The *Local Government Parking Management Handbook* (Kodama and Willson 1996) is a good primer on the development and implementation of parking management strategies.

A PARKING MARKET

Parking quantity requirements could be dropped entirely from zoning codes, and decisions about the proper supply of off-street parking could be left to market forces. Additionally, on-street and public stalls could be priced at market rates. A significant amount of funds could be generated by charging fees for what is now free parking. Under current conditions, with no direct charge to the driver for 99 percent of parking (Shoup 1997), the private parking industry takes in about $5 billion a year from parking fees on its 1 percent of the market (Rudnitsky 1996).

Shoup has proposed creating "parking benefit districts" (Shoup 1997). In these districts, residents would receive free stickers allowing them to park at the curb. Additionally, the city could sell a number of permits to nonresidents. The fees from the nonresident permits could fund neighborhood improvements. There are some questions about the constitutionality of this approach. It may be that the city could not sell permits to on-street stalls, but only to off-street spaces in the district.

In busy commercial areas, business associations could be funded from meter fees collected in excess of the city's standard rate. Careful study about the price elasticity of demand for parking should be conducted before significantly raising the commercial area's meter fees. Shoppers may opt to drive to malls with unpriced parking.

The goal of these programs is that the funds from curb-parking fees benefit the neighborhood affected by the curb parking. Transitioning from subsidized parking to an open market for parking must be done with a great deal of care to avoid creating undue advantages for areas that retain their subsidies. Well-designed advance research and a city- or regionwide integrated plan are needed.

MAXIMUMS

In some cases, a city may wish to establish maximums on the amount of parking a building may supply based on the capacity of the street system, air quality, the desired minimum density of buildings, and the impact of automobiles on other resources. If the maximums are set to restrict what developers would otherwise provide, and if buildings are allowed to sell or combine their rights to stalls within a district, then market forces theoretically will distribute parking to those who most desire it. Care should be taken to construct the program so that it encourages shared parking. For example, if two buildings are given a maximum of 10 stalls each, they may be induced to share the spaces if the reward for doing so is a 21-stall total. (Of course, by sharing, they may not *need* as many stalls. They can then sell the right to their excess stalls).

In this case, demand data are not strictly necessary. Instead, the municipality must determine the maximum amount of parking a district may provide without undue nuisance. Christopher Alexander suggests that one possible standard is to limit the amount of space used for parking to 9 percent of the district's total land area (Alexander et al. 1977, 120). Here are some other possible approaches: (1) limit the square footage of parking to a percentage of habitable built space (i.e., a parking-to-habitable-area ratio); (2) limit the parking based on shared parking–demand calculations (ULI's *Shared Parking* and ITE's *Shared Parking Planning Guidelines*); (3) develop traffic-mode split standards (e.g., specify a desired percentage of employees arriving by transit and set a maximum number of parking stalls per building to achieve the standard); and (4) set an absolute maximum for districts based on air-quality standards and/or street capacity.

Summary

The vitality of our cities has been eroded by the institutionalized focus on "free" and easy parking. Demand for parking should be analyzed under conditions where costs are visible to the user and alternatives are readily available. Additionally, demand should be measured at the level of the block or district to reflect shared use and the possibility that people may visit more than one building after parking their cars.

Municipalities have a legitimate interest in managing parking. In fact, the scope of recognized public nuisance from parking has increased since the time cities first sought and gained court approval to regulate parking in order to eliminate street congestion. Because of this increased scope, alternatives to zoning requirements mandating the private provision of parking should be considered.

In all of the preceding alternatives, a city may shift its focus from regulating the quantity of parking stalls to improving the quality of the public space. Incorporating a bus shelter into the facade of a store may increase the store's customer base, reduce parking requirements, and provide a more pleasant sidewalk. A city's investment in pedestrian counts may persuade a restaurant owner and his or her lender that little or no off-street parking is required and that the money might be better spent on a sidewalk café, a well-designed facade, and contributions to streetscape improvements. District parking may satisfy an office's need for employee parking and reduce the amount of pavement in the district. Finding revenue-producing uses for a parking lot may induce a developer to reduce the number of parking stalls and provide for pedestrians and vendors (Chapter 8). (See Chapter 13 for the required number of bicycle stalls and stalls for the mobility-impaired.)

CHAPTER 13

Dimensions and Circulation

Consistency requires you to be as ignorant today as
you were a year ago.
—BERNARD BERENSON, 1952

The following tables and diagrams offer minimum, maximum, and ideal standards for various aspects of parking lot design.

Misuse of Standards

Standards are not a substitute for thought. They must be used within the whole context of the design. A few of the most common misuses of standards follow.

- *The minimum as maximum.* When a minimum dimension is given, it does not mean it is the best dimension, only that it is the least one can use in most cases without significant problems. Often a few more inches makes the difference between OK and great.

- *Standards as the unmitigated truth.* Standards are informed judgments meant to be generally applicable. If your particular application is significantly different, do some research to understand the basis of the standard. Then you may modify the standard to better fit your situation.

- *It's not interesting unless I break the standards.* Good standards represent experience about what makes something safe and gracious, and minimums often imply the dimension that just barely makes an action feasible. Simply breaking the rules could easily make things worse.

- *My standard trumps your judgment.* Pedestrians have lost space to auto traffic in many cases simply because the auto-traffic advocates have adopted standards, while pedestrian advocates used judgment tailored to the case.

- *Escalating standards.* In 1929, recommended stall widths were 7 feet (2.13 m) and under. Today a stall width under 7 feet is unacceptable. Parking stall dimensions are based on vehicle sizes. As traffic lanes and parking spaces have increased in size to accommodate the largest vehicles, it has become easier to operate large vehicles (Figure 13.1). This encourages more people to buy larger vehicles (other things being equal), and in response, stall dimensions increase.[1] Part of the reason European parking stalls are smaller than stalls in the United States is that respect for and investment in pre-automobile cities has limited the growth in parking stall size and thus limited the growth in car size.

Figure 13.1 Copyright Tribune Media Services, Inc. All Rights Reserved. Reprinted with permission.

Parking Lots

Bay and Stall Dimensions

There are number of different approaches to the sizing and dimensioning of parking facilities. Table 13.1 incorporates a service approach that allows a designer to vary dimensions based on the expected use of the lot. It assumes a mix of small and large cars close to the 1995 national average. To use Table 13.1, three initial decisions must be made: (1) the appropriate stall width based on the expected turnover of the lot (Table 13.2), (2) if and how small car stalls will be provided (see following), and (3) the angle of parking. Slightly smaller dimensions are recommended in certain conditions by Smith in her level-of-service approach (Chrest, Smith, and Bhuyan 1996, chapter 2).

SPECIAL CONDITIONS

Table 13.5 lists some special conditions for vehicle stall dimensions. Parking for other vehicles should be based on the vehicle's length, width, and turning radii (Tables 13.3 and 13.4).

SMALL CAR STALLS

It is estimated that in 1995, half the cars on the road in the United States were small cars, 5 feet 9 inches wide by 14 feet 11 inches long (1.75 by 4.55 m) or smaller (Chrest, Smith, and Bhuyan 1996, 30). Many local regulations allow a specified percentage of stalls to be designated for small or compact cars. However, the average difference in size between small and large cars has been decreasing so that it is often confusing for motorists to decide if they are driving a small or standard car. I recommend that small car stalls be designated in three different conditions:

1. In employee parking lots, stalls for compact cars may constitute up to 40 percent of the general stalls. This standard supplies compact stalls for 80 percent of the expected

Table 13.1 Stall and Module Dimensions

		Stall Width		Stall Depth Parallel to Aisle		Aisle Width *Min.* (AW) ft	Minimum Modules	
		Par. to Car (Sw) ft	Par. to Aisle (WP) ft	to Wall (VPw) ft	to Interlock (VPi) ft		Wall to Wall (W₂) ft	Interlock (W₄) ft
Two-Way Aisle								
	90°							
Mix	G	10.00	10.0	18.4	18.4	24.0	60.8	60.8
	A	9.00	9.0	18.4	18.4	24.0	60.8	60.8
	B	8.75	8.8	18.4	18.4	24.0	60.8	60.8
	C	8.50	8.5	18.4	18.4	24.0	60.8	60.8
	D	8.25	8.3	18.4	18.4	24.0	60.8	60.8
Small	A	8.00	8.0	15.1	15.1	22.3	52.4	52.4
	B	7.75	7.8	15.1	15.1	22.3	52.4	52.4
	C	7.50	7.5	15.1	15.1	22.3	52.4	52.4
	D	7.25	7.3	15.1	15.1	22.3	52.4	52.4
Large		9.00	9.0	18.7	18.7	24.0	61.3	61.3
One-Way Aisles								
	75°					(+2 ft min. for 2-way aisle—see note)		
Mix	G	10.00	10.4	19.4	18.6	20.8	59.6	58.0
	A	9.00	9.3	19.4	18.6	21.0	59.9	58.2
	B	8.75	9.1	19.4	18.6	21.1	60.0	58.3
	C	8.50	8.8	19.4	18.6	21.2	60.0	58.4
	D	8.25	8.5	19.4	18.6	21.2	60.1	58.4
Small	A	8.00	8.3	16.2	15.4	20.0	52.5	50.8
	B	7.75	8.0	16.2	15.4	20.1	52.5	50.9
	C	7.50	7.8	16.2	15.4	20.1	52.6	50.9
	D	7.25	7.5	16.2	15.4	20.2	52.7	51.0
Large		9.00	9.3	19.7	18.9	20.9	60.4	58.7
	70°							
Mix	G	10.00	10.6	19.5	18.4	18.2	57.2	55.0
	A	9.00	9.6	19.5	18.4	18.6	57.5	55.3
	B	8.75	9.3	19.5	18.4	18.7	57.6	55.4
	C	8.50	9.0	19.5	18.4	18.7	57.7	55.5
	D	8.25	8.8	19.5	18.4	18.8	57.8	55.6
Small	A	8.00	8.5	16.4	15.3	17.9	50.6	48.4
	B	7.75	8.2	16.4	15.3	18.0	50.7	48.5
	C	7.50	8.0	16.4	15.3	18.0	50.8	48.6
	D	7.25	7.7	16.4	15.3	18.1	50.9	48.7
Large		9.00	9.6	19.8	18.7	19.1	58.7	56.4

Table 13.1 Stall and Module Dimensions (*Cont.*)

		Stall Width		Stall Depth Parallel to Aisle		Aisle Width *Min.* (AW) ft	Minimum Modules	
		Par. to Car (Sw) ft	Par. to Aisle (WP) ft	to Wall (VPw) ft	to Interlock (VPi) ft		Wall to Wall (W₂) ft	Interlock (W₄) ft
One-Way Aisles (*Cont.*)								
	65°							
Mix	G	10.00	11.0	19.4	18.0	15.7	54.4	51.7
	A	9.00	9.9	19.4	18.0	16.1	54.9	52.2
	B	8.75	9.7	19.4	18.0	16.2	55.0	52.3
	C	8.50	9.4	19.4	18.0	16.3	55.1	52.4
	D	8.25	9.1	19.4	18.0	16.4	55.2	52.5
Small	A	8.00	8.8	16.4	15.0	15.7	48.5	45.8
	B	7.75	8.6	16.4	15.0	15.8	48.6	45.9
	C	7.50	8.3	16.4	15.0	15.9	48.7	46.0
	D	7.25	8.0	16.4	15.0	16.0	48.8	46.1
Large		9.00	9.9	19.7	18.3	16.6	56.0	53.2
	60°							
Mix	G	10.00	11.5	19.1	17.5	13.2	51.4	48.2
	A	9.00	10.4	19.1	17.5	13.7	51.9	48.7
	B	8.75	10.1	19.1	17.5	13.8	52.0	48.8
	C	8.50	9.8	19.1	17.5	13.9	52.2	49.0
	D	8.25	9.5	19.1	17.5	14.0	52.3	49.1
Small	A	8.00	9.2	16.3	14.7	13.6	46.1	42.9
	B	7.75	8.9	16.3	14.7	13.7	46.2	43.0
	C	7.50	8.7	16.3	14.7	13.8	46.4	43.2
	D	7.25	8.4	16.3	14.7	13.9	46.5	43.3
Large		9.00	10.4	19.5	17.8	14.1	53.1	49.8
	55°							
Mix	G	10.00	12.2	18.7	16.9	11.7	49.2	45.6
	A	9.00	11.0	18.7	16.9	11.2	48.7	45.1
	B	8.75	10.7	18.7	16.9	11.4	48.9	45.2
	C	8.50	10.4	18.7	16.9	11.5	49.0	45.4
	D	8.25	10.1	18.7	16.9	11.7	49.2	45.5
Small	A	8.00	9.8	16.0	14.2	11.5	43.5	39.8
	B	7.75	9.5	16.0	14.2	11.6	43.7	40.0
	C	7.50	9.2	16.0	14.2	11.7	43.8	40.1
	D	7.25	8.9	16.0	14.2	11.9	44.0	40.3
Large		9.00	11.0	19.1	17.2	11.7	49.9	46.1

Table 13.1 Stall and Module Dimensions (*Cont.*)

		Stall Width		Stall Depth Parallel to Aisle		Aisle Width *Min.* (AW) ft	Minimum Modules	
		Par. to Car (Sw) ft	Par. to Aisle (WP) ft	to Wall (VPw) ft	to Interlock (VPi) ft		Wall to Wall (W₂) ft	Interlock (W₄) ft
One-Way Aisles (*Cont.*)								
	50°							
Mix	G	10.00	13.1	18.2	16.2	11.4	47.8	43.7
	A	9.00	11.7	18.2	16.2	11.0	47.4	43.3
	B	8.75	11.4	18.2	16.2	11.0	47.4	43.3
	C	8.50	11.1	18.2	16.2	11.0	47.4	43.3
	D	8.25	10.8	18.2	16.2	11.0	47.4	43.3
Small	A	8.00	10.4	15.7	13.6	11.0	42.4	38.2
	B	7.75	10.1	15.7	13.6	11.0	42.4	38.2
	C	7.50	9.8	15.7	13.6	11.0	42.4	38.2
	D	7.25	9.5	15.7	13.6	11.0	42.4	38.2
Large		9.00	11.7	18.6	16.4	11.3	48.4	44.1
	45°							
Mix	G	10.00	14.1	17.5	15.3	11.0	46.1	41.5
	A	9.00	12.7	17.5	15.3	11.0	46.1	41.5
	B	8.75	12.4	17.5	15.3	11.0	46.1	41.5
	C	8.50	12.0	17.5	15.3	11.0	46.1	41.5
	D	8.25	11.7	17.5	15.3	11.0	46.1	41.5
Small	A	8.00	11.3	15.2	12.9	11.0	41.4	36.9
	B	7.75	11.0	15.2	12.9	11.0	41.4	36.9
	C	7.50	10.6	15.2	12.9	11.0	41.4	36.9
	D	7.25	10.3	15.2	12.9	11.0	41.4	36.9
Large		9.00	12.7	17.9	15.6	11.0	46.8	42.1

1. Figures 13.2 and 13.3 define dimensions used in Table 13.1.
2. Stalls angled between 90 and 60° confuse whether the aisle is one-way or two-way. Do not use angles between 90 and 75°. Some designers advocate using 75° stalls with two-way aisles because the right-hand-side parking maneuver is easier into an angled stall. However, making a left-hand turn to park in a 75° stall is difficult. A minimum of 22 feet is necessary for two-way aisles, and 24 to 25 feet allows ample walking space and occasional left-hand parking. Stalls at angles between 45 and 0° (parallel parking) are not generally advisable because they are often space-inefficient and confusing. The formula used to calculate Table 13.1 is given in Table 13.3; if special circumstances warrant, stall dimensions or angles other than those given may be calculated.
3. In the interest of legibility, metric dimensions are not given. The dimension in meters may be derived by dividing feet by 3.28. However, it may be better to recalculate, using Table 13.3 and appropriate metric stall dimensions.
4. Stall stripes are often painted 6 to 10 inches shorter than the stall depth to encourage drivers to fully pull into the stall.
5. The chart uses a minimum aisle width of 11 feet. This dimension is minimally sufficient to allow passage of cars and pedestrians. In high-turnover or special situations such as lots primarily serving the elderly or children, a pedestrian walkway and/or a wider aisle should be provided.
6. Sources: Adapted and recalculated from Ricker 1957; Weant and Levinson 1990; Box 1992; and Chrest, Smith, and Bhuyan 1996.
7. See Table 13.4 and Figure 13.4 for the design vehicles and clearances used to calculate this table.

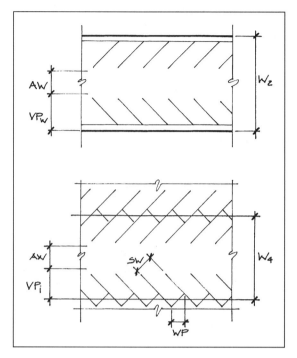

Figure 13.2 Module variables.

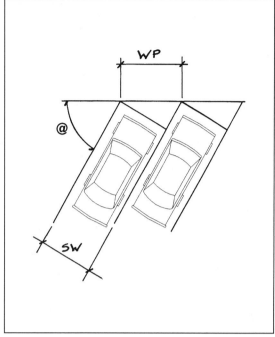

Figure 13.3 Stall widths.

Table 13.2 Turnover Categories and Stall Widths

Name		Stall Width Parallel to Car	Application
Mix*	G	10.00 ft (3.05 m)	Grocery stores and others that use shopping carts[†]
	A	9.00 ft (2.74 m)	Very high turnover rates—post office, convenience stores Areas with a high percentage (>20%) of passenger trucks
	B	8.75 ft (2.67 m)	High turnover rates—general retail
	C	8.50 ft (2.59 m)	Medium turnover rates—airport, hospitals, residential
	D	8.25 ft (2.52 m)	Low turnover rates—employee parking
Small	A	8.00 ft (2.44 m)	Same as categories above
	B	7.75 ft (2.36 m)	
	C	7.50 ft (2.29 m)	
	D	7.25 ft (2.21 m)	

* The mix of cars includes about 40% small cars, based on 1995 U.S. averages.

[†] There are a variety of grocery cart models ranging in width from approximately 18 to 32 inches. I recommend "hairpin" double stripes at least 2 feet wide for lots that use grocery carts. This 2-foot width is included in the 10-foot centerline-to-centerline dimensions.

Table 13.3   Formulas for Parking Stall and Module Dimensions

	Formula
Sw =	Given
WP =	Sw/sin @
VPw =	W cos @ + (L + cb) sin @
VPi =	.5Wcos @ + (L + cb) sin @
AW =	For lots with @ < critical angle,
	AW = R' + c − sin @[(r − Os)^2 − (r − Os − i + c)^2]$^{.5}$ − cos @(r + tr + Os − Sw)
	For lots with @ > critical angle,
	AW = R' + c + sin @[(R^2 − (r + tr + Os + i − c)^2]$^{.5}$ − cos @(r + tr + Os + Sw)
W$_2$ =	AW + 2VPw
W$_4$ =	AW + 2Vpi

Critical Angle

Mixed Stalls		**Small Car Stalls**		**Large Car Stalls**	
Stall Width	**Critical Angle**	**Stall Width**	**Critical Angle**	**Stall Width**	**Critical Angle**
10.00	57.6	8.00	51.6	9.0	55.0
9.00	54.8	7.75	50.7		
8.75	54.0	7.50	49.8		
8.50	53.2	7.25	48.8		
8.25	52.4				

Critical angle = arccot {[(R^2 − (r + tr + Os + i − c)^2)$^{.5}$ + ((r − Os)^2 − (r − Os − i + c)^2)$^{.5}$]/2Sw}.

Critical angle chart assumes design vehicles listed in Table 13.4.

Sw = stall width parallel to car; WP = stall width parallel to aisle; VPw = stall depth from wall parallel to aisle; VPi = stall depth from interlock parallel to aisle; AW = aisle width min.; W2 = module wall to wall; W4 = module interlock to interlock; @ = stall angle; W = design vehicle width; L = design vehicle length; cb = curb clearance .5 ft; R ft = design vehicle wall-to-wall rear radius; c = car clearance; Os = design vehicle side overhang; r = design vehicle curb-to-curb rear radius; i = walkway between cars; tr = design vehicle rear width.

For 90° lots, use 85% of the AW value given by the aisle width formula (see Weant and Levinson 1990, 160).

Aisle width formula from Edmund R. Ricker, *Traffic Design of Parking Garages,* Eno Foundation, 1957.

Table 13.4   Design Vehicle Dimensions

Type	**Mix**	**Small Car**	**Large**	**Passenger truck**
Length (L) inches	215 (5.46 m)	175 (4.45 m)	218 (5.54 m)	212 (5.39 m)
Width (W) inches	77 (1.96 m)	66 (1.68 m)	80 (2.03 m)	80 (2.03 m)
Wall-to-wall front radius (R) feet	20.5 (6.25 m)	18 (5.49 m)	20.75 (6.33 m)	
Wall-to-wall rear radius (R') feet	17.4 (5.31 m)	15 (4.57 m)	17.5 (5.34 m)	
Curb-to-curb rear radius (r) feet	12 (3.66 m)	9.6 (2.93 m)	12.25 (3.73 m)	
Rear width (tr) feet	5.1 (1.55 m)	4.6 (1.4 m)	5.08 (1.55 m)	
Side overhang (Os) feet	0.63 (.192 m)	0.46 (.14 m)	0.75 (.228 m)	0.66 (.201 m)
Walkway between cars (i) feet	2 (.61 m)	2 (.61 m)	2 (.61 m)	2.85 (.87 m)
Car clearance (c) feet	1.5 (.46 m)	1.5 (.46 m)	1.5 (.46 m)	

SOURCES: Weant and Levinson 1990, 157; passenger truck data from Dare 1985.

number of small cars based upon the 1995 U.S. average. When a survey has been conducted or if there is reason to believe that the number of small cars varies from the average, then the supply of compact stalls should be adjusted. In order to build smaller parking lots, businesses could offer rewards to employees who drive compacts. One hundred small car stalls and aisles use about 5300 square feet (~493 m²) less land than needed for 100 standard stalls.[2]

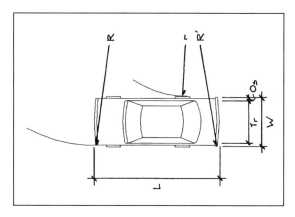

Figure 13.4   Vehicle design variables.

2. At stadiums or other lots in which someone directs traffic to parking areas, cars may be sorted by size. Often, stall markings are not used in these conditions to preserve flexibility. Designers should calculate the number of vehicles that may be parked under various expected conditions (e.g., compacts only, mixed, large only) and provide bays that have as little wastage under each condition as possible. A

Table 13.5   Stall Dimensions for Special Conditions

	Width	**Length**	**Clr. Height**
Designated large	9 ft (2.74 m)	18.5–20 ft (5.79–6.1 m)	
Passenger truck[1]	9 ft (2.74 m)	18.5 ft (5.64 m)	
Handicap car[2]	8 ft (2.44 m) + 5 ft (1.52 m) aisle	17.5 ft (5.34 m)	
Handicap van[2]	8 ft (2.44 m) + 8 ft aisle	17.5 ft (5.34 m)	8.16 ft (2.49 m)
Universal[3] (handicap car or van)	11 ft (3.35 m) + 5 ft (1.52 m) aisle		8.16 ft (2.49 m)
Valet[4]	7.5 ft (2.29 m)	17 ft (5.18 m)	
Europe typical[5]	7.83–8.16 ft (2.39–2.49 m)	15.58–16.42 ft (4.75–5 m)	
Bicycle[6]	2.5 ft (.76 m)	6 ft (1.83 m)	
Motorcycle[6]	3.33 ft (1.02 m)	7 ft (2.13 m)	

SOURCES: [1] Dare 1985.
[2] ADAAG.
[3] Bulletin #6.
[4] Burrage 1957, 242.
[5] Hunnicutt 1982, 650.
[6] Weant and Levinson 1990, 167.

68-foot-long bay, for example, provides nine 7.5-foot-wide stalls or eight 8.5-foot-wide stalls.

3. In general-service lots, up to 40 percent of the stalls may be for compacts (again, this should be adjusted for local conditions). Alternatively, very large cars could be given special stalls. By removing them from the mix of cars, the general stalls and aisles could be made smaller. For example, if 5 to 10 percent of stalls were designated for large cars, a stall width two sizes smaller could be used for the remainder of the lot, and aisles could be approximately 6 inches (~15 cm) smaller. (The large-size cars, classes 10 and 11, made up 7 percent of the market in 1993. See Chrest, Smith, and Bhuyan 1996, 33). These large car stalls should be the least convenient so that smaller cars do not occupy them. Since there is limited experience with this approach, consult a traffic engineer to tailor dimensions to expected local conditions.

LANES

Table 13.6 shows widths for various traffic lanes. All of these dimensions are for public streets. Local regulations and standards often specify similar dimensions for parking lot lanes. The Uniform Fire Code requires that fire lanes be a minimum of 20 feet (6.09 m) wide, have a height clearance of at least 13.5 feet (4.11 m), have a 40-foot (11.98-m) minimum radius on curves, and have a maximum dead-end length of 150 feet (46.26 m).

Table 13.6   Lane Widths

Type	Width	Notes
Fire lane	20 ft (6.1 m) min. typ.	
Curb parking lane	6–8 ft (2.03 m)	10 ft (3.05 m) when also a traffic lane
Parking + traffic lane	18 ft (5.49 m) min.	
No-parking one-way	10 ft (3.05 m) min.	
No-parking two-way	16 ft (4.88 m) min.	

Driveway Location

The existing street and pedestrian network must be evaluated before designing a parking lot to determine the best location for entrances and exits. Local codes normally limit the size, number, and location of access points. Considerations in locating access points include the following:

- Avoid crossing busy pedestrian routes.
- Minimize the number and size of curb cuts to reduce conflicts with pedestrian and street traffic.
- Integrate driveways into the street system. Use alleys when possible. Otherwise, place driveways away from intersections. Entrances must be "upstream" from exits.
- Avoid left turns across traffic if possible (provide turn lanes where volume is significant).
- Keep internal traffic flow simple.
- Avoid requiring cars to back up onto sidewalks in order to exit a parking stall.
- Entry control devices require at least a two-space off-street reservoir (See following to calculate queuing for large lots).

Driveway Width

Driveway width should be kept to a minimum to limit sidewalk curb cut lengths and to minimize pavement. However, sufficient width must be given to accommodate traffic flow. See Table 13.7.

Number of Driveway Lanes

For large lots, the standard method for determining the number of lanes entering or exiting a lot is based on the highest demand for the lot during any 15-minute period. The method follows, but some thought may be given to the use of this standard. For example, using the following charts for a stadium parking lot suggests that they should be designed so

Table 13.7 Driveway Widths

Type	Entry Lanes	Exit Lanes	Total Width	Corner Radii
Commercial[1]				
Typical	1	1	22–30 ft (6.71–9.15 m)	15 ft (4.57 m)
Large volume	1 @ 14–16 ft (4.29–4.88 m)	2 @ 10–11 ft (3.05–3.35 m)	34–36 ft (10.37–10.98 m)	15 ft (4.57 m)
Very high volume	2 @ 10–11 ft (3.05–3.35 m)	2 @ 10–11 ft (3.05–3.35 m)	40–44 ft (12.20–13.41 m)	20 ft (6.09 m)
Residential[2]				
Driveway for 1 car			8 ft (2.44 m) max.	
Driveway for 2 to 10 cars			12 ft (3.66 m) max.	

SOURCES: [1]Box 1992, 206.
[2]Untermann 1984, 202.

that they can empty in 30 minutes. Perhaps adjacent merchants would prefer that people stay a bit longer. Adjacent roads could be a bit smaller and cheaper if the crowd were metered out more slowly, and perhaps more people would use transit and the lot could be smaller. Limited exit capacity may be an adjunct to increased parking fees for jurisdictions wishing to reduce auto travel in downtowns.

The rate at which cars may enter a lot is affected by the angle of approach to the lot (in order of ease, straight approach, left turn to entrance, right turn to entrance) and drivers' familiarity with the lot (e.g., commuters are more familiar with a lot than are tourists). Rates up to 1000 cars per lane per hour are possible. Entrance fee and control booths reduce the entrance rate by 50 to 83 percent. Attendants can park 8 to 16 cars per hour per attendant (Box 1992, 207).

The standard formula for the number of lanes is $N = (S \times R)/(P \times U)$, where N is number of lanes, S is number of stalls, R is the percent of lot capacity moving at peak hour (Table 13.8), P is the peak hour factor (Table 13.9), and U is the design capacity of the lane (Table 13.10).

Table 13.8   Design Percent of Lot Capacity Moving at Peak Hour (R)

	Morning Peak		Afternoon Peak	
Land Use	In	Out	In	Out
Office	40–70%	5–15%	5–20%	40–70%
Medical office	40–60%	50–80%	60–80%	60–90%
General retail	20–50%	30–60%	30–60%	30–60%
Convenience retail	80–150%	80–150%	80–150%	80–150%
Hospital visitors	30–40%	40–50%	40–60%	50–75%
Hospital employees	60–75%	5–10%	10–15%	60–75%
Residential	5–10%	30–50%	30–50%	10–30%
Hotel/motel	30–50%	50–80%	30–60%	10–30%
	Before event		After event	
Special event	80–100%		85–200%	

SOURCE: Adapted from Chrest, Smith, and Bhuyan, 1996.

Table 13.9   Peak Hour Factors (PHF)

Condition	PHF
Special events	.5–.65
Single lane	.75 max.
Two lanes	.85 max.
Three lanes	.95 max.

SOURCE: Adapted from Weant and Levinson, 1990.

Table 13.10   Design Capacity for Lanes (*U*)

	Entrance Vehicles/Hour/Lane		Exit Vehicles/Hour/Lane	
Control device	Design Rate	Max. Rate	Design Rate	Max. Rate
No stop	800	1,050	375	475
Automatic ticket dispenser	525	650		
Push-button ticket dispenser	450	525		
Coin/token-operated gate	150	200	150	200
Fixed fee to cashier with gate	200	250	200	250
Fixed fee to cashier with no gate	250	350	250	350
Variable fee to cashier			150	200
Validated ticket to operator			300	350
Machine-read ticket			375	425
Coded-card reader	350	400	350	400
Proximity card reader	500	550	500	550

SOURCE: Adapted from Weant and Levinson, 1990, 186.
NOTE: This table assumes an easy or straight approach with no sharp turns.

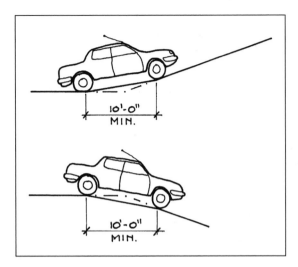

Figure 13.5   Slopes at grade changes. Change grade by a maximum of 10° increments with 10 feet (3.05 m) minimum between changes of grade.

Queuing

Entrance routes for lots at which people tend to arrive at the same time (e.g., employee parking, special events) should have off-street queuing space to avoid having cars block the sidewalk and street. Alternatively, work hours can be staggered and special events can have incentives for arriving early. The formula to estimate the number of cars queued is $L = i^2/(1 - i)$, where L = number of vehicles waiting, i = peak hour volume/maximum service rate (Tables 13.8 and 13.10) (Weant and Levinson 1990, 186–187).

Grades

Table 13.11 and Figure 13.5 show maximum recommended grades within parking lots. Care should be taken to minimize the grades of routes used by the mobility-impaired. Ramps may have a maximum slope of 1 in 12 (i.e., 1 unit of rise per 12 units of run) over a maximum length of 30 feet between landings.

Table 13.11   Grades in Parking Lots

Grade	Condition
6% max.	Continuous slope in parking lot
12% max., 30 ft long	Nonparking automobile ramps with pedestrians allowed
15% max.	Nonparking automobile ramps with signs banning pedestrians
>6% change	A vertical curve transition is required; see Figure 13.5
1% min. / 2% rec.	Slope to drain asphalt
.5% min. / 2% rec.	Slope to drain concrete
2% (1:50) max.	Slope within accessible stalls

SOURCE: Adapted from Chrest, Smith, and Bhuyan, 1996; ITE, 1982; and Untermann, 1984.

End Islands

In lots with more than 200 cars or difficult conditions, islands should be created at the end of bays to ensure sight distances, provide adequate turning radii, protect vehicles at the end of parking bays, and limit parking encroachment into cross aisles. End islands also help delineate circulation and may be used to plant trees, pile snow, or store grocery carts. They provide places for light poles, fire hydrants, low signage, and other equipment. Striped pavement in and of itself is not very effective in discouraging use of these areas for auto parking, and drivers turning into an aisle often cut the corner, putting themselves on the wrong side of the aisle. Curbs or bollards are often needed to establish the end island.

The character of these islands is a significant design feature. They line the cross street and act as gateways to each bay of parking. Figure 13.6 shows typical end islands. The size and geometry of the islands should be adjusted for particular conditions. Design considerations include the following:

- A typical car has an inside turning radius of about 15 feet (4.57 m), and end islands with smaller radii may cause cars to turn wide—into the opposing lane.

- Care should be taken with the placement of the radii to avoid exposing the end of an adjacent car and its disembarking passengers to "clipping" from turning cars.

- Cars parking next to the island need a walking aisle of at least 24 inches (.6 m) between them and any landscaping.

- Adequate sight distance becomes greater as car speed increases and when the road is curved. For example, a car making a right turn onto a 20 mph (32 kph) aisle (typical small-lot speeds) needs to be able to see about 250 feet (~76 m) upstream; turning onto a 35 mph

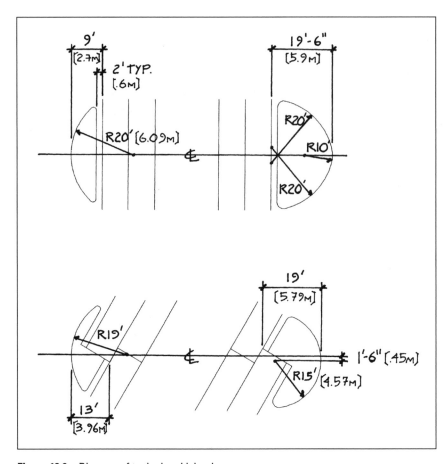

Figure 13.6 Diagram of typical end islands.

(56 kph) aisle, the driver needs to see about 550 feet upstream to judge the safety of making the turn (Stover and Koepke 1989, table 1). Thus the depth of the island should increase for higher-speed or curved aisles/ roads.

- End islands may also be increased in size to provide space for trees or other amenities.

Stall Markings

Marking stalls aids in the even distribution of vehicles within a lot and is necessary for stalls for the handicapped.

Painted or applied stripes are typical. Street reflectors offer higher visibility and can be felt if a tire crosses them. Changes in pavement color and material can also help designate stalls. Painted or applied stall stripes are usually 4 inches (~10 cm) wide and about 6 inches (~15 cm) shorter than the stall to encourage drivers to pull fully into the stall. Reflective and ridged stripes are available that provide increased visibility and a tactile presence to pedestrians and drivers.

There is disagreement about the effectiveness of double stripes to encourage centering of cars. A study by Paul Box (1994b) of shopping center, motel, and office building parking lots found no significant difference in parking efficiency between single and double stripes and thus recommends avoiding the expense of paired lines. However, for stalls for the mobility-impaired, possibly grocery store lots, and in other conditions where the usable width of the between-doors aisle is large and critical for pedestrian access, the aisle should be marked with two stripes and cross-hatching.

The design manuals of the 1950s suggest that stall marks be continued up walls to help drivers locate the stall. Careful placement of parking meters, trees, bollards, and other vertical elements can provide the same function.

Overhangs, Wheel Stops, and Bumpers

Wheel stops, curbs, bumpers, and bollards are used to protect structures, limit parking encroachment onto pedestrian pathways or planting areas, and signal to drivers when they have fully pulled into a stall. Sometimes they are used to prevent driving across rows of empty stalls, because this cutting across is perceived as a hazardous activity. Backing up from parking stalls, however, generates more parking lot accidents (Box 1981), and thus cars should not be prevented from pulling through stalls when possible.

The Institute of Transportation Engineers discourages wheel stops in parking lots because they may present a tripping hazard, interfere with snowplowing, and trap trash (ITE Committee 5D-8, 1990). Wheel stops should be used to protect a wall, column, or other item only at a location where pedestrians are unlikely to walk. Where wheel stops are used, an overhang of about 2.5 feet (.76 m) for 90° front-in parking and about 4.5 feet (1.37 m) for 90° back-in parking should be provided beyond the wheel stop. Concrete and recycled plastic wheel stops come in a range of sizes. Typically, a 6-foot (~1.8 m) stop is used for each stall, and 6 inches (~15 cm) is the maximum height for a wheel stop. Wheel stops should not be shared between adjacent stalls because it creates confusion and blocks pedestrian circulation in the aisle.

Curbs are often used in lieu of wheel stops. Curbs present a smaller tripping hazard than wheel stops because the action of stepping up or down is easier than the action of stepping over and because they appear at an expected location. Curbs along walkways should be designed as steps, with rounded, skid-resistant, and contrasting-color nosings. Curbs require the same overhang setbacks as wheel stops.

Some vehicles overhang their wheels farther than the overhang setbacks recommended here, and cars occasionally ride up or over curbs and wheel stops. Thus, curbs and wheel stops should not be used when positive limitation is required. Bollards at least 36 inches (~.9 m) tall or bumpers can be used to protect buildings, trees, fire hydrants, or other structures within harm's way.

Bicycle Parking

Some cities require that places to park and secure bicycles be provided whenever automobile parking is required. For example, Albuquerque, New Mexico, requires that buildings provide a number of bicycle stalls equal to 10 percent of the number of required car stalls, with a minimum of three bike stalls.

Bicycle stalls require either a lockable enclosure or secure stationary racks that support the frame and to which the frame and both wheels can be locked. A space with minimum dimensions of 6 feet (1.83 m) long, 2.5 feet (.76 m) wide, and with a minimum overhead clearance of 7.5 feet (2.28 m) is necessary for each stall. An access aisle 5 feet (1.52 m) wide at a minimum is needed beside or between each row of bike stalls.

Ideally, bike stalls should be covered to protect the bikes from rain and the heat of the sun. The parking area should be well lighted, close to the entrance of the building (50 feet [15.2 m] maximum), and visible to passersby and/or building occupants. Bikes may also be parked in secured areas within a building.

The State of Oregon's Department of Transportation developed a set of questions to help evaluate bike parking racks (ODOT 1992), including the following:

- Can the rack support children and adults sitting, standing, or jumping on it without bending? Is the rack safe for children to play near?

- Can rack capacity be expanded as needs increase?

- Is there adequate lighting?

- Does the rack allow a bike to be easily and securely locked to it without damage to the bike? Will the bike stand up even if bumped?

Commercial Truck Parking

There are an estimated 185,000 commercial truck stalls near interstates at truck stops. On a typical night, 90 percent of these spaces are occupied, and a study by the Federal Highway Administration (1996) estimates that currently another 28,400 stalls are needed to make certain that exhausted truck drivers have a safe and secure place to pull off the highway.

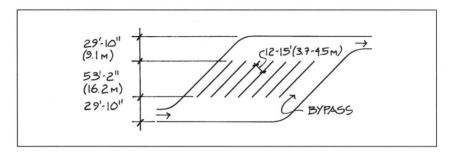

Figure 13.7   Commercial truck parking layout.

This same report advises that public highway rest stops are not a direct substitute for private truck stops. The rest stops are used primarily during the day for short rests, while the truck stops provide longer nighttime parking. Significant factors in the preference for truck stops are the added security of the truck stop and the services offered.

Figure 13.7 shows the preferred layout of stalls for single-trailer trucks. This pattern is up to 70 percent more land-efficient than parallel parking (Federal Highway Administration 1996, xxiii). More than half of truck stop lots currently have no markings, thus providing the flexibility to accommodate double- and triple-trailer rigs, but complicating parking and unparking maneuvers.

Lots Accessible to the Mobility-Impaired

The first case brought into federal court that resulted in a civil penalty under Title III of the Americans with Disabilities Act (ADA) was for failure to make parking accessible. Parking is a critical element of accessibility.

The ADA is a civil rights law. The Department of Justice has the charge of enforcing the law; people who believe they have been discriminated against may sue the property owner. The guidelines issued by the government are not a building code that is subject to state or local approval or variances.

The information in this book was compiled from publications of the Architectural and Transportation Barriers Compliance Board (Access Board) and other sources as noted. It should be viewed as the opinion of the author. The law and best practices continue to evolve. The designer should review materials and conditions that apply directly to the project at hand. Lots owned by government agencies generally follow Title II rules, which are usually more stringent than the Title III rules for privately owned lots discussed subsequently.

Required Number of Accessible Stalls

Whenever parking is supplied, no matter how the total amount of parking was determined, a portion of the stalls must be accessible to people with mobility impairment (hereafter called "accessible stalls"). Local codes may exceed the federal requirement for required number of accessible stalls shown in Table 13.12. The more stringent rule governs. When a facility has more than one lot, the required number of stalls is determined lot by lot. In employee or contract lots, accessible stalls must be provided, but "accessible spaces may be used by persons without disabilities when they are not needed by (persons) with disabilities" (Bulletin #6). When the use of a facility (e.g., a senior center) indicates that more accessible stalls are needed than are required by Table 12.3, a study should be conducted to determine an adequate supply of accessible stalls.

Location of Stalls

The location of accessible stalls must give mobility-impaired persons preferential treatment in terms of access and must not discriminate against them in terms of amenities (e.g., if the general stalls have hail-protection canopies, the accessible stalls must also). The shorthand rule is that accessible

Table 13.12   Required Number of Accessible Stalls

General Case

Total in Parking Lot	Required Minimum Number of Accessible Spaces	Source
1–25	1	ADAAG 4.1.3 (5) (a)
26–50	2	
51–75	3	
76–100	4	
101–150	5	
151–200	6	
201–300	7	
301–400	8	
401–500	9	
501–1000	2% of total	
1001 and over	20 + 1 per 100 over 1000	

No. of Accessible Spaces	Required Minimum Number of Van-Accessible Spaces	Source
1–8	1	ADAAG 4.1.3 (5) (a)
9–16	2	
17–24	3	
25–32	4	
33 and over	1 additional van-accessible per 8 accessible spaces	

Special Cases

Place	Requirement	Source
Medical outpatient units	10% of total stalls in lots serving visitors and patients.	ADAAG 4.1.2 (5) (d) and Bulletin #6
Medical units that specialize in persons with mobility impairments	20% of total stalls in lots serving visitors and patients.	ADAAG 4.1.2 (5) (d) and Bulletin #6
Valet parking	No stalls required. However, an accessible loading zone is required, and it is strongly recommended that self-park stalls be provided.	Bulletin #6

stalls should be located with the shortest possible route to the entrance(s). Relevant U.S. regulations include the following:

"**Accessible parking spaces serving a particular building shall be located on the shortest route of travel from adjacent parking to an accessible entrance. In parking facilities that do not serve a particular building, accessible parking shall be located on the shortest accessible route of travel to an accessible pedestrian entrance of the parking facility. In buildings with multiple accessible entrances with adjacent parking, accessible parking shall be dispersed and located closest to the accessible entrances.**" (ADAAG 4.6.2)

"**Accessible spaces can be provided in other lots or locations, or in the case of parking garages, on one level only when equal or greater access is provided in terms of proximity to an accessible entrance, cost and convenience. . . . The minimum number of spaces must still be determined separately for each lot . . .**" (Bulletin #6)

Van-Accessible Stalls

See Table 13.5 for required dimensions of van-accessible stalls and Table 13.12 for the required number of stalls. These stalls must be marked "van-accessible," but this does not restrict the stall to vans only (Bulletin #6).

Notes on the Layout of Stalls

Two accessible stalls may share an access aisle. However, this should be done only when the stalls are at 90° and allow both front-in and back-in parking (Title II modification to ADAAG, 14.2.6(1) (b)).

Curb ramps or other obstructions may not be within the stall's access aisle, but may begin at the curb face when vehicles overhang a curb (Chrest, Smith, and Bhuyan 1996, 212).

Car overhang may not obstruct the clear width of a sidewalk access route. Wheel stops and/or a reinforced signpost may help limit car overhang.

Signage

"Accessible parking spaces shall be designated as reserved by a sign showing the symbol of accessibility. . . . (Van) spaces . . . shall have an additional sign 'van-accessible' mounted below the symbol of accessibility" (ADAAG 4.6.4).

ADAAG requires that the sign not be obscured by a car or parked van. Centering the sign on the access aisle may help its visibility.

Equipment

Equipment such as parking meters, automated teller machines, pay stations, and ticket dispensers must have accessible controls. Most such equipment is now designed with operating mechanisms that are considered accessible, and the designer's major role is to place the controls at a proper level and to provide clear access to the controls.

For example, ADAAG 14.2(2) controls the design and placement of parking meters in public right-of-ways: "Parking meter controls shall be 42 in (1065 mm) maximum above finished public sidewalk . . ." and "Where parking meters serve accessible parking spaces, a stable, firm, and slip-resistant clear ground space a minimum of 30 in by 48 in (760 mm by 1220 mm), shall be provided at the controls. . . . Parking meters shall be located at or near the head or foot of the parking space so as not to interfere with the operation of a side lift or a passenger side transfer."

Existing Lots

Bulletin #6 of the Access Board suggests that existing lots must be made accessible when it is possible to do so: "ADAAG established minimum requirements for new construction or alterations. However, existing facilities not being altered may be subject to requirements for access. Title III of the ADA, which covers the private sector, requires the removal of barriers in places of public accommodation where it is 'readily achievable' to do so. This requirement is addressed by regulations issued by the Department of Justice. Under these regulations, barrier removal must comply with ADAAG requirements to the extent that is readily achievable to do so. For example, when restriping a parking lot to provide accessible spaces, if it is not readily achievable to provide the full number of accessible spaces required by ADAAG, a lesser number may be provided. The requirement to remove barriers, however, remains a continuing obligation; what is not readily achievable at one point may become achievable in the future."

When alterations are made (e.g., realigning striping or resurfacing, but not routine maintenance), whatever is altered must be made accessible unless technically infeasible (ADAAG 4.1.6 (1)) *and* improvements to the path of travel to the lot must be made, up to a cost equal to 20 percent of the project budget (Title II, Rule 36.403 (f)).

Passenger Loading Zones

There must be at least one passenger loading zone for the mobility-impaired whenever designated loading zones are provided. There must be an access aisle at least 5 feet wide and 20 feet long (1.53 by 6.10 m) adjacent and parallel to the vehicle pull-up space. A clear height of 9 feet 6 inches (2.90 m) is required at the loading zone and along the vehicle route to, from, and within the zone. The vehicle space and the access aisle shall be level with surface slopes not exceeding 1:50 (2 percent) in all directions (ADAAG 4.6.6). Neither curb ramps nor street furniture may occupy the access aisle space (Bulletin #6).

Curb Parking and Loading Zones

Table 13.13 gives dimensions for accessible curb stalls, bus stalls, and stalls for other vehicles. Local regulations may require different dimensions.

Table 13.13 Curb Parking

	Stall Length	Other	Source
Accessible loading	22 ft min. (6.71 m)	Platform 5 ft (1.53 m) wide, 20 ft (6.10 m) long, 9.5 ft (2.90 m) clear height	ADAAG 4.6.5 and 4.6.6
Truck loading	30–60 ft (9.15–18.29 m)	Add truck length per additional truck	Weant and Levinson
Drop-offs/taxi	50 ft (15.24 m)	Add 25 ft (7.62 m) per additional vehicle	Weant and Levinson
Paired (length per pair)	44–50 ft (13.41–15.24 m)	20 ft (6.10 m) stalls	Hunnicutt, 666 Hunnicutt, 666
Compact	19 ft (5.79 m)		Hunnicutt, 666
End stall	20 ft (6.10 m)		Hunnicutt, 666
Interior stall	22 ft–24 ft (6.71–7.32 m)		Hunnicutt, 666

Length of Curbside Bus Loading Zones

	Wheel Position from Curb		One 40-ft Bus (~12.2 m)	Additional per Bus
	6 Inches (~15 cm)	1 Foot (~30.5 cm)		
Upstream of intersection	L + 85 ft +(~25.9 m)	L + 65 ft +(~19.8 m)	105–125 ft (~32–38 m)	L + 5 ft +(~1.5 m)
Downstream of intersection Street width >39 ft (~11.9 m)	L + 55 ft +(~16.8 m)	L + 40 ft +(~12.2 m)	80–95 ft (~24.4–29 m)	L
Street width 32–39 ft (~9.75–11.9 m)	L + 70 ft +(~21.3 m)	L + 55 ft +(~16.8 m)	95–110 ft (~29–33.5 m)	L
Midblock Street width >39 ft (~11.9 m)	L + 135 ft +(~41.2 m)	L + 100 ft +(~30.5 m)	140–175 ft (~42.7–53.4 m)	L
Street width 32–39 ft (~9.75–11.9 m)	L + 150 ft +(~45.7 m)	L + 115 ft +(~35 m)	155–190 ft (~47.25–58 m)	L

SOURCE FOR BUS LOADING: Adapted from Homburger and Quinby, 1982. "Urban Transit" in *Transportation and Traffic Engineering Handbook*, 2nd edition.

L = length of bus.

Circulation Patterns

The circulation though a parking lot is critical to its performance. Overall goals are to create a simple, legible route that allows drivers to easily circulate past all available stalls on their way in and past as few stalls as possible on their way out. It is prudent to avoid dead-end aisles when possible, although even in high-turnover lots, parking cul-de-sacs for 10 to 12 cars may function well. Circulation patterns should be reviewed to remove choke points—places that many cars must pass through. Additionally, stalls for the mobility-impaired need to be placed as near to entrances as possible, fire lanes often are required by local codes, and conflicts between cars and between pedestrians and cars should be minimized. Usually there are trade-offs between these goals. For the layout of vast lots, see the Urban Land Institute's *Parking Requirements for Shopping Centers.* Following are some possible layouts for smaller lots. In general, any of these patterns is more efficient if the aisles run the long dimension of the lot.

The Parking Row

Perhaps the most common unit of parking is the two-way aisle with 90° stalls and exits at both ends. (See Figure 13.8.)

Advantages:

- Accessible stalls are easily incorporated into the design.

- The wide aisles increase separation between cars and pedestrians in the aisle.

- The two-way aisles allow drivers to exit efficiently.

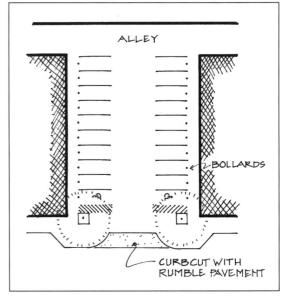

Figure 13.8 Two-way bay.

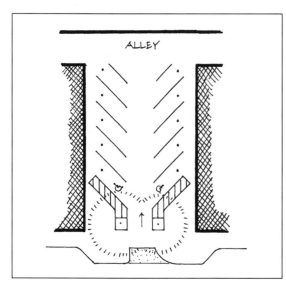

Figure 13.9 One-way slot.

• This design does not require aisle directional signs and markings.

Disadvantages:

• Two-way traffic may increase the conflict between pedestrians and cars.

• This pattern does not fit into all constrained sites.

One-Way Slot

See Figure 13.9 for an example.

Advantages:

• This pattern can be fitted into narrow sites.

• One-way entrance and exit simplifies circulation and reduces required curb-cut width.

• Pedestrian/car conflict is reduced.

• Angled parking is perceived as the easiest in which to park.

Disadvantages:

• Drivers cannot recirculate within the lot.

• Signage of one-way entrance and exit required.

• Stalled or slow vehicle blocks entire system.

• Requires an alley or must run block face to block face.

Herringbone

The one-way slot can be expanded into multiple one-way bays with the herringbone pattern. (See Figure 13.10.) The advantages and disadvantages are similar to the one-way slot except that because cars cannot recirculate within the

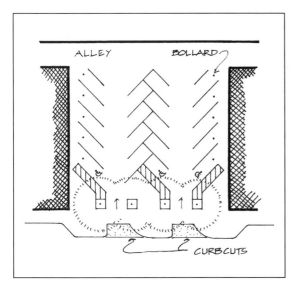

Figure 13.10   Herringbone pattern.

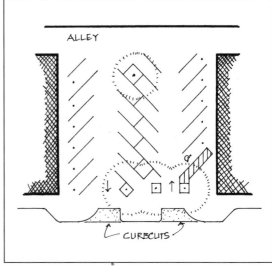

Figure 13.11   One-way loop.

lot and cannot pass by all the stalls, there may be significant inefficiency in parking.

One-Way Loop

The advantages and disadvantages of the one-way loop are similar to the one-way slot. The exit should be downstream of the entrance. A cross aisle can be added to allow cars to recirculate within the lot (Figure 13.11).

Dead-End Lots

Dead-end lots should be limited to 10 to 12 cars for public parking and 40 cars for low-turnover employee or contract parking and should have back-out stubs at the dead end. (See Figure 13.12.)

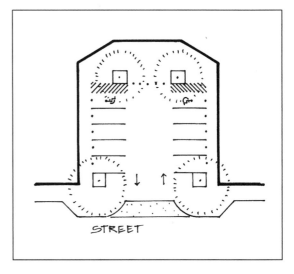

Figure 13.12   Dead-end lots.

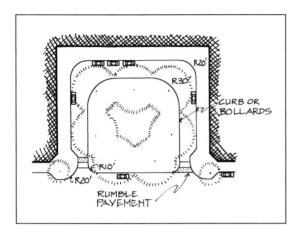

Figure 13.13   Drop-off turnaround.

Advantages:

- All stalls are along edges, allowing pedestrians to avoid crossing traffic.
- With a small lot the curb-cut width can be minimal.

Disadvantages:

- The size must be limited to reduce conflicts due to excessive turnover.

Drop-off Turnarounds

See Figure 13.13 for an example.

Advantages:

- Removes the activity of dropping off and picking up from the street.
- Allows architectural design of the place of arrival and departure.

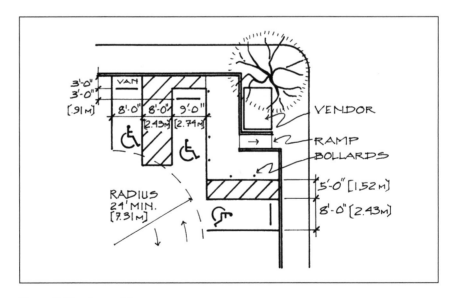

Figure 13.14   Accessible corners.

(Adapted from Chrest, Smith, and Bhuyan 1996.)

Disadvantages:

- Can be less time- and land-efficient than on-street drop-offs.

Accessible Corners

The corners of parking lots can provide good access routes to accessible stalls. (See Figure 13.14.) The advantages and disadvantages are dependent on the layout of the entire lot and must be evaluated on a case-by-case basis.

Entrance Aisle

Lots that are likely to generate significant traffic, such as grocery store lots or other high-turnover large lots, should have entrance aisles. (See Figure 13.15.) These aisles provide a place to slow down cars as they enter the car commons and allow space for cars waiting to exit the lot. They can also provide direct pedestrian paths that do not cross parking areas.

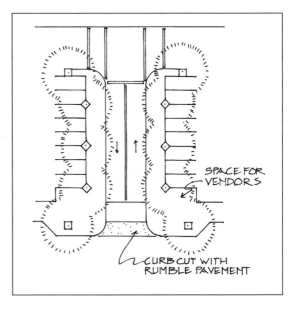

Figure 13.15 Entrance aisle.

Resources

Associations

American Trucking Association
2200 Mill Road
Alexandria, VA 22314-4677
e-mail: Trucking@CAIS.COM

American Concrete Institute
P.O. Box 9094
Farmington Hills, MI 48333
313-532-2600

Architectural and Transportation Barriers Compliance
   Board (Access Board)
1331 F Street NW, Suite 1000
Washington, DC 20004-1111
202-272-5434 (voice), 202-
   272-5449 (TTY), 202-272-
   5447 (fax), 800-872-2253
   (technical assistance)
e-mail: pubs@access-board.gov

Asphalt Institute
Research Park Drive
P.O. Box 14052
Lexington, KY 40512-4052
606-288-4960

Eno Foundation
One Farragut Square South,
   Suite 500
Washington, DC 20006-4003
202-879-4700
www.enotrans.com

I Madonnari Italian Street
   Painting Festival
Children's Creative Project
1235-B Veronica Springs Road
Santa Barbara, CA 93105
805-569-3873

Institute of Traffic Engineers
525 School Street SW, Suite 410
Washington, DC 20024-2797
202-554-8050

International Association for
the Child's Right to Play
(formerly International Playground Association)
Box 7701 NCSU
Raleigh, NC 27695-7701
919-737-2204

International Parking Institute
(IPI)
701 Kenmore Avenue,
Suite OO
P.O. Box 7167
Fredericksburg, VA 22404-
7167
540-371-7535

International Society of
Arboriculture
P.O. Box GG
Savoy, IL 61874-9902
www.ag.uiuc.edu/~isa/
welcome.html

National Council for the Traditional Arts (formerly National
Folk Festival Association)

1320 Fenwick Lane, Suite 200
Silver Spring, MD 20910
303-565-0654
e-mail: oldtime1@aol.com

National Parking Association
(NPA)
1112 16th Street NW, Suite
300
Washington, DC 20036
202-296-4336

Portland Cement Association
5420 Old Orchard Road
Skokie, IL 60077
847-966-6200
http//www.portcement.org

Project for Public Spaces, Inc.
153 Waverly Place
New York, NY 10014
212-620-5660
e-mail: pps@pps.org
www.pps.org

State of California South Coast
Air Quality Management
District (SCAQMD)
21865 East Copley Drive
Diamond Bar, CA 91765-
4182
909-396-2000

Further Reading on Selected Topics

Environmental Topics

Baker, Robert F., and Eileen Connolly. "Mix designs and air quality emissions tests of crumb rubber modified asphalt concrete." *Transportation Research Record,* 1995, no. 1515, pp. 18–27.

Chiazze, L. Jr., D. K. Watkins, and J. Amsel. "Asphalt and risk of cancer in man." *British Journal of Industrial Medicine,* 1991, vol. 48, no. 8, pp. 538–542.

Glick, R. H., M. L. Wolfe, and T. L. Thurow. 1993. "Effectiveness of native species buffer zones for nonstructural treatment of urban runoff." *Water Resources Abstracts,* section SW 3070.

Kostecki, P. T., E. J. Calabrese, and E. J. Fleischer. "Asphalt batching of petroleum contaminated soils as a viable remedial option." *Petroleum Contaminated Soils: Remediation Techniques, Environmental Fate and Risk Assessment,* vol. 1, 1989, pp. 175–186.

Lenhart, J. H. "Processed deciduous leaves for stormwater treatment." *Land Water,* 1997, vol. 41, no. 2, p. 54.

Prey, Jeffrey. "On-site controls for urban stormwater pollution." *Public Works,* 1994, vol. 125, no. 7, pp. 52–53.

Rosenfeld, Arthur H., Joseph J. Romm, Hashem Akbari, and Alan C. Lloyd. "Painting the Town White—and Green." *Technology Review,* Feb./March 1997, pp. 52–59.

Waller, H. Fred, and Richard W. May. "Waste Materials in Pavements." *ASTM Standardization News,* August 1993, pp. 30–35.

Festivals

Getz, Donald. 1991. *Festivals, Special Events and Tourism.* New York: Van Nostrand Reinhold.

Handelman, Don. 1989. *Models and mirrors: towards an anthropology of public events.* Cambridge and New York: Cambridge University Press.

Thompson, Sue Ellen & Barbara W. Carlson. 1994. *Holidays, Festivals and Celebrations of the World Dictionary.* Detroit: Omnigraphics Inc.

Wilson, Joe and Lee Udall. 1982. *Folk Festivals: A Handbook for Organization and Management.* Knoxville: University of Tennessee Press.

Parking Bibliographies

Municipal Parking Garages, Annotated References, 1946–1950. Municipal Reference Library, Detroit Public Library, 1950.

Bibliography on Automobile Parking in the United States. The Libraries of the Federal Works Agency, Washington, DC, August 1946.

Play

Forbush, William Byron, and Harry R. Allen. 1939. *The Book of Games for Home, School and Playground.* Philadelphia: John C. Winston Co.

Frost, Joe L. 1992. *Play and Playscapes.* Albany, NY: Delmar Publishers Inc.

Handbook for Public Playground Safety. U.S. Consumer Product Safety Commission, Washington, DC, 20207

Moore, R. C., Goltsman, S., and Iacofano, D., eds. 1988. *Play for All Guidelines: Planning, Design and Management of Outdoor Play Settings for All Children.* Champaign, IL: Sagemore Publishing.

Opie, Iona, and Peter Opie. 1969. *Children's Games in Street and Playground.* Oxford, U.K.: Clarendon Press.

Trees

Matheny, Nelda P., and James R. Clark. 1994. *A Photographic Guide to Evaluation of Hazard Trees in Urban Areas.* Savoy, IL: International Society of Arboriculture.

Miller, Robert W. 1997. *Urban Forestry.* Madison, Wisconsin: University of Wisconsin.

Phillips, Leonard E., Jr. 1993. *Urban Trees*. New York: McGraw-Hill.

Schein, Richard D. 1993. *Street Trees: A Manual for Municipalities*. State College, PA: TreeWorks.

Woonerfs

Engel, Ulla. "Effects of Speed Reducing Measures in Danish Residential Areas," *Proceedings of Conference on Road Safety and Traffic Environment in Europe*. Gothenburg, Sweden, September 1990, 95–135.

Eubank, Brenda. "A Closer Look at the Users of Woonerven." *Public Streets for Public Use,* ed. Anne Vernez Moudon. New York: Columbia University Press. Morningside Edition, 1991.

Hass-Klau, Carmen, Inge Nold, Geert Bocker, and Graham Crampton. *Civilized Streets: A Guide to Traffic Calming*. Brighton, England: Environmental and Transportation Planning, 1992.

Ichikawa, Kiyoshi, Kioshi Tanaka, and Hirotada Kamiya. "Living Environment and Design of 'Woonerf,' " *International Association of Traffic and Safety Sciences,* 8 (1984) 40–51.

Kraay, Joop H. "Woonerfs and Other Experiments in the Netherlands." *Built Environment,* 1986, 12:1/2, 20–29.

Polus, Abishai. *Evaluation of the Characteristics of Shared Streets,* Report no. 85-72. Haifa, Israel: Transportation Research Institute, 1985.

Notes

Introduction

1. See Wilbur Smith and Associates. *Parking in the City Center*. New Haven, Conn.: Wilbur Smith and Associates, 1965, p. 59. Reprinted in John B. Rae. *The Road and the Car in American Life*. Cambridge, Mass: MIT Press. 1971, p. 220. Also see Catherine G. Miller. *Carscape: A Parking Handbook*. Columbus, Indiana: Washington Street Press.

2. See Richard W. Willson. 1995. For typical suburban developments, he found average peak parking utilization rates of 56 percent.

3. For example, see James Howard Kunstler. 1996. *Home From Nowhere*. New York: Simon and Schuster.

4. For example, the Albuquerque, New Mexico, code requires one stall per every 200 square feet of shop space. A stall with its attendant access requires 300 to 400 square feet of land.

Chapter 1

1. The existence of Inca roadways in a place that did not know the wheel suggests that the vehicle is not a necessary prerequisite for roads. However, the road may have arisen in the Old World in response to the invention and use of vehicles.

2. On smooth streets over short distances, bicycles of the 1890s could go up to twice the speed of a horse and carriage.

Chapter 2

1. See *Republic Aviation Corp. v. National Labor Relations Board,* 324 U.S. 793, 803 n. 10 (1945).

2. See *Lechmere, Inc. v. NLRB,* 914 F.2d 313 (1st Cir. 1990).

3. Thucydides vii.63.

Chapter 3

1. The parking street and the curb parking were metered. The courtyard was posted for a two-hour limit of free parking, and the lot provided free indefinite parking. The hierarchy of use was measured in turnover rates and occupancy rates during 40 hours of observations that included weekends and weekdays. The parking street and courtyard had nearly twice the utilization per stall as the lot. Curb parking had approximately 1.7 times the utilization of lot stalls.

Chapter 4

1. For example, Weant and Levinson 1990, p. 244, cite studies showing up to a 63 percent reduction in accidents in cases where parking was changed from angle to parallel.

2. A collection of more than five to seven things is perceived as "many things," and it becomes harder to remember where your car is among the many. See G. Miller, "The Magical Number 7, plus or minus 2: Some Limits on Our Capacity for Processing Information," in *Readings in Perception,* D. Beardslee and M. Wertheimer, eds. New York, 1958, p. 103.

Chapter 6

1. For a more detailed discussion of design for handicapped pedestrians see Robert C. Reuter, 1994, "Pedestrians with Disabilities," in *Design and Safety of Pedestrian Facilities,* ITE 5A-5, 1995.

2. Pleasant walking environments can increase walking distances up to 30 percent. See Olaf Lovemark, referenced in Pushkarev and Zupan 1975, 74.

3. For a discussion of stores in tunnels, see *European Experience in Pedestrian and Bicycle Facilities,* reprinted from the International Road Feder-

ation Annual Report 1974, U.S. Department of Transportation, April 1975. Also see Untermann 1984, 38.

4. © 1995 Institute of Transportation Engineers. Used by permission.

Chapter 8

1. The Galveston Historical Foundation, which conducts the festival, requires that vendors' booths and costumes look Dickensian. Approximately half the vendors were locals and half were traveling professional festival vendors. There were 185 vendors at the festival. I received a 15.67 percent response rate to a questionnaire mailed after the event. The event is held primarily in the streets of downtown Galveston. The Galveston Historical Foundation had conducted a booth design contest in previous years, and of those who had participated in the festival during those years, over 90 percent thought it should be reinstituted.

2. D. M. Susin et al. (1993) discuss injury rates associated with playground surfaces. They observe that (1) playground equipment injuries are relatively uncommon given how much the equipment is used, and (2) playground equipment–related injuries occur on asphalt at a rate 3 to 5 times greater than on gravel, grass, sand, and mats. These more forgiving surfaces have similar injury rates. Concrete was not discussed in the article.

Chapter 9

1. For examples of recent European public art and a set of criteria to evaluate public art proposals, see Susanne H. Crowhurst Lennard and Henry L. Lennard. 1995. *Livable Cities Observed.* Gondolier Press. For a discussion of contemporary American public art and why it is a source of controversy, see Erika Doss. 1995. *Spirit Poles and Flying Pigs.* Washington D.C: Smithsonian Institution Press.

2. For a discussion of the design of artwork for a public space, see John H. Owen Jr. 1987 and 1991. "A Successful Street Design Process," in *Public Streets for Public Use.* Anne Vernez Moudon, ed. New York: Columbia University Press.

3. Molajoli, Bruno. 1990. "Museums," in *Time Savers Standards for Building Types, Third Edition.* Editors Joseph De Chiara and John Callender. New York: McGraw-Hill. Copyright © 1990. Used by permission of the McGraw-Hill Companies.

4. Patricia Failing writes about how the lack of agreement between artist and site owner on the permanence of the art led Richard Serra to withdraw his project for the Fine Arts Museum of San Francisco in "Proposed Sculpture in Museum Parking Lot," *ARTnews*. October 1994.

Chapter 11

1. This system has been shown to remove 95 percent of total suspended solids, over 80 percent of oil, grease, and petroleum hydrocarbons, just less than 60 percent of total phosphorus, and about 80 percent of copper, lead, and zinc (Unified Sewerage Agency, Hillsboro, Oregon, 1994). Compare to Table 11.1.

Chapter 12

1. For example, on average, households with incomes above $40,000 a year own 2.3 automobiles. The average household with an income below $10,000 a year owns 1.0 cars. Residential zoning codes have the same parking requirement for both households.

2. Photographs can be used instead of maps, but a method to record the time and date must also be established. Photographs have the advantage that they can be reviewed later to glean other information (e.g., where are store employees parking?).

3. See California AB 2109. There are more detailed exemptions (e.g., the office must be in a nonattainment air-quality area, and the parking must be leased by the employer in order for the requirement to be mandatory).

Chapter 13

1. The 1970s to 1980s downturn in average car size was a response to external factors (oil embargo fuel price increases, national fuel-efficiency standards, etc.). Recently, car sizes are tending to cluster near the middle ranges. See Chrest, Smith, and Bhuyan.

2. This calculation is based on 60° parking in low-turnover lots.

Bibliography

(AAMA) American Automobile Manufacturers Association. 1994. *AAMA Motor Vehicle Facts and Figures '94*. Detroit, MI: Public Affairs Division, AAMA.

(AASHTE) American Association of State Highway and Traffic Engineers. 1990. *A Policy on Geometric Design of Highways and Streets*. Washington, DC.

Adams, John. 1995. *Risk*. London, England: University College London Press.

Adkins, Lesley, and Roy A. Adkins. 1994. *Handbook to Life in Ancient Rome*. New York: Facts On File, Inc.

Akbari, Hashem, Susan Davis, Sofia Dorsano, Joe Huang, Steven Winnett, editors. 1992. *Cooling Our Communities: A Guidebook on Tree Planting and Light-Colored Surfacing*. U.S. Environmental Protection Agency and Lawrence Berkeley Laboratory. GPO Document #055-000-00371-8.

Alexander, Christopher, et al. 1977. *A Pattern Language*. New York: Oxford University Press.

(ATBCB) Architectural and Transportation Barriers Compliance Board. *Americans with Disabilities Act Accessibilities Guidelines for Buildings and Facilities; Final Guidelines* (ADAAG). 36 CFR Part 1191, July 26, 1991.

———. 1994. *Bulletin #6: Parking.*

Berenson, Bernard. 1952. *Italian Painters of the Renaissance. Venetian and North Italian Schools.* London and New York: Phaidon.

Bertha, Brian. 1964. Appendix A. *The Low-Rise Speculative Apartment* by W. Smith. Research Report 25. Berkeley, CA: Center for Real Estate and Urban Economics, University of California. Quoted in Shoup 1997.

Box, Paul C. "Parking Lot Accident Characteristics." *ITE Journal,* December 1981.

———. 1992. "Parking and Terminals." *Traffic Engineering Handbook,* fourth edition. Englewood Cliffs, NJ: Prentice-Hall.

———. 1994. "Avoiding Tort Claims in Parking Lots." *Public Works,* vol. 125, no. 1.

———. 1994b. "Effect of Single vs. Double Line Parking Stall." *ITE Journal,* May 1994, pp. 27–29.

Boyd, John Taylor Jr. "The Garage in the House." *Country Life* 33, May 1917, p. 56.

Brand, Stewart. 1994. *How Buildings Learn: What Happens to Them After They're Built.* New York: Penguin Books.

Buchanan, Colin, et al. 1963. *Traffic in Towns.* London: HMSO.

Bulletin #6. *See* ATBCB.

Burrage, Robert H., and Edward G. Mogren. 1957. *Parking.* Saugatuck, CT: The Eno Foundation for Highway Traffic Control.

Calabresi, Guido, and Alvin K. Klevorick. 1984. *Three Tests for Liability in Torts.* Working Paper #26. Yale Law School.

Calthorpe, Peter. 1993. *The Next American Metropolis: Ecology, Community and the American Dream.* New York: Princeton Architectural Press.

Cantrell A. "Annual Refining Survey." *Oil and Gas Journal,* 82, March 26, 1984.

Chase, R. M., G. M. Liss, D. C. Cole, and B. Heath. 1994. "Toxic Health Effects Including Reversible Macrothrombosis in Workers Exposed to Asphalt Fumes." *American Journal of Industrial Medicine,* vol. 25, no. 2, pp. 279–289.

Chidister, Mark. 1986. "The Effect of the Context on the Use of Urban Plazas." *Landscape Journal* 5(2):115–127.

Childs, Mark. 1995. "The Architecture of Festivals." Paper presented at the 1995 Making Cities Livable Conference. Carmel, CA.

———. "The Living End." *Planning,* May 1996.

Chrest, Anthony P., Mary S. Smith, and Sam Bhuyan. 1996. *Parking Structures: Planning, Design, Construction, Maintenance and Repair.* New York: Chapman & Hall.

Dare, Charles E. "Consideration of Special Purpose Vehicles in Parking Lot Design." *ITE Journal,* May 1985.

De Crescenza, Luciano. 1988. *Thus Spake Bellavista.* London: Pan Books.

Dewar, Robert. 1992. "Driver and Pedestrian Characteristics." *Traffic Engineering Handbook,* fourth edition. Englewood Cliffs, NJ: Prentice-Hall.

During, Alan Thein. 1996. *The Car and the City.* Seattle: Northwest Environmental Watch.

Ellis, Rafaela. "Test Your Parking Lot Smarts." *Car & Travel,* July/August 1996.

Emanuel, Steven L. 1994. *Torts.* Larchmont, NY: Emanuel Law Outlines.

Eno Foundation. 1942. *The Parking Problem.*

Evans, L. 1985. *Car Size and Safety: Results from Analyzing US Accident Data.* Research Publication GMR-5059. Warren, MI: GM Research Laboratories.

Federal Highway Administration. 1978. *A Pedestrian Planning Procedures Manual.* Report No. FHWA-RD-79-45 and No. FHWA-RD-79-47.

———. 1983. *Model Parking Code Provisions to Encourage Ridesharing and Transit Use.*

———. 1996. *Commercial Driver Rest and Parking Requirements.* Report No. FHWA-MC-96-0010.

Fenester, J. M. "The Longest Race." *American Heritage,* November 1996.

Flink, James J. 1970. *America Adopts the Automobile 1895–1910.* Cambridge, MA, and London: MIT Press.

———. 1990. *The Automobile Age.* Cambridge, MA: MIT Press.

Francis, Mark, and Randolph T. Hester Jr. 1990. *The Meaning of Gardens.* Cambridge, MA, and London, England: MIT Press.

Gebhard, David. 1992. "The Suburban House and the Automobile." *The Car and the City: The Automobile, the Built Environment and Daily Urban Life.* Martin Wachs and Margaret Crawford, editors. Ann Arbor: University of Michigan Press.

Gehl, Jan. 1987. *Life Between Buildings: Using Public Space.* New York: Van Nostrand Reinhold.

Gordon, John Steele. "Engine of Liberation." *American Heritage,* November 1996.

Gruen Associates. 1986. *Employment and Parking in Suburban Business Parks: A Pilot Study.* Washington, DC: Urban Land Institute.

Hackman, Lonnie, and Norene D. Martin. 1969. *The Parking Industry: Private Enterprise for the Public Good.* Washington, DC: National Parking Association.

Hall, Edward T. 1966. *The Hidden Dimension.* Garden City, NY: Doubleday & Company.

Hanson, Susan, editor. 1995. *The Geography of Urban Transportation.* New York: The Guilford Press.

Hass-Klau, Carmen. 1990. *The Pedestrian and City Traffic.* London and New York: Pinter Publishers.

Highway Research Board. 1971. *Parking Principles.* Special Report 125.

(ITE 5A-5) Institute of Transportation Engineers Technical Council Committee 5A-5. 1995. *Design and Safety of Pedestrian Facilities.* Washington, DC.

(ITE 5D-8) Institute of Transportation Engineers Technical Council Committee 5D-8, 1990. *Guidelines for Parking Facility Location and Design.* Washington, DC.

(ITE 6F-52) Institute of Transportation Engineers Technical Council Committee 6F-52, 1995. *Shared Parking Planning Guidelines.* Washington, DC.

Itoh, Teiji. 1980. *Space and Illusion in the Japanese Garden.* New York, Tokyo, and Kyoto: Weatherhill/Tankosha.

Jackson, J. B. 1980. *The Necessity for Ruins.* Amherst: The University of Massachusetts Press.

———. 1994. *A Sense of Place, a Sense of Time.* New Haven and London: Yale University Press.

Jacobs, Allan B. 1993. *Great Streets.* Cambridge, MA, and London, England: MIT Press.

Joardar, S. D., and J. W. Neill. 1978. "The Subtle Differences in Configuration of Small Public Spaces." *Landscape Architecture,* 68(11):487–491.

Kangas, Scott E. 1996. "The Fundamentals of Parking Lot Protection." *Security Management,* July 1996, pp. 44–50.

Kaplan, Rachel, and Stephen Kaplan. 1989. *The Experience of Nature: A Psychological Perspective.* Cambridge, England: Cambridge University Press.

Kelling, G., and M. Moore. 1988. "The Evolving Strategy of Policing." U.S. Department of Justice, National Institute of Justice.

Kemmis, Daniel. 1995. *The Good City and the Good Life: Renewing the Sense of Community.* Boston, New York: Houghton Mifflin Company.

Kielbaso, J. James, et al. 1988. *Trends in Urban Forestry Management, Baseline Data Report,* vol. 20(1). International City Management Association, Washington, DC.

Kirkpatrick, Susan A. 1997. " '90s Campus Parking: Meet the Demand—Provide a Better Service—Reduce the Cost." *The Parking Professional,* October 1997, pp. 16–21.

Knoblauch, R. C., et al. 1988. "Investigation of Exposure Based Pedestrian Areas." FHWA Report No. FHWA/RD 88/038.

Kodama, Michael R., Dr. Richard Willson. 1996. *Local Government Parking Handbook: Using Demand-Based Parking Strategies to Meet Community Goals.* The Mobile Source Air Pollution Reduction Review Committee. Contact Michael Kodama 818-846-6272.

Kostof, Spiro. 1991. *The City Shaped.* Boston, Toronto, London: Little, Brown & Company.

———. 1995. *A History of Architecture.* New York, Oxford: Oxford University Press.

Kuzemka, Katherine. "Measuring Your Parking Meter Program." *The Parking Professional,* November 1997, pp. 16–23.

Leopold, Luna B. 1994. *A View of the River.* Cambridge, MA: Harvard University Press.

Liebs, Chester H. 1985. *Main Street to Miracle Mile: American Roadside Architecture.* Baltimore and London: The Johns Hopkins University Press.

Lincoln Institute of Land Policy. 1995. *Alternatives to Sprawl.*

Longstreth, Richard. 1997. *City Center to Regional Mall.* Cambridge, MA, and London, England: MIT Press.

Lynch, Kevin. 1971. *Site Planning,* second edition. Cambridge, MA: MIT Press.

———. 1984. *Theory of Good City Form.* Cambridge, MA, and London, England: MIT Press.

Lyndon, Donlyn, and Charles W. Moore. 1994. *Chambers for a Memory Palace.* Cambridge, MA, and London, England: MIT Press.

Marcus, Clare Cooper, and Carolyn Francis. 1990. *People Places: Design Guidelines for Urban Open Space.* New York: Van Nostrand Reinhold.

MacArthur, R. H., and E. O. Wilson. 1967. *The Theory of Island Biogeography.* Princeton: Princeton University Press.

McClintock, Miller. 1925. *Street Traffic Control.* New York: McGraw-Hill.

McPherson, E. Gregory, James R. Simpson, and Klaus I. Scott. 1997. "Benefits from Shade Trees in Parking Lots." Briefing paper of the Western Center for Urban Forest Research and Education, University of California, Davis.

McShane, Clay. 1994. *Down the Asphalt Path: The Automobile and The American City.* New York: Columbia University Press.

Mayo, James M. 1993. *The American Grocery Store: Business Evolution of an Architectural Space.* Westport, CT, and London, England: Greenwood Press.

Means, Larry W., John Lutz, Thomas E. Long, and Karen M. High. 1995. "Memory for Parking Location in Large Lots." *Psychological Reports,* 1995, pp. 76, 775–779.

Melnick, Mimi, and Robert A. Melnick. 1994. *Manhole Covers.* Cambridge, MA: MIT Press.

Merrill, Jean. 1964. *The Pushcart War.* New York: Grosset & Dunlap.

Messenger, Todd, and Reid Ewing. 1996. "Transit-Oriented Development in the Sunbelt: Get Real (and Empirical)!" Paper presented at 75th annual meeting of the Transportation Research Board, Washington, DC.

Miller, Catherine G. 1988. *Carscape: A Parking Handbook.* Columbus, IN: Washington Street Press for the Irwin-Sweeney-Miller Foundation.

Miller, Gerald. *The Impacts of Parking Prices on Commuter Travel.* Washington, DC: Metropolitan Washington Council of Governments, December 1991.

Miller, Robert W. 1997. *Urban Forestry: Planning and Managing Urban Greenspaces.* Upper Saddle River, NJ: Prentice-Hall.

Molajoli, Bruno. 1990. "Museums." *Time Savers Standards for Building Types,* third edition. Joseph De Chiara and John Callender, eds. New York: McGraw-Hill.

Moore, Charles W., William J. Mitchell, and William Turnbull Jr. 1988. *The Poetics of Gardens.* Cambridge, MA, and London, England: MIT Press.

Moore, R. I., and S. J. Older. 1965. "Pedestrians and Motors Are Compatible in Today's World." *Traffic Engineering,* Sept. 1965, cited in ITE 5A-5 1994.

Mumford, Lewis. 1954. *In the Name of Sanity.* New York: Harcourt, Brace & Co.

National Committee on Uniform Traffic Laws and Ordinances. 1987. *Uniform Motor Vehicle Code and Model Traffic Ordinance,* Washington, DC.

Newman, Oscar. 1972. *Defensible Space: Crime Prevention Through Urban Design.* New York: Collier Books.

Newman, Peter, and Jeffrey R. Kenworthy. 1989. *Cities and Automobile Dependence.* Aldershot, England: Grower Technical.

O'Brien, David. 1993. *Street Trees for Cities and Towns.* Sydney, Australia: Imago Press.

(ODOT) Oregon Department of Transportation. 1992. *Bicycle Parking Facilities.*

(PBQD) Parsons Brinkerhoff Quade and Douglas Inc., Cambridge Systematics Ltd., and Calthorpe Associates. 1993. *The Pedestrian Environment,* vol. 4A. Portland, OR: 1000 Friends of Oregon.

Pfeiffer, Christina Ann. 1986. *Analyses of Landscape Design and Maintenance Requirements in Urban Parking Lots.* Thesis, Master of Science, University of Washington.

Phillips, Leonard E. Jr. 1993. *Urban Trees: A Guide for Selection, Maintenance, and Master Planning.* New York: McGraw-Hill.

Pielou, E. C. 1979. *Biogeography.* New York: John Wiley & Sons.

Pietrucha, M. T., and C. W. Plummer. 1992. "Design Considerations for Pedestrian Sensitive Geometric Features." *1992 Compendium of Technical Papers,* Institute of Transportation Engineers. Washington, DC.

Pisarski, A. 1996. *Commuting in America II: The Second National Report on Commuting Patterns and Trends*. Lansdowne, VA: Eno Transportation Foundation.

Polanis, S., and K. Price. "Parking Regulations in Southeastern Cities: A Summary Report." *ITE Journal,* June 1991, pp. 31–34.

Prey, Jeffrey. "On-Site Controls for Urban Stormwater Pollution." *Public Works,* vol. 125, no. 7, 1994, pp. 52–53.

Pushkarev, Boris, and Jeffrey M. Zupan. 1975. *Urban Space for Pedestrians*. Cambridge, MA, and London, England: MIT Press.

Rae, John B. 1971. *The Road and the Car in American Life*. Cambridge, MA, and London, England: MIT Press.

Ricker, Edmund R. 1957. *Traffic Design of Parking Garages*. Westport, CT: Eno Foundation.

Rudnitsky, Howard. "Take-Away Game." *Forbes,* July 29, 1996.

Sammis, Bryon T. "A Businessman's Point of View on Off-Street Parking Facilities." *Transportation Quarterly,* vol. 2, no. 2, April 1948.

Scharf, J. Thomas, and Thompson Westcott. 1884. *History of Philadelphia 1609–1884*. Philadelphia: C. H. Everts & Co.

Schein, Richard D. 1993. *Street Trees: A Manual for Municipalities*. State College, PA: Treeworks.

Shoup, Donald C. 1995. "An Opportunity to Reduce Minimum Parking Requirements." *Journal of the American Planning Association* 61(1):14–28.

———. 1997. "The High Cost of Free Parking." *Journal of Planning Education and Research* 17:3–20.

Shulman, Seth. "The Lowdown on Blacktop." *Technology Review,* Feb./March 1995.

Smith, Robert A. 1972. *A Social History of the Bicycle: Its Early Life and Times in America*. New York: McGraw-Hill.

Sosin, D. M., P. Keller, J. J. Sacks, and M. Kresnow. "Surface-Specific Fall Injury Rates on Utah Playgrounds." *Ameri-*

can Journal of Public Health., vol. 83, no. 5, 1993, pp. 733–735.

Southworth, Michael, and Eran Ben-Joseph. 1997. *Streets and the Shaping of Towns and Cities.* New York: McGraw-Hill.

Spirn, Anne Whiston. 1984. *The Granite Garden: Urban Nature and Human Design.* New York: Basic Books, Inc.

Stover, Vergil G., and Frank J. Koepke. "End Islands as an Element of Site Design." *ITE Journal,* November 1989, pp. 33–38.

Sucher, David. 1995. *City Comforts: How to Build an Urban Village.* Seattle: City Comforts Press.

Svec, Otto Ph.D., P.E. "Recycled Tires Can Improve Asphalt." *Canadian Consulting Engineer,* July/August 1996, p. 23.

Tillson, George W. 1912. *Street Pavements and Paving Materials.* New York: John Wiley & Sons.

Trust for Public Land. 1994. *Healing America's Cities.* San Francisco.

Unified Sewerage Agency of Hillsboro, OR. 1994. *CSF Stormwater Treatment System: Independent Three Year Performance Summary.* 2035 N.E. Columbia Blvd., Portland, OR.

United States Department of Justice. 1995. *Crime in the United States, 1994. Uniform Crime Reports.*

Untermann, Richard K. 1984. *Accommodating the Pedestrian: Adapting Towns and Neighborhoods for Walking and Bicycling.* New York: Van Nostrand Reinhold.

(ULI) Urban Land Institute. 1982. *Parking Requirements for Shopping Centers.* Washington, DC: Urban Land Institute.

Venturi, Robert, Denise Scott Brown, and Steven Izenour. 1972. *A Significance for A&P Parking Lots, or Learning from Las Vegas.* Cambridge, MA: MIT Press.

Vieyra, Daniel I. 1979. *Fill 'er Up.* New York: Macmillan Publishing Co., Inc.

Wachs, Martin, and Margaret Crawford, editors. 1992. *The Car and the City*. Ann Arbor: The University of Michigan Press.

Waller, Fred H., and Richard W. May. "Waste Materials in Pavements." *ASTM Standardization News,* August 1993.

Weant, Robert A., and Herbert S. Levinson. 1990. *Parking*. The Eno Foundation.

Whyte, William H. 1980. *The Social Life of Small Urban Spaces*. Washington DC: The Conservation Foundation.

————. 1988. *City: Rediscovering the Center*. New York: Doubleday.

Willson, R. 1995. "Suburban Parking Requirements: A Tacit Policy for Automobile Use and Sprawl." *Journal of the American Planning Association* 61(1):29–42.

Xiao, Qingfu, Gregory McPherson, James R. Simpson, and Susan L. Ustin. 1997. "Rainfall Interception by Sacramento's Urban Forest." In preparation at the Western Center for Urban Forest Research and Education, University of California, Davis.

Index

Union Iron Products Company advertisement.

(*The American City Magazine,* July 1920, p. 84.)